Golf Travel by Design

*How You Can Play the World's Best Courses
by the Sport's Top Architects*

By the Editors of *The Golf Insider*

The Globe Pequot Press

GUILFORD, CONNECTICUT

Cover photos: Greg Norman, courtesy of Great White Shark Enterprises Inc.; aerial view: Jasper Park Lodge Golf Club, courtesy of Fairmont Hotels & Resorts; and inset photo: Whistling Straits, courtesy of Kohler Co.

Spot photos: ©2002–2003 www.clipart.com

Cover and text design by Casey Shain
Project Editor: Jan Cronan

Library of Congress Cataloging-in-Publication Data
Golf travel by design: how you can play the world's best courses by the sport's top architects/by the editors of The golf insider.—1st ed.
      p. cm.
   Includes bibliographical references and index.
   ISBN 0-7627-2379-3
      1. Golf courses—Guidebooks. 2. Golf courses—Design and construction.
   3. Golf course architects—Biography. I. Golf insider.

GV975.G57 2002
796.352'06'8—dc21

Manufacturered in the United States of America
First Edition/First Printing

The prices and rates listed in this book were confirmed at press time. We recommend, however, that you call establishments before traveling to obtain current information.

Contents

Foreword

consider myself very fortunate to have made my living doing something I love, which is playing golf. I am also fortunate that my job has enabled me to play the greatest courses on earth, including some that most people never have the opportunity to experience, such as Cypress Point. But the golfer who loves the game enough to travel to play it can find great courses all over the globe. Alister MacKenzie is one of my favorite golf course designers of all time—he laid out Cypress—and while you may not be able to play it, you can experience some of his best work, whether you go to California or visit Australia, my home. A. W. Tillinghast is another favorite of mine, and this year the U.S. Open was played on one of his great designs, a public course that costs less to play than the cart fee in many places. No matter what your budget is, if you travel, you can find wonderful courses by the greatest designers of all time and experience them for yourself.

You can't love the game of golf and play it for years without falling in love with the design process as well. There are so many elements, some obvious and some subtle, that make the difference between a mediocre golf course and a good one, or between a good one and a great one. Yet not enough golfers appreciate the design side of the golf experience, even though it is what they are paying for when they tee up. Perhaps they would begin to appreciate it more if they understood how much the design affects the way a course should be played. Practice and lessons are a very important part of golf, but many golfers could lower their handicaps immediately by picking up a book like this one.

When you stand on the tee and look down the fairway, the designer is telling you something. I've been influenced in my own work by my favorite classic designers—MacKenzie and Tillinghast. MacKenzie used aiming bunkers to define his fairways on longer holes. They are out of reach off the tee for most players, but they show you where to go. People think of bunkers only as hazards, but in this case they are actually there to help you. At the same time, fairway bunkers that are in play usually tell you something: Don't

GREAT WHITE SHARK ENTERPRISES INC.

play to this side of the fairway. It sounds simple, but so many amateur players automatically grab the driver out of their bag with no thought as to how they are going to play the hole.

For many years I have looked at holes backward by knowing where the pin is, then determining from what point I want to hit my approach shot to the green, and then choosing the appropriate club off the tee in order to get to that point. Many architects work backward as well, and if you can understand their intent, it will help you make smart decisions from tee to green.

But there is more to appreciating golf course design than cold, analytical scoring. When you go for a walk in the park, you do it to experience nature or beauty. But some parks are better than others, and the great parks, like Central Park in New York, become world famous because their design is so pleasing and simple. It's the same way with golf courses. No matter how you score or how good a golfer you are, you are always going to enjoy a well-designed course better, because it is more fun, more beautiful, and more rewarding. Golf is an expensive passion, and there are a lot of golf courses in the world. This book is as much about travel as it is about design. *The Golf Insider* and *Golf Travel By Design* are the best tools for the traveling golfer to identify the world's best courses and resorts.

I am honored to be included in this book alongside the greatest golf course designers in history, people like Pete Dye and Donald Ross. In recent years I have devoted a very substantial portion of my time to golf course design, and I'm glad to see that many of my courses have been well received. Today I get a bigger thrill out of building a golf course than shooting the low score or winning a championship. It's a passion for me right now. I hope that with the help of this book, you will visit and enjoy all my courses, but I also urge you to visit the many wonderful designs that inspired me and explore the work of contemporary architects who will continue to produce fine golf courses for decades to come. Let the editors of *The Golf Insider* and their book be your road map to one great golf vacation after another. You will come away with an appreciation for what great golf course design is. Armed with this knowledge, you will play the best golf of your lifetime when you visit the great courses described in the following pages.

Greg Norman

Greg Norman is widely recognized as one of the game's all-time greatest players and takes great pride in the fact that he is one of golf's global ambassadors, playing competitively on many of the world's tours, including the PGA Tour, the European Tour, and the Australasian Tour. He has enjoyed one of the greatest careers in golf history and was a 2001 inductee into the World Golf Hall of Fame. Norman, whose nickname is the Great White Shark, has spent much of his professional career as the number-one-ranked player in the world and has sat atop the PGA Tour's money list many times. He has won eighty-seven golf tournaments worldwide, including the 1986 and 1993 British Open Championships, in addition to eighteen titles on the PGA Tour. He was the first player ever to surpass $10 million in career winnings. He has designed golf courses around the world, including the United States, Ireland, the Bahamas, Australia, and the Far East.

Acknowledgments

I n writing *Golf Travel By Design,* we were greatly assisted by the generous contributions of many individuals and organizations who gave freely of their knowledge, experience, and, in many cases, photography. We would like to thank the United States Golf Association, whose archives and public museum at Golf House in Far Hills, New Jersey, contain a wealth of information and images on the history of the game; renowned golf course designers Greg Norman and Rees Jones, who never hesitated to take time out of their busy schedules to offer sage advice; Laura Fairweather and her staff at Fairmont Resorts, who operate some of the most luxurious golf resorts in North America while remaining dedicated to the historical accuracy of their courses throughout the United States and Canada; Brad King, editor of *Links Magazine,* for arranging interviews with several of the architects and providing general support of the newsletter; Dove Jones and the staff at Perry Golf, a golf travel specialist, for helping us so many times throughout the years with detailed arrangements to visit the great courses of the British Isles; Karen Moraghan, the quintessential golf industry insider, for her advice and assistance with photography and resort contacts; Nancy Berkley, author and women's golf advocate, for reminding us of the importance of the forward tees; Mike Klemme, owner of Golfoto, the nation's premier golf course photographer, and one of the few people who has visited so many great courses around the world that even we are jealous; and most importantly of all, the loyal readers of *The Golf Insider,* the most well-traveled group of golf lovers on earth, whose questions, comments, and travel feedback keep teaching us about golf travel month after month after month.

TROON NORTH, COURTESY OF © MIKE KLEMME/GOLFOTO

Introduction

Golf is more than a game, it is your passport to the world. Unlike almost every other sport, it is not played on a standardized field or court or track. It is played in the mountains, the desert, the jungle, the rain forest, and inside volcanic craters. It is played on cliffs, prairies, islands, and farmland. It has even been played on the moon. There are short courses and long courses, old courses and new courses, some with ten holes and some with nineteen, some par 68, some par 73. One costs $500 to play; another is free. Some are shared with elk, some with alligators, others with kangaroos, sheep, even giraffes. Some are shared with people walking their dogs and some, with no one at all.

Golf can take you places. It can introduce you to new experiences and new people, from the players you are paired with to the locals sharing stools at the pub. It can be played in the dark, above the Arctic Circle, and on an African safari. Golf is an adventure, and no matter how well or how poorly you play, it can bring you a lifetime of memories.

In the following pages you will discover some wondrous courses, in all types of settings all over the globe. We hope you are able to visit each and every one of them, because we think golf is an excuse for exploration. We also know that the point of exploration is to learn something, either about ourselves or our surroundings. Similarly, to make the most of your golf travels, you should learn something about golf architecture. It is intrinsic to the history and development of the sport, and it will help you appreciate the spirit of the game and the spirit of exploration that comes with it.

But there are more selfish reasons to learn about golf course design.

As Greg Norman points out, understanding this topic will let you play better golf. This is even more important for the traveling golfer, because you'll be spending time and money to visit courses you've never played, or even seen, before. In these cases your only substitute for experience is understanding the architect's intent.

However important scoring is to you, there is an even greater reason to learn a little about golf course design. Understanding what architects do, and which of them do it best, can help ensure that your next golf vacation is the best it can be. In a way, golf travel is like going to the movies. If you like most of Steven Spielberg's films, you'll probably like the next one he makes. It's no guarantee, but it improves your odds. Same thing with golf courses. Most people find they like the work of particular golf course designers, and dislike that of others. But just like movie directors, even the best golf course designers can't make hits all the time; they produce the occasional flop. So in addition to helping you find the best designer for you, this book helps you find his best courses to visit, so you won't waste precious time or money.

Golf is a game, and it is supposed to be fun. It is the most fun when you play a beautiful course you enjoy, and one that is suited for your game. Royal County Down in Northern Ireland, for instance, is one of the world's greatest courses, both beautiful and strategic. It is also extremely difficult. Very good players will absolutely love it, while high-handicappers would best be served visiting a gentler seaside links layout. The course is great, but it's not for everyone. The Stadium course at PGA West, on the other hand, is an expensive and very, very difficult course that is not fun for players of any ability. At the opposite end of the spectrum lies Pinehurst Number Two, a course that players of all skill levels will relish a round on. If you do not know what makes each of these courses suited for different types of players, how will you decide which one to visit? Or which one to skip?

We wrote this book so that you can plan and enjoy the very best golf vacations or simply play the best available golf when you travel. Our golf travel newsletter, *The Golf Insider*, has a simple motto: "If you play golf, play the best and skip the rest." There are so many courses out there, you might as well play great ones all the time. But you cannot play them all.

For that reason, the hardest part in writing this book was not picking which designers and courses to include, but choosing which to leave out. An argument can be made that Mother Nature herself was the first golf course architect, carving out the sandy dunes along the Scottish coast with wind and sea, designing layouts such as the Old course at St. Andrews, the birthplace of golf, so that players simply had to pick out tee and hole locations and go have a game. Since then, thousands of people have tried to improve on Mother Nature, and while most have failed, many succeeded. But we did not include all of these success stories in this book. Why? Today about 90 percent of the golf courses being built in the United States are for public access, but this was not always the case. For much of the sport's formative years, almost all golf courses were private clubs. While private clubs in much of the world, including the United Kingdom, welcome visitors, most American private clubs do not. Since this book is about golf travel, we included the architects who designed courses you can play. Legendary architects such as A. W. Tillinghast and the design duo of Seth Raynor and C. B. Macdonald laid out some of the world's great courses, but most of us will never be able to play the vast majority of them, which are ultraprivate. And some of the most famous courses on earth, public or private, were designed not by golf course architects, but by lovers of the game who did little or no additional work. You won't find the fabled Pebble Beach Golf Links in the following pages. Its creator, Jack Neville, was a real estate salesman who never laid out another hole. Very private Pine Valley, widely ranked as the world's top course, was similarly designed by an unheralded hotelier name George Crump.

It was equally difficult to select the courses. Donald Ross alone put his name to more than 400 of them. We included five. Some are left out because frankly, even the best designers don't always do good work. But time has a funny way of changing golf courses, and few courses, especially older ones, are still the same today as their designers built them. Many Ross courses have been "renovated," often for the worse, leaving little of the original character. This happens to other designers as well. In other cases, some of the famous architects we've included have improved other people's work, and for the most part we omitted these, because it is usually impossible to tell where one designer stopped and another started. But the main reason we included the following courses is because they are very, very good, and they are accessible.

Make no mistake about it, this is a travel book, one that happens to be about golf and the design of the great courses you can visit. When most people travel, for any reason, they learn something in the process—something about history, or the arts or food or language. It is the same with golf. If you like to lie on the beach, you might take a vacation to whatever Caribbean island gives you the best deal, without caring about its culture, history, or atmosphere. In golf you can buy a package trip to Myrtle Beach or Scottsdale, and not care what courses you play, and still enjoy yourself and your game. But if you love golf and are the type of traveler who picks a particular destination for a reason, you should approach golf travel the same way, and this book is for you.

How to use this book

Some of the golf courses described in the following pages are at resorts, others are public courses with no associated lodging, and a handful are private or semi-private courses that allow guests to visit, albeit sometimes on a limited basis. In every case, we have included the necessary information to arrange a trip, including lodging suggestions either associated with the course or nearby. For courses located abroad, we have included additional information, such as recommended tour operators specializing in golf travel to the area. There is also information on how to get to the destination, the best time of year to go, other courses nearby that are profiled in this book, and statistical information on the courses, including yardage, slope, and course rating. These days, even the most remote golf courses in the most remote regions often have useful and informative Web sites, and we have included those Web addresses whenever possible.

There are two different—but equally useful—ways to take advantage of the information presented in this book. If you have played some of the courses we've profiled, find the ones that you enjoyed playing and read up on the architect who designed them. You will probably find that what you liked about the course is, at least in part, due to the designer's architectural style. You can then use the book to locate and plan trips to other courses he has designed.

Alternatively, if you are planning a trip to a particular destination, such as Scotland, northern California, Myrtle Beach, or elsewhere, you can use this book to research the courses that are in the area where you are going. Since almost all of the courses covered here are well above average quality, you can pick some "must-play" courses and build a wonderful golf trip around them.

More than one hundred golf courses are profiled in this book. When a featured course is mentioned elsewhere in the book, it is highlighted in italicized, boldface type. This indicates that you can read more about that course; refer to the alphabetical index for the page number.

Rates

The following symbols are used to describe the cost of greens fees. The listed price is always based upon the highest rate, typically for high-season weekends. In some regions, especially hot weather destinations that are crowded in the winter and deserted in the summer, rates can drop by more than 50 percent from those shown when playing at off-peak times. The value rating "V" indicates courses that are unusually inexpensive or offer exceptionally good quality golf for the fee it commands, which means the best courses can be good values even though they are expensive.

$	Greens fees less than $50
$$	$51-$100
$$$	$101-$150
$$$$	$150-$300
$$$$$	$300 and up
$$$$$+	Well in excess of $300, often indicating a course that also requires a hotel stay to play

There are almost 30,000 golf courses across the globe. None of us is ever going to play them all, so we might as well play the best. If you love golf, and you love travel, the world is your oyster, and this book will steer you to the pearls of the golf world. Hit 'em straight!

Larry Olmsted
Robert Pedrero
The Golf Insider

The Golf Insider is a newsletter devoted entirely to golf travel. Unlike traditional golf publications, we accept no advertising, and offer unbiased, firsthand evaluations of every course and resort. Each issue reviews not only established courses but also the latest new layouts. Written by the world's leading golf experts, the newsletter is designed to help you plan the golf adventures of a lifetime. Whether you are looking for a quick weekend getaway, a memorable family trip, or a pilgrimage to the game's hallowed grounds, The Golf Insider *can help (877-526-6331, www.thegolfinsider.com).*

ABCs of Golf Course Architecture

A s you read about the individual architects in the following pages, you will find descriptions of their styles, and of the way they used natural and human-made features ranging from trees, sand, grass, and rocks to deserts, oceans, and mountains. Most of this is self-explanatory if you play golf, but the following primer on golf course architecture will summarize the major elements, and provide definitions of the terms used in the book.

The world's first golf courses were seaside links courses in the British Isles. Every golf expert has a different opinion of what constitutes a so-called true links course, and these definitions are so divergent as to be worthless. The term itself derives from the land—linksland, the sandy soil left along the coast as the sea receded. Ironically, it was not the natural beauty of this coastal land that compelled the Scots to lay out golf holes here, it was the fact that this sandy acreage supported little useful vegetation and thus was of no value for agriculture, the mainstay of the local economy. The characteristics associated with links courses are sandy soil, dunes, fescue grasses, dry hard fairways and greens, and omnipresent wind. Another typical links course trait is an out-and-back routing—nine holes running away from the clubhouse and nine holes returning, with no more than two holes parallel to each other. While some purists think this is a vital design trait, it is more so by necessity than design. Linksland was typically narrow and followed the coast, and the golf course was laid out so as to avoid intruding into the more valuable interior land. Many older courses were built first as nine-hole designs, so it was natural to utilize the entire exposure to the ocean. When a second nine was added later, there was little choice but to return to the starting point. It is safe to say that not every course along the ocean is a links, and not every links course lies along the ocean.

It is a misperception among golfers who have never visited the British Isles that links courses offer stunning coastal settings. There is a

One of golf's most prolific designers, Robert Trent Jones Jr. has built courses all over the globe. ROBERT TRENT JONES II, LLC

big difference between coastal courses and clifftop layouts such as Pebble Beach. At almost all the great links, rows of sandy dunes and (in some cases) public beaches separate the course from the sea, which you often cannot see at any point during the round. You can sometimes hear the waves and taste the salt air, but the sea usually remains hidden from sight. Those expecting the crashing surf of Hawaii will surely be disappointed. Kingsbarns, a new course near St. Andrews that opened in 2000, made headlines because it was the first course in all of Scotland to offer ocean views from all eighteen holes.

On the earliest links courses, bunkers were not built—they were naturally occurring, usually dug by animals such as sheep seeking shelter from the wind, which is why small, deep "pot" bunkers are so prevalent in Scotland and Ireland. These were filled with sand simply because the soil

Golfing Terminology

A few terms used in the following pages may not be part of every golfer's lingo, so we have explained exactly what they mean.

Course Rating: The course rating is one of the two common measurements of the difficulty of a course, and is expressed as a potential golf score, such as 70 or 73.2. It indicates what a zero-handicap or "scratch" golfer should statistically expect to score when playing the rated set of tees (each set usually has a different course rating). Thus a player carrying a zero handicap and playing her best would expect, on average, to shoot even par on a par-72 course with a 72 rating. A par-72 course with a 75 rating is much more difficult, and zero-handicap players would be expected to shoot three strokes over par. The course rating allows all golfers to compare the relative difficulty of courses and is a much more accurate indication for players close to zero handicaps. For example, a course such as Pinehurst Number Two has very tricky greens, and better players who typically need only two putts per hole will often need three here. Less skilled players, however, often use three putts and will do so here as well, but their scores will not be higher than expected due to the increased difficulty.

Handicaps: Golf handicaps are usually positive numbers between 1 and 36, and refer to the number of strokes that a player typically exceeds par by when playing well. While the basis for handicaps varies with the difficulty of the course, in general terms, on an average course with a par of 72, a 15-handicap player will be expected to shoot an 87 when he is playing his best. Handicaps are used to make players equal in matches, so that when a 13-handicap plays an 18-handicap, the 13 gives the 18 a five-stroke scoring advantage prior to play so they begin the match on even footing.

Scratch player or scratch golfer: This is golf slang for a player who carries a handicap of zero, meaning that on a good day on an average course that player should shoot a score equal to par.

beneath the grass surface was sand. When golf courses began to be constructed inland, bunkers, which had become a characteristic hazard of the game, were artificially re-created.

At the end of the nineteenth century, the English began to build golf courses closer to the major cities and away from the coast, which yielded a form of design known as the parkland course. A few experts proclaim any course that is not a links course is a parkland design, but most of us agree that parkland has become its own distinct style. These courses are typically carved from woodlands, while seaside links are almost always devoid of trees. Since they have no coast to follow, parkland designs often have many parallel fairways, with holes being built in a back-and-forth routing rather than out-and-back nines. For instance, the first hole might play away from the clubhouse, the next hole back toward the clubhouse, and so on, and so

Shaped Shots: Most players do not hit the ball straight, they "hook" (curve left) or "slice" (curve right). Normally, this is an error. But better golfers can hit shots that curve left to right or vice versa on purpose, usually in order to get around a tree or another obstacle or to counteract the slope of the green. Such controlled curves are called shaped shots. Some designers lay out courses so that shaped shots are required occasionally to score well.

Shot Values: This refers to how much the golf course design requires players to hit more exacting shots, such as shaped shots or shots with an unusual degree of accuracy. For example, a wide open golf hole that allows the player to land anywhere in the fairway and then hit a straight approach to the green has low shot values. A hole that requires hitting a precise part of the fairway to open an angle onto the green and then favors a particular side of the green is said to have high shot values because each shot must be precise.

Single-digit player or single-digit handicapper: A player with a handicap between 0 and 10, considered a very good amateur golfer, but not as good as a scratch player. Single-digit players often opt to play the back tees, the longest and most difficult set. The industry average handicap is in excess of 18.

Slope Rating: This is the other indication of difficulty and is aimed at the higher-handicap player. While scratch players and single-digit handicappers will find the course rating useful, "average" players can use the slope rating to judge how difficult a course will be for them from a particular set of tees. The slope rating is a three-digit number, such as 132. It is derived from a complicated formula, but it expresses the relative difficulty of a course for an 18-handicap player, which is approximately the industry average. The higher the slope rating, the more difficult the course, and in broad terms, a slope rating under 120 is low or easy, 120 to 130 is normal, and over 130 is more difficult, with most slope ratings ranging from about 110 to 155. So while exceptionally skilled players should look at the course rating to compare courses, the average player should use the slope.

on. Parkland courses are usually built on more traditional heavier soil, but some of the best are built on linkslike sand. These were the first courses that were truly designed, allowing architects complete creative control and making more use of creeks and other water hazards. Since the United States has far more terrain suited to parkland golf than links golf, the creation of the inland design, credited largely to Willie Park in England, ushered in what is now known as the Golden Age of Golf Course Design in this country.

Another type of course is the heathland, which is a cross between links and parkland, built inland on sandy alluvial soil with some vegetation—most notably shrubs and pine trees, but not hardwoods. For those who classify heathland courses separately from parkland, Pinehurst Number Two would fit this description, as would Pine Valley, the famed sandbelt courses of Melbourne, Australia, and some of the more famous English inland courses such as Sunningdale. Whatever terms you prefer, it has become clear that the vast majority of the world's best courses, coastal or inland, are built on sand.

Great designers such as Greg Norman can visualize a course routing by exploring the existing land. GREAT WHITE SHARK ENTERPRISES INC.

In the 1920s the advent of the steam shovel and other motorized earthmoving equipment gave designers far more latitude in what they could do and launched what we call the modern age of golf course design. Some believe this continues today, although we consider Robert Trent Jones Sr. and his contemporaries in the 1940s, 1950s, and 1960s as the modern designers, and those since the 1970s as postmodern. Whether you agree or not, the evolution of earthmoving equipment, along with substantial technological advances in irrigation, drainage, and agronomy, allowed designers to tackle styles of courses previously unheard of—most notably desert golf—or to re-create other styles of design in locations unsuited for them by nature. Perhaps the ultimate expression of postmodern design is Tom Fazio's Shadow Creek, a traditional Carolinas-style parkland design that is very heavily wooded and hilly but was built at great expense on a flat desert tract in Las Vegas, both beautiful and completely artificial to the region. Some find it the consummate image of humanity's conquest of nature, others an expensive gimmick, but it is without doubt a beautiful golf course.

From the player's point of view, the biggest change in golf as it moved from the shores of Scotland to the forests, deserts, and prairies of the United States was the flight path of the ball. Because of the often strong wind, players in the British Isles developed a style of play favoring low ball flight, keeping the ball out of the wind whenever possible. Early golf course architecture reflected this, almost always allowing a safe path to the green along the ground. This encouraged "bump-and-run shots," which landed well short of the green and bounced or rolled onto the putting surface. Once earthmoving was introduced, and with it water hazards, the higher-ball-flight American-style game gained popularity. On the country's more common parkland courses, where wind is less of an issue, shots are flown all the way to the green, landing from a high trajectory. While most of us who learn the game in the United States develop this target-oriented style, it is important to remember that the best golf course designs reward multiple strategies; to score well, it is best to have as many different shots that produce the same result as possible, so that hazards, wind, or water can be negotiated.

Important Architectural Terms

Aiming bunkers: Sand traps placed in the fairway so far from the tee that they cannot be reached, whose purpose is to frame the fairway and give a line off the tee. When in doubt, if a bunker is too far to reach, aim at it, and you will seldom find yourself in a bad position.

Arroyo: Streambeds, often dry, found in the desert and canyons of the American Southwest, forming ditchlike natural hazards.

Blind shot: A situation where the player cannot see the target and has to hit blindly, usually over an obstacle such as a ridge or mound.

Bulkheading: Whereas natural lakes and ponds typically run right up to the edge of the fairway, human-made bodies of water often sit below it, requiring some sort of edge to contain the water and keep the ground from eroding toward it. The most obvious form of bulkheading is the use of vertical wooden slats or railroad ties, but rocks are often used as well.

Championship course: A term that unfortunately holds little meaning today. In the British Isles many famous clubs had two courses—a championship layout where tournaments and club contests were held, and an easier course. This is the case at Royal County Down, Royal Troon, Lahinch, and many others, and the designation meant something. It could also refer to a place where important tournaments such as the Amateur Championship were held. Today it is strictly a marketing term meant to impress traveling golfers. It implies that a course is of the caliber to host such tournaments, even though it doesn't, which often is untrue. This term should be ignored when reading travel promotional materials.

Crowned greens: Putting greens that are higher in the middle than the edges, encouraging balls to roll off them if not landed in the center.

Desert golf: Just as every seaside course is not a links, not every layout in the desert is a desert course. Before water restrictions, architects built grassy parkland layouts in the desert just like anyplace else. Desert courses are the newer versions that use a limited amount of grass and incorporate the barren desert surroundings in play.

Dogleg: A hole that bends, usually in the shape of an elbow, rather than just offering a straight fairway from tee to green. Usually a dogleg left or right, but the occasional par-5 is a double dogleg that bends first one way, then the other, creating an S- or Z-shaped fairway.

Elevated green: When the approach to the green is uphill, so that the putting surface is well above the location from which shots are played to it. Also called a tabletop green.

Elevated or plateau fairways: Fairways that are raised above the surrounding rough or waste area; if your shot misses one or rolls off it, you'll play the ball from below the level of the fairway.

Flashed bunkers: Sand hazards that end right at the fairway and are typically shallow and flat—as opposed to the more traditional style, which is deeper, is surrounded by mounding, and has a raised lip. Flashed bunkers are often more visually dramatic.

The hottest young designer in golf, Tom Doak made Pacific Dunes the most important course to be built in this country in decades.

Forced carry: A design requiring you to play a shot over a penal hazard of a certain distance. If a lake sits in front of the tee, for instance, you'll need sufficient length to reach the fairway.

Fringe: The narrow band of transition between the very short grass of the putting surface and the higher grass of the fairways or rough.

Gorse: A thick, thorny bush common in the British Isles, which flowers brilliant yellow in the summer yet swallows balls mercilessly.

Grass bunker: A depression filled with grass rather than sand.

Grasses: Several different types of grasses are found on golf courses, which directly affect play. Fescue is the traditional links grass and has a short, close-knit blade system, resulting in a hard surface that makes the balls travel farther; still, it can be harder to hit off for those unfamiliar with it. Bent grass is the typical grass found in the United States north of the snowbelt and is widely considered the best choice, especially for greens, where it rolls true according to the slope of the ground with little interference from grain. Bermuda grass is a spongy surface found in nearly all warm-weather climates and the Tropics. It's very beautiful to the eye but grows in a particular direction and thus has distinct grain, which affects putts—sometimes so dramatically that they can break uphill. There are many different species of all these grasses.

Green complex: The putting surface and the area around it that affects play. This usually includes greenside bunkers, sand, or grass. The most common use is with an elevated green, where the surrounding bunkers, slopes, and hillocks all form a complex that leaves players who miss the green itself on a slope, or in a hollow or hazard.

Heather: A low, thick ground cover, often tinted purple, that is found throughout the British Isles and elsewhere. Balls disappear into heather without a trace.

Heroic design: A type of architecture that bridges the penal and strategic schools of design in that the player must choose how much of a hazard to carry in order to maximize benefit. An example is the eighteenth hole at Pebble Beach, where golfers hit their tee shots across the water to a fairway curving away; the longer the carry, the closer they get to the green, producing a shorter second shot.

Limited-turf design: A newer style of course, derived from desert golf, which minimizes the amount of grass used, often by separating the tees and fairways with waste area and replacing the rough with waste area. The less grass is used, the less expensive and easier a course is to maintain.

Penal Design: An architectural style in which errant shots are lost, without the opportunity for recovery. The famous seventeenth hole at the TPC Sawgrass, with its island green, is the ultimate example of penal design: There is no option but to play to the green, and missing incurs a penalty.

Peninsula green: A green set on a point of land jutting into a water hazard, so that shots missing it on three sides are lost.

Redan: The most famous style of hole, a par-3, usually relatively long (190 or more yards) with a green set diagonally to the line of play from front right to back left and a deep bunker in the front on the left side. This allows both multiple pin positions of varying difficulty and numerous risk-reward options for the player, who can opt to always play to the center, always play to the safe front edge, or play for the pin. The hole gets progressively more difficult as the pin is moved back and left, since it both gets longer and brings the bunker into play. When the hole is set up with the green running left to right, and the bunker on the right, it is known as a reverse redan. The original redan is found at Scotland's North Berwick, but the hole has been replicated on hundreds of courses.

Routing: The layout or path of the holes that constitute the course. This path can be "out and back," with nine holes away and nine holes returning, or two distinct loops, a front nine and back nine, both of which start from and return to the clubhouse. It can also be a non-returning layout that does not go out and back, but wanders.

Shaved collar: A style of green that has no fringe; instead, where the fairway or rough is at the same height as the putting surface, allowing balls to be putted from well off the green.

Strategic design: A school of architecture emphasizing the importance of placing shots in certain specific locations, not just in the fairway, and often offering more than one approach to play a hole, with risk-reward options. For instance, a dogleg par-5 that can be reached in 2 by a long tee shot over a hazard at the bend is a strategic hole, because you can choose between two distinct routes of varying risk and reward.

Target golf: A style of play and design made popular in the desert, where grass is planted sparingly and, as a result, players hit lofted shots from one target to the next—from tee to fairway to green—all of which are typically separated by the hazards of raw desert. Target golf can be found anywhere, such as on an island hole in a lake, where the penalty for missing the target is severe and the ball must be flown, not rolled, to the target.

Tiers: Greens that are divided into more than one level with a severe slope between them, creating the effect of a set of steps. Most typical are two- or three-tiered greens. Because landing on a different tier from the hole means putting up or down a severe slope, multitiered green put an emphasis on precise distance control on the approach shot—landing on the wrong tier often results in 3 putts, or more.

Waste area: An open expanse of sand or rocky soil, sometimes with some grass growing in it, that is not a bunker but rather a surface, used in lieu of either fairway or rough. These are usually found between the tee and the front edge of the fairway, or parallel to the fairway where rough would normally be found. Unlike bunkers and other hazards, it is legal to ground a club during practice swings in a waste area.

The Forefathers

Golf course design evolved over hundreds of years, and new trends and even entirely new styles continue to develop to this day. Innovators were defined not by the years they lived in, but rather by what effect their designs had on the game. Those who developed the major architectural styles and elements we take for granted today were the forefathers of golf course design. They laid the foundation for the architects who followed in their footsteps, and in the most sincere form of flattery, their work is regularly copied today.

The forefathers stretch from Old Tom Morris, who laid out many of the great links courses of the British Isles with nothing but hand labor, to Robert Trent Jones Sr., who ushered in the modern era and—for better or worse—commercialized golf course design, changing the nature of the game forever. In between were Donald Ross and Stanley Thompson, who popularized the game in the United States and Canada, respectively. Alister MacKenzie took an academic approach to golf course design and revolutionized strategic play, while Harry Colt mastered parkland golf and spread the game throughout England, setting the stage for an American golf course revolution.

Every one of the courses described in the following section is a classic in the truest sense of the word, from the most revered links of Scotland and Ireland to heathland gems Down Under and historic tournament venues in the States. They are, for the traveling golfer, the stuff that dreams are made of.

Honorable Mention

Some other notable designers who helped develop the game include:

Willie Park. Credited with inventing the parkland style of inland course, Park did not build many courses, yet by taking the game far from the sea he opened up much of the landlocked world to golf. His greatest masterpiece that you can visit is England's Old course at *Sunningdale* outside London.

A. W. Tillinghast. A masterful designer who spearheaded the Golden Age of American Golf and built some of the finest private courses and tournament venues in the United States, including both courses at Winged Foot in New York, the San Francisco Golf Club, and New Jersey's fabled Baltusrol. For the traveling golfer, Tillinghast's pinnacle work is his series of courses at Bethpage State Park on New York's Long Island, perhaps the finest collection of municipal courses in the nation, highlighted by Bethpage Black, site of the 2002 U.S. Open and one of the game's great bargains.

C. B. Macdonald and **Seth Raynor.** This formidable design team secured a page in golfing history by building the nation's first eighteen-hole course, the Chicago Golf Club, and what is considered the nation's first strategic design, the National Golf Links on Long Island. Macdonald studied in Scotland, visited all the great links courses, and, after returning to the States, incorporated the best features of the British Isles, regularly re-creating redans and other classic holes he loved from his travels. Unfortunately, the vast majority of this duo's work is private. The finest examples you can play are the Yale University course in New Haven, Connecticut, and the fantastic Mid-Ocean Club in Bermuda.

Old Tom Morris (1821–1908)
The Father of Golf Course Architecture

The first renowned golf course architect, Old Tom Morris—whose name distinguished him from his famous son, Young Tom—set the stage for the name-brand designers we have today. Like most golf professionals of his time, Old Tom was a club maker by trade, a player by passion, and became a designer because of his keen understanding of the game. He played in the first thirty-six British Opens, including many at the Prestwick course he mostly designed, winning the championship four times; he remains the oldest player ever to do so. More than just a famous professional or designer, he is regarded by many Scots as the father of golf itself, so much did he do to popularize the game. He was the premier club maker in St. Andrews, where he lived most of his life, and is revered there to this day. His knowledge was coveted, and various club membership committees paid to have him come lay out their courses. At the time Old Tom the designer commanded the rate of one pound per day, plus expenses.

Playing the Fabled Links

As a designer, Morris did little to impress current critics, and it can be argued that he barely delved into the finer points of golf course design, because it was the fashion at the time to place tees and greens such that the "fairway" was the natural valley between rows of sandy dunes. Nonetheless, he designed or renovated seventy-five courses in his lifetime, a stunning number considering how few there were, and his creations include many of the game's greatest venues. In Old Tom's day there was only coastal links golf, and due to his fame, he had the choicest locations to work with. One reason he does not enjoy more respect among critics is that all of his courses have been renovated or tampered with, to varying degrees. But the spectacular settings and, in many cases, the basic routings remain intact. The natural features he made wide use of remain, so that when you play one of these fabled links, you can expect to find certain things:

- **Difficult par-3s.** It may be that Old Tom himself was not long off the tee and was a poor putter, so it was to his advantage to use his accuracy on these types of holes. Or it may have been the demands of the natural terrain where he worked. Whatever the reason, golfers who look for 1-shotters as a reprieve will not find them on most Morris designs.

- **Blind shots.** These were more common on older links to begin with, but Morris seemed to use them wherever possible. His masterpiece at Royal County Down has several tee shots over blind ridges; his courses include some of golf's most famous blind par-3s, such as the Himalayas at Prestwick and the Dell at Lahinch, not to mention the blind approach on the famed Alps at Prestwick.

MORE THAN JUST A FAMOUS PROFESSIONAL

OR DESIGNER, HE IS REGARDED BY MANY

SCOTS AS THE FATHER OF GOLF ITSELF, SO

MUCH DID HE DO TO POPULARIZE THE GAME.

- **Small, domed greens.** Although not to the degree used by his famous protégé Donald Ross, the style that has come to be attributed to Ross can be found first at Royal Dornoch, where Morris was designer and greenskeeper and Ross apprenticed.

- **Pot bunkers.** Again, Morris relied more on existing natural features than did the designers who came after him, and pot bunkers, which were the work of animals seeking shelter from the fierce winds, were often found on the land. But he used them well, especially the duo that make up the famous "spectacle" bunkers at Carnoustie.

Golf travelers who visit any of Old Tom Morris's better-known designs are in for what most avid players consider a once-in-a-lifetime treat, a pilgrimage to the great championship courses of the British Open Rota. This brings in two additional hazards that Old Tom had little control over: wind and rough. It is the nature of the rough in the British Isles to be untended, and on these layouts it regularly grows knee-high and thick. Howling winds can affect shots dramatically, in terms of both distance and direction. But one characteristic that many visitors do not expect and are grateful for is the dry fairways, which—despite ample rain—get rock hard by the popular summer tourist season, mostly from the wind. This translates into the longest tee shots many golfers will ever hit.

You will have to cross the Atlantic to play one of Old Tom's designs. For the traveling golfer this is much more a blessing than a curse.

PRESTWICK GOLF CLUB, *Prestwick, Scotland*

Host of more British Opens than any other course, quirky Prestwick breathes history.

If Prestwick were built today, it would almost certainly be deemed gimmicky. But it was not built today, and the course has history on its side. Prestwick hosted the very first British Open, and for decades this tournament was held only here. Although Prestwick is now deemed too short for today's long-hitting pros and is not on the Rota of British Open courses, it has still hosted the event more times than any other course. Old Tom himself won the Claret Jug here on multiple occasions.

There are those who like their golf neat and clean with no surprises, and for them, Prestwick is unsettling with its blind shots, huge bunkers, and odd holes. But nowhere is there more ample proof that golf has no right or wrong or grand design, and in the same tradition of the game that dictates *Play it as it lies*, Old Tom laid out his holes as the land lies—and a spectacular piece of land it is.

The course is not long, but it demands accurate placement, and on many tees, beginning with the very first, an iron can be a smart play. The famous holes begin with three, which features the immensely huge and deep Cardinal bunker, which was among the first to be bulkheaded with

Bring a Tie

If you go to play Prestwick, it is almost as important that you bring a jacket and tie as your clubs. While some Open venues, most notably the uptight and overrated Royal Troon nearby, relegate visitors to a cafeteria-like section of the clubhouse, at Prestwick you are welcomed to lunch in the Captain's Room—as long as you are properly dressed. This is an event worth visiting for in and of itself. One large table is shared by members and visitors alike, with the gregarious former regaling the latter with colorful stories of the club. Prestwick is not stuffy in the least, and if all you have is a golf shirt, you will still eat, drink, and play well . . . you just won't make it to the big table.

railroad ties—an innovation often credited to Pete Dye a century later, who revived the tradition. The Bridge, a par-4 that doglegs around a creek (or *burn* to the Scots), has earned a reputation as one of the best, if not the best, risk-reward par-4s on the planet. It offers two distinct routes to the green, a short risky one or a much longer and eminently safe path. Himalayas is a totally blind par-3 playing 206 yards over a series of high hills guarding the green; the Wall is a long par-5 with a blind third shot over its towering namesake ridge. The oddest hole of all is an original Tom Morris work, the Alps, a par-4 with a blind approach that must carry not just the mountain in front of the green but also the hidden trap beyond it— so vast that it is known as the Sahara bunker.

It is these unique holes, one after another, that make Prestwick one of the most fun and memorable courses in the British Isles. The traveler will find that it offers other advantages. It is among the most welcoming of the famed Scottish courses to guests, and certainly the least pretentious of such historical stature. Tee times are always allotted on an odd basis in the United Kingdom, with certain times reserved for two-ball and four-ball matches. But the green fees allow unlimited play, and if tee times are available it is possible for speedy players to play a full three rounds—fifty-four holes—given the late Scottish summer sunset. Few courses are so rewarding to play more than once in a row, and it is worth the effort. While Prestwick has no women members or women's tees, it does allow female play, and women are encouraged to tee it up from wherever they see fit. For first-time visitors, more than at any other venue save the Old course at St. Andrews, a caddie is a must.

+44 1292-477-404, www.prestwickgc.co.uk

Golf Course Info: No practice area, caddies, walking only.

$$$ (unlimited daily play), 6,544–6,678 yards, one tee.

Lodging Info: Prestwick is a small town but offers a full array of dining and lodging choices. The top choice in the area is the luxurious full-service Turnberry resort (twenty minutes away), one of the top golf resorts in the world, with two courses of its own, including the famed Ailsa, another British Open venue and the finest of all the Scottish seaside courses (800–WESTIN–1, www.turnberry. co.uk).

Getting There: Prestwick has its own small airport with limited service from London, but most international visitors arrive via Glasgow.

When to Go: Golf is played year-round; summer is high season, but spring often has the best weather in Scotland, where it can and does rain any time of year.

European Travel Tips: Like many top courses in the British Isles, Prestwick is technically a private club and has limited tee times daily for visitors. It can be quite arduous to arrange your own itinerary: The time difference and international calling can make it difficult to contact many European courses, each has certain days reserved for competitive member play, and some have days reserved for women members. For this reason, many travelers make all their tee time, lodging, and transportation arrangements in the U.K. through specialized golf tour companies, of which the best are Perry Golf (800–344–5257, www.perry golf.com) and Wide World of Golf (800–214–GOLF, www.wideworldofgolf.com).

Golf Travel by Design Courses Nearby: Muirfield (ninety minutes); Eden course at St. Andrews (two hours).

ROYAL COUNTY DOWN, *Newcastle, Northern Ireland*

Considered by some experts to be the finest golf course on earth, this beautiful but very challenging test demands the ability to hit every shot in golf.

The courses of Northern Ireland are beautiful and enjoy arguably the finest golfing coastline in the British Isles, but among even this elite group Royal County Down stands out. There is something magical about the setting, with the stunningly beautiful mountains and sea linked by rolling hillsides of emerald-green grass, yellow gorse, purple heather, and white sand. It is often said that nature herself designed the best old links courses, but nowhere is nature felt as strongly as at Royal County

The Ultimate Test

More than one expert has called Royal County Down the ultimate test of golf. It is about as difficult and demanding as a course can be without crossing the line into unfair. To make pars here, you have to be both long and straight off the tee *and* able to hit a variety of approach shots—including long irons and fairway woods, often with a particular shape. For this reason, very good players love the course, which forces them to hit a wide variety of shots and execute time and time again in a stunning setting.

Down, which has a raw, almost primal atmosphere. It seems as if the tees and greens were simply placed in available spots in the dramatic rolling setting; everything else serves as an almost insurmountable obstacle to scoring.

Low-handicap players love the course because it requires a precise outcome on every shot, and every shot is different. Players are called to hit it straight, long, high, low, and to shape shots on occasion, testing every facet of the game. Unlike some penal modern courses that are difficult for the sake of being difficult, there is a point to Royal County Down, a reward for playing the proper shot. At the same time, it is an extremely difficult course, one that many high-handicappers will not enjoy despite the physical grandeur of the setting—the base of Slieve Donard, the highest peak in the Mourne Range.

Even more than at other Morris designs, blind shots are called for often, usually over aiming rocks placed on the heather- and gorse-covered ridges. Five holes require blind tee shots, including three of the first six; others require blind approaches. Gorse and thick rough, even by Irish standards, await those who stray from the very narrow fairways, which would be tough to hit even without the strong ocean winds. The 129 famed "eyelash" bunkers reflect the raw surroundings, with jagged edges and tall grass growing right into the bunker sand itself, making it possible to play a bunker shot here and escape from the rough at the same time. Old Tom Morris and Royal County Down take nature at its fiercest and most beautiful and throw it all at the traveling golfer looking for the ultimate test.

+44 1396-723-314

Golf Course Info: No practice area, walking only, caddies.

$$–$$$, 6,179–7,451 yards, three tees.

Lodging Info: $$–$$$. The large, modern Slieve Donard hotel next to the clubhouse features a pool, health club, pub, and restaurant (+44 2843–723–681, www.hastingshotels.com). A more intimate choice favored by visiting golfers in the know is the Glassdrumman Lodge, an upscale bed-and-breakfast serving a very fine dinner, twenty minutes away (+44 2844–768–585).

Getting There: Flying into Belfast (via London or Dublin) is the most convenient, but the majority of visitors fly into Dublin or Shannon and drive north.

When to Go: The best conditions can be found from mid-March through the end of October; in March and April the course is quite empty.

European Travel Tips: See Prestwick.

Golf Travel by Design Courses Nearby: Royal Portrush (two hours).

MUIRFIELD OLD COURSE, *Gullane, Scotland*

The most exclusive of the British Open venues is also the most balanced, with one fine hole after another.

Muirfield sits near Edinburgh on the Firth of Forth, the body of water nearly every golfer who visits Scotland crosses en route to St. Andrews, the birthplace of the game. But despite its convenient location, most skip over Muirfield, often in the misguided belief that it does not allow outside play. It does have one of the most restrictive policies of any British Open venue, but it is well worth the effort required to visit on a Tuesday or Thursday when some outside tee times are offered.

Muirfield is the home of the Honourable Society of Edinburgh Golfers, which is regarded by most experts as the oldest club in the world. The club was founded nearly a century and a half before its members enlisted Old Tom Morris to build Muirfield, having outgrown their former course. As a result, it became the first course besides Morris's Prestwick to host the British Open.

In true Morris style Muirfield is defended by tenacious bunkers, which sit amid natural bowls in the fairways to draw in shots landing near them. Fairways are on the narrow side, and the rough is quite thick by Scottish standards. What sets the course apart from other links is its unusual routing. Two circular nines are set within one another, so that all the holes are near the clubhouse. Also, no more than three consecutive holes ever play in the same direction; the frequent winds seem to change direction from hole to hole. All in all it is a very unusual links, parklandlike in character without the high sand dunes; many holes are in view at all times.

For those who dislike the blind shots common to Morris's designs, or the seemingly random and chaotic bounces intrinsic to links golf, Muirfield is quite a departure. It is recognized as being exceedingly fair, and while it has many subtleties, it welcomes first-timers and rewards a straightforward approach on nearly every hole. There are many apparent "shortcuts" that will lead greedy players into the ample bunkers, but those steering for the center of the fairway here will seldom regret it.

MUIRFIELD AT A GLANCE

+44 1620-842-977

Golf Course Info: Practice area, walking only, caddies.

$$$, 6,601–6,963 yards, two tees.

Lodging Info: $$. There are several choices in Gullane, but the traditional choice for visiting golfers is Greywalls, a small hotel with a good restaurant immediately adjacent to the course (+44 1620–842–144). The proximity to Edinburgh allows the option of staying in the city.

Getting There: Muirfield is just 20 miles from the Edinburgh airport.

When to Go: Golf is played year-round. Summer is high season, but spring often has the best weather in Scotland, where it can and does rain at any time of year.

European Travel Tips: See Prestwick.

Golf Travel by Design Courses Nearby: Eden course (forty-five minutes); Prestwick (ninety minutes).

LAHINCH OLD COURSE, *Lahinch, Ireland*

Near the stunning Cliffs of Moher, Lahinch anchors the southwest coast of Ireland, which has one of the best collections of fine golf courses in the world.

For many golf travelers, Lahinch is the first course they play on the Emerald Isle, mainly because it sits just half an hour from the Shannon airport. It would be worth a trip even if was much harder to get to, but it makes a wonderful spiritual—as well as geographical—welcome to links golf. This is because Lahinch is one of the easiest-to-navigate, least-punishing of the great seaside courses, one even a high-handicapper can love. It is Old Tom Morris's version of Pinehurst Number Two and Augusta, courses that are highly touted for their ability to please players all across of the ability spectrum.

The Easiest Ace in Golf?

More than one American visitor has returned home from Lahinch thinking that the luck of the Irish intervened in a round here. Local legend has it that some enterprising Lahinch caddies have an accomplice, usually a younger brother, wait secretly near the green on the Dell, the most famous blind par-3 in the world. The accomplice runs out from hiding after the player, inevitably an American tourist, has hit. The unseen accomplice places the ball in the hole, ensuring a hole-in-one and, accordingly, a larger tip.

Lahinch's gentle nature is due to a modest length, ample landing areas, and less fierce rough and bunkering than will be found at many older links. By no means uninspired, however, it has what is probably the most famous blind hole in all of golf: the par-3 sixth, known as the Dell. Here the green sits inside a natural amphitheater formed by a ring of mounds, which you hit over. Although no sign of the flagstick is visible from the tee, there is a white aiming rock on the top of the mound that is moved along with the pin position.

But before you reach the Dell, you have to conquer the equally compelling Klondyke, the par-5 fifth. This requires a drive down a narrow valley between tall dunes, in true links fashion. The unusual part is that the fairway is completely blocked 350 yards from the tee by a towering dune, requiring you to hit a blind long iron or fairway wood over the monstrous obstacle (or lay up in front of it and play for bogey). It is hard to avoid a letdown after two of the most spectacular back-to-back holes in golf, so the seventh hole's fairway offers up a huge, deep, rocky crater with a bunker at the very bottom—a bunker from which escape itself is worthy of celebration. The back nine is less unusual but no less fun, playing through a gorgeous sandy dunescape with occasional views of the ruins of a nearby castle.

Like many of the great links courses of the British Isles, including Morris's **Royal County Down** and **Muirfield,** Lahinch offers a second eighteen-hole course to relieve congestion. Like most such venues, the second or wee course is not in a league with the championship or Old course. In almost every case, with a few notable exceptions, the "second" course at these world-class venues should be skipped for another go at the main event.

+353 658–1003, www.lahinchgolf.com

Golf Course Info: Practice area, walking only, caddies.

$$, 5,497–6,735 yards, three tees.

Lodging Info: $–$$. Several small hotels are available nearby, the most full featured of which is the fifty-five-room Aberdeen Arms in Lahinch (+353 658–1100). Less than 30 miles from the Shannon airport sits one of Ireland's finest accommodations at Dromoland Castle, which also has its own rather mundane eighteen-hole course (+353 6136–8444).

Getting There: Lahinch is 30 miles from Shannon International Airport.

When to Go: Golf season is year-round, but the best weather is from April through November. Renovations are often undertaken in early spring.

European Travel Tips: See Prestwick.

Golf Travel by Design Courses Nearby: Ballybunion New course (sixty minutes); Doonbeg (thirty minutes).

ROYAL DORNOCH, *Dornoch, Scotland*

The northernmost of the world's great links courses, where Old Tom Morris passed on his secrets to protégé Donald Ross, who would become the Father of American Golf.

There are still some hidden gems among the coastal courses of the British Isles, but most of the famed and revered links receive heavy outside play from traveling golfers. An exception is Royal Dornoch, which still evades most golfers' itineraries due to its seemingly remote location, although it can be easily incorporated with a visit to St. Andrews. Dornoch lies on Scotland's rugged northeast coast, 60 miles beyond Inverness, the nearest city of any size.

It is obvious to any Dornoch visitor familiar with Pinehurst Number Two that Donald Ross borrowed a page in his design ideology from this course, where the greens are elevated atop natural plateaus, making them hard to hold. This, plus an uncharacteristic lack of bunkering, a short length, and wide-open fairways, gives Dornoch the same qualities intrinsic to Ross's famed Number Two: It welcomes and entertains players of all abilities while challenging the best to score well. In fact, the dramatic plateau green on Foxy, Dornoch's most famous hole, the fourteenth, has been replicated by both Ross and other U.S. designers. But unlike the wooded Carolinas, this is true linksland. The first eight holes run straight out along bluffs, with several along the sea. It is a traditional links routing that is awe-inspiring to see. If you undertake the journey to Royal

While most links courses are separated from the sea by dunes, Royal Dornoch runs right to the water's edge. LARRY OLMSTED

Dornoch, you will find the most user-friendly links course in Scotland—and at less than 6,300 yards from the championship tees, even high-handicappers will remember it fondly.

Although only about four hours from St. Andrews, the absence of a nearby town and the wild coast give Dornoch the air of a wilderness. Indeed, another of its unique traits is that the weather here is even more unpredictable than in the rest of Scotland, with the usual high winds but also very rapid changes, making it possible to play in sun, rain, sleet, fog, and sun again, all in nine holes.

ROYAL DORNOCH AT A GLANCE

+44 1862–810–219

Golf Course Info: Practice areas, walking only, caddies.

$$, 5,552–6,271 yards, three tees.

Lodging Info: $–$$. Dornoch is a small town, and the only choice of note is the Dornoch Castle hotel, with just seventeen rooms (+44 1862–810–216). A more unusual nearby option for high rollers is Skibo Castle, where singer Madonna held her lavish wedding in 2000. Although a private club, Skibo allows outside guests one visit as nonmembers, and the nightly rate of about 1,000 pounds per couple includes deluxe lodging, all meals, drinks, and activities, including use of Skibo's fine Donald Steel–designed eighteen-hole course (+44 1862–894–600).

Getting There: Dornoch is most easily coupled with St. Andrews, about a four-hour drive to the south. It is nearly six hours from the Edinburgh airport.

When to Go: Golf season is year-round, but the best weather is from April through November. Due to its northern location, the course has more varied

Not Quite the End of the Road

For years Royal Dornoch has been considered the most remote of the great Scottish courses, at least on the mainland. Offshore island courses such as Old Tom's Machrihanish can be even more difficult to reach, yet Dornoch, on the northeastern coast several hours beyond St. Andrews, has been too far out of the way for many American visitors. But soon it will seem close in comparison to the new Cape Wrath golf club, another 60 miles up the coast, at the end of the country. Cape Wrath is the latest public project from Mike Keiser, the owner of Bandon Dunes, whose theory is that if you can build a good enough course, people will come no matter how remote it is. So far he has been right.

weather than elsewhere in Scotland, although temperatures are not appreciably lower.

European Travel Tips: See Prestwick.

Golf Travel by Design Courses Nearby: None.

ROYAL NORTH DEVON/WESTWARD HO!,
Devon, England

England's first links course is a living museum, virtually unchanged since the routing was completed.

I f you somehow visited the Old course at St. Andrews without knowing where you were, you would be quite unimpressed at first glance. Until you get out on the course and unravel its secrets—the multiple options on almost every hole, the hidden bunkers and deceptively eager burns—it appears flat and featureless. Much the same can be said for England's oldest links course, Royal North Devon, also named Westward Ho!

The course occupies a vast treeless expanse, which immediately distorts spatial perception. Hidden amid this seemingly open plain are a unique variety of obstacles, including treacherous bunkers, unseen ditches, and wee burns (creeks). The most memorable hazard is one reminiscent of

Morris's Cardinal bunker at Prestwick. The large and deep Cape bunker blocks the fairway on the fourth hole and must be carried, wooden bulkhead and all, from the tee.

Living hazards include the most livestock you will ever encounter on a course, mostly sheep and horses; the course occupies common land and is open to grazing. A more nefarious resident will be found on the back nine. Great sea rushes are a unique type of wild grass that can grow 6 feet high and sport rock-hard spikes that have been known to actually puncture golf balls. The rushes are used in lieu of rough on the first few holes of the back nine, except that a ball hit into them might as well be lost.

Westward Ho! remains a mystery even to those who have played it, and features many strategic subtleties that only time and patience will discover. At the same time, it is good fun for players of all abilities the very first time out, because there are few intimidating driving holes. It is very resistant to scoring—in its first century of existence, members managed to better par on only four occasions—yet it is more tricky than overpowering. It is also one of the great bargains of the United Kingdom, with weekday green fees well under the $50 mark.

ROYAL NORTH DEVON AT A GLANCE

+44 1237-473-817

Golf Course Info: Practice areas, walking only, caddies.

$, 5,650–6,590 yards, three tees.

Lodging Info: $$. The most convenient choice is the Culloden House hotel, located near the course (+44 1237–479–421).

Getting There: Westward Ho! is surprisingly hard to reach, located 60 miles from Plymouth, the nearest sizable city. It sits on England's extreme southwestern tip, not far from Land's End.

When to Go: Golf season is year-round, and the weather is considerably milder than in Scotland or the north, although it remains quite windy and occasionally receives heavy rain. Spring through fall is the best time to visit.

European Travel Tips: See Prestwick.

Golf Travel by Design Courses Nearby: None.

Other notable Old Tom Morris courses you can play

- **Carnoustie (Open course),** Angus, Scotland
- **Nairn,** Nairn, Scotland
- **Machrihanish,** Campbeltown, Scotland
- **Crail,** Crail, Scotland

Donald Ross (1872–1948)
The Father of American Golf Design

Although born in Scotland, Donald Ross did not begin designing golf courses until he immigrated to the United States, where he quickly became the preeminent golf course architect of his time. This was no easy feat, as he lived and worked through what is known as the Golden Age of American Golf Architecture. But both the quality and quantity of Ross's work (there are a staggering 413 courses attributed to him) make him the premier golf course designer in American history. While his peers worked mainly on private country club layouts, Ross pioneered high-quality public golf at resort settings such as Pinehurst, the Broadmoor, and the Sagamore. As a result, traveling golfers today have the ability to enjoy his work more than that of his contemporaries.

Both Extremely Challenging and Extremely Fair

Ross learned his trade as an assistant greenskeeper at Scotland's Royal Dornoch and apprenticed with the Father of Golf Course Design, Old Tom Morris himself. Ross then set out for America to make his fortune, and shortly after his arrival was hired by visionary developer James Walker Tufts to assist with the expansion of the Pinehurst resort in North Carolina. The rest is golf history. Ross lived his entire adult life in Pinehurst, creating new courses and fine-tuning his existing ones, but the demand for his services carried him throughout North America.

More than any other designer, Ross's layouts have extremely broad appeal to all types of players. Time and again he managed to walk the finest line in golf architecture, crafting routings that were not daunting on the surface and thus fun for lesser players, yet still challenged the world's best golfers to score well. Anyone can make a difficult golf course, but only the most talented designers can create a course that is both extremely challenging and extremely fair. No public course is as good an example of this balance as Ross's masterpiece, Pinehurst Number Two. It is for this reason that the course continually makes the Top Ten list of almost every golf publication. From a travel perspective Number Two is a true must-play course that resides at the grandest of all American golf resorts. From a design perspective it is a masterpiece, showcasing all the traits Ross is known for. Almost every designer has trademarks, but few are as recognizable as Ross's. These include:

- **An easy opening hole.** Ross knew that golfers were often unprepared to hit a heroic shot off the first tee, where they may have arrived harried or unable to warm up properly. He felt the first hole should provide this warm-up, welcoming the player to the course in good spirits. In many cases his first was the course's easiest, but at the very least it would be of moderate length, with a wide, receptive landing area, and an absence of penal hazards.

BUT BOTH THE QUALITY AND QUANTITY OF

ROSS'S WORK MAKE HIM THE PREMIER GOLF

COURSE DESIGNER IN AMERICAN HISTORY

- **Bunkering as the hazard of choice.** As a member of the strategic, rather than penal, school of design, Ross presented hazards that could be seen and avoided with well-struck shots. But in the event that these hazards were not skirted, they would allow an opportunity for a heroic recovery or—in the worst case—cost the player one, not two shots. For this reason, his courses are amply bunkered but tend to lack water, thick rough, and other ball-swallowing hazards.

- **Shotmaking variety.** Ross believed a quality course should "call for long and accurate tee shots, accurate iron play, precise handling of the short game and, finally, consistent putting. These abilities should be called for in a proportion that will not permit excellence in any one department of the game to largely offset deficiencies in another." In other words, his courses were meant to require every shot in the bag. Big hitters could not overpower the course, and short-game wizards could not steal par. For this reason, when you play a Donald Ross course you will usually find a wide variety of tee shots, hole lengths, and approach angles. He does not hesitate to design par-5s that suggest an iron layup off the tee or build greens so that they can only be approached successfully from one side of a deceptively wide fairway. When playing Ross courses, do not assume that a par-4 or even -5 automatically requires hitting a driver. Look at the way the hole is shaped; playing from the correct side of the fairway is often more important than length.

- **Small, domed greens.** No other facet of Ross's design aesthetic is as well documented as his demanding greens, which are often described as "inverted saucers" or "turtle backs." While the stereotypical mental image of a Ross green is a circle that is higher in the middle than anywhere else, falling off to the edges in every direction, this is a bit of an oversimplification. Ross did indeed use such designs liberally, but he had many variations, including more standard oval or kidney-shaped greens that would be divided into two parts by a "hogback" ridge. He often honored his Scottish roots by leaving the front of the green open and accessible, flush with the fairway, to welcome a running shot. In these cases it's the back and sides that fall away dramatically, punishing shots hit long more than those left short. Rather than adding extensive greenside sand bunkers, Ross often chose simple grass bunkers or hollowed-out collection areas, thereby leaving tricky chips, pitches, and putts back to the putting surface.

In all these cases, what Ross was doing was reducing the effective target area of the green, a mental and optical trick. In the case of the pure domed greens, only shots hit to the center would hold, regardless of pin locations. Those that missed this bull's-eye would roll off, because the green sloped downward in all directions. The divided hogback-ridged greens called for the player to hit the side the pin was on in order to have a reasonable chance to 2-putt.

Ross's trademark green complexes are the key to the dichotomy of his designs. At Pinehurst Number Two the average player can spray a tee shot in a variety of directions without losing it. The approach shot looks straight-forward, but even when you hit the green, it rarely holds, resulting in what appears to be a "near miss." This empowers the high-handicapper, creating the illusion that you're constantly close to reaching greens in regulation and thus playing well. The truth is that most of the difficult greens require an approach shot from a particular angle, making precise placement of the tee shot important, as is a very accurate approach. Since even the best players can fail to hit these perfect shots back to back, low-handicappers find making pars more difficult than they are accustomed to. By employing these tricky greens, Ross ensures a memorable round for every player.

While many designers today use large, severely undulating greens to make putting more difficult, it is worth noting that Ross's greens were meant to challenge the approach more than the putt itself. They were built under the assumption that the speed of the green would remain constant, but technology has made putting surfaces faster, so Ross's greens appear more severe today than when they were built. If you're traveling to play Ross courses, the secret is to play to the center or most receptive part of the green, regardless of hole position, and take your chances putting rather than attacking the flag. The latter often results in a shot deflected away from the edges of the green.

Finally, golf travelers can expect two characteristics from Ross courses that are common to layouts of his era. Since most were built without motorized earthmoving equipment and had few homes on them, the courses are compressed, with tees close to the preceding greens, making them easy to walk. Second, a wide range of tee boxes were uncommon in that era, so women golf travelers will find that rather than playing the same hole from 100 yards up the fairway, they play farther back—but the par of the hole is often adjusted accordingly. This means that longer par-4s become par-5s for women. Many Ross courses boast pars of 74 or 75 from the forward tees.

Always Fun to Play

All of Ross's design elements result in one thing: courses that are fun to play. There are no shortages of well-designed courses that aim to punish poorly hit shots—the kind where a struggling golfer can lose a dozen balls and feel beaten up after a round. No matter how poorly you are playing, though, a Ross course will be less frustrating than most highly rated designs. While you may score just as badly, it will not take the high emotional toll of a tough penal layout.

The traveling golfer has ample opportunities to test Ross's domed greens—his layouts can be found at many top resorts, especially throughout New England and the Middle Atlantic states. When you visit a Donald Ross course, you are walking on American golf's hallowed ground. His courses have hosted large numbers of majors and amateur championships. Ross was a founder and the first president of the American Society of Golf Course Architects, and he remains the most admired in his field. The Donald Ross Society, which strives to preserve and restore his work, has some 1,200 members, including acclaimed designers such as Tom Doak and Jack Nicklaus. A recent movement toward historically accurate restoration of his layouts make many courses more authentic than they have been since Ross left us.

PINEHURST NUMBER TWO, *Pinehurst, North Carolina*

Rich in history and southern flavor, Pinehurst is the world's largest golf resort: eight courses under one roof—and two more on the way!

Only a handful of golf destinations transcend the game and achieve a level of spirituality visitors cannot help but get swept up in. The Old course at St. Andrews and Pebble Beach are two examples; each player coming down the fairway is walking in the footsteps of golf history. Pinehurst is another such place.

With eight eighteen-holes courses, a ninth under construction, and a tenth on the drawing board, Pinehurst is nothing less than the largest golf resort in the world. This is a case in which bigger *is* better, because the eight courses at Pinehurst include not just Donald Ross's seminal work but also some of the very best work of other top designers, including Rees Jones and Tom Fazio. While the courses here are indisputably parkland style, the defining factor at Pinehurst is the unusually sandy, well-drained soil, remarkably similar to terrain that makes the great seaside links courses of the British Isles so spectacular. Few inland sites in the world rival the sandhills of the Carolinas (as the area is known) for prime golf course territory. A weeklong visit is the minimum required to pay homage to the home of American golf, but if a shorter trip is all time allows, the must-play choice is Pinehurst Number Two (all the courses are numbered).

When Ross arrived, Pinehurst had most of its first course; he redesigned it, however, and Number One is now considered one of his designs. Number Two was the first course at Pinehurst he built from scratch. It has hosted more championships than any other in the United States and is a true championship venue, where bogeys come easily and birdies only with great effort.

Nonetheless, Ross's landmark is so well balanced that it is perhaps the easiest course in the world for a high-handicapper to play with a single ball—losing one is all but impossible. There is just one small water hazard on the course, and it is barely in play. The pine forests that line the fairways are simply pines, without a trace of underbrush or high grass in which to hide a ball. No matter how far you slice it into the trees, you'll find your tee shot sitting on a bed of dried pine needles, waiting to be extricated—at the cost of a wasted stroke. At first glance, Pinehurst Number Two suggests nothing of its greatness, appearing very ordinary. Yet from the receptive tee shot on the first hole, a Ross tradition, it reveals the trademarks of his work. Fairways are wide, but more than a hundred bunkers lie in wait. The green complexes are his most famous, and so tricky to chip onto that John

A Test for Champions

Many modern courses have intentionally been built long and tough from the back tees in the hope of attracting a tournament, while others simply grab for any marketing advantage and advertise themselves as "championship" designs, a meaningless term. But if one course can honestly claim the title, it is Pinehurst Number Two, which has hosted more important championships than any course in the United States. It is one of the only layouts to have hosted both of this country's traveling majors, the PGA Championship (in 1936) and the U.S. Open (in 1999). The course was also been the site of the 1951 Ryder Cup, the 1962 U.S. Amateur, the 1994 U.S. Senior Open, and several important regional amateur events. Number Two will again be the site of the U.S. Open in 2005.

Daly, after several foiled attempts to get his ball onto the putting surface, withdrew from the 1999 U.S. Open in midround. Fortunately for the traveling golfer, Pinehurst has one of the nation's best caddie programs; taking a caddie to help navigate Number Two is almost a prerequisite. He or she can point out the house Ross lived in, which still sits alongside his most treasured course.

Pinehurst's Number One and Number Three are also Ross designs, carved from the same sandy pine forest, but are much shorter and less stern tests, both with par of 70 and less than 6,000 yards (Number Two stretches 6,741). Both are rated most difficult from the women's tees. Number Four was also done by Ross, but it was so extensively renovated in 2000 by Tom Fazio that it now bears his name. While much of the Ross routing is intact, there are a few new holes, several more pot bunkers (bringing the total to a whopping 140), and a new lake. It features much more elevation change than the relatively flat Number Two. Besides Pinehurst, the region has three more Ross designs, the best of which is Pine Needles, recent host of the U.S. Women's Open. While featuring most of the Ross trademarks, it is unusual in its use of water hazards, a rarity on a Ross parkland course.

The other golf highlights at Pinehurst are Rees Jones's *Number Seven,* his first important solo effort, and Number Eight, or Centennial, the only course here with a name. Opened in 1996 to mark the resort's one hundredth birthday, it is one of the best routings by the top living architect, Tom Fazio. Numbers Five and Six are less heralded but solid par-72 designs. Ellis Maples's Number Five has the most water at the resort; Number Six sits on the most rugged, hilly terrain with thick vegetation and has the hardest nine holes here, the back side. Numbers Nine and Ten, both expected to open in 2003, will sit on property previously owned by the family of Robert Trent Jones Sr., 5 miles from the main clubhouse, and will anchor a new resort village with additional shops and restaurants.

Pinehurst is a huge resort, occupying more than 5,500 acres, and has much to offer beyond its 144 holes of golf. There is a large choice of lodging, including the classic Carolina Hotel, the largest property and the main building at the resort. There are also two smaller properties. The upscale Holly Inn is a seventy-five-room boutique property that opened back in the 1890s and was recently completely renovated. The Manor is a more casual forty-five-room country-style inn. Each of the properties has one or more restaurants and bars. Most guests at Pinehurst are on a Modified American Plan that includes breakfast and dinner at the many restaurants throughout the resort. Finally there are one-, two- and three-bedroom condos along the fairways of Number Three and Number Five, with full kitchens—perfect for either families or foursomes. All resort guests have equal access to the eight courses; other amenities include a world-class tennis center, stables, championship croquet courts, a 200-acre lake and beach, and a large, brand-new, state-of-the-art spa. The Pinehurst Advantage Golf School is one of the nation's best, and the resort is also home to a branch of the acclaimed Dave Pelz Scoring Game School. Before playing Numbers One through Five, which all radiate from the main clubhouse, golfers can warm up on Donald Ross's "Maniac Hill," believed to be the sport's first driving range.

The village of Pinehurst is a community that lives and breathes golf. It's located within the larger town of Southern Pines, which houses several more notable golf courses and additional shops and eateries. While the Carolinas are chock-full of quality golf courses, most are along the coast. Pinehurst sits in the interior highlands and is among the easiest of the game's elite resorts to get to. It is within driving distance of most of the East Coast, has a commuter airport right in town, is served by Amtrak, and has several larger airports within an hour. Golf is played year-round, but frost delays and occasional snow can occur in winter.

PINEHURST RESORT & CLUB AT A GLANCE

(800) ITS-GOLF, www.pinehurst.com

Golf Course Info: Practice area, caddies, walking allowed.

Number One: $$, 5,297–6,128 yards, three tees. *Slope rating* 115–117. *Course rating* 68.0–70.5.

Number Two: $$$$+, 5,035–6,741 yards, three tees. *Slope rating* 124–131. *Course rating* 69.6–72.8.

Number Three: $$, 5,232–5,682 yards, two tees. *Slope rating* 115–117. *Course rating* 67.2–69.9.

Number Four: $$$$, 5,217–6,658 yards, four tees. *Slope rating* 115–130. *Course rating* 67.8–72.1.

The opening hole of the Sagamore showcases Lake George behind the green.
COURTESY OF THE SAGAMORE

Number Five: $$, 5,248–6,640 yards, four tees. *Slope rating* 117–131. *Course rating* 68.0–72.3.

Number Six: $$, 5,430–6,603 yards, three tees. *Slope rating* 124–130. *Course rating* 70.1–71.9.

Number Seven: $$$$, 4,996–6,692 yards, three tees. *Slope rating* 122–135. *Course rating* 69.7–72.7.

Number Eight: $$$$, 5,177–6,698 yards, four tees. *Slope rating* 120–129. *Course rating* 67.9–72.4.

Resort Info: $$–$$$$. Pinehurst is primarily a Modified American Plan resort, and most guests receive dinner and breakfast with accommodations. Lodging choices include Manor Inn (a casual bed-and-breakfast, least expensive); Carolina Hotel (a large grand hotel with the most facilities, middle tier of prices); the Holly Inn (a small boutique property, most expensive); and a wide range of condominiums. Amenities: spa, fishing, boat rentals, lawn games, tennis, horseback riding.

Getting There: Southern Pines is served by US Airways commuter service and Amtrak, and the resort offers ground transportation from both. The Raleigh, Greensboro, and Charlotte airports are all within two hours. It is located four and a half hours from Washington, D.C., by car.

When to Go: Golf is played year-round, but spring and fall are high season, followed by the hot, humid summer months and winter, when frost delays and snow are possible. Early spring and late fall offer the best values, with the promise of good weather.

Travel Deals: Pinehurst offers a wide range of golf packages, most of which include a Modified American Plan. Less expensive packages include golf on courses One, Three, Five, and Six, with various additional surcharges for Two, Four, Seven, and Eight. If playing the four most desirable courses is your goal, more expensive packages that waive the surcharges are a better deal. Due to its popularity, most packages limit guests to one round on Number Two per visit.

Golf Travel by Design Courses Nearby: Mike Stranz's Tobacco Road (thirty minutes).

THE SAGAMORE, *Bolton Landing, New York*

**This Adirondack resort occupies its own island.
It's equally popular for its golf and its proximity to
the swank horse racing at Saratoga Springs.**

The Sagamore is the classiest resort in the popular tourist region of Lake George, sitting on a private island in the large lake. Amenities include dinner cruises, swimming, and croquet, but the real gem here is the Donald Ross course, built in 1929 and painstakingly renovated to its original design by acclaimed architect and author Geoffrey Cornish using Ross's blueprints. With the possible exception of famed Pinehurst Number Two, this is Ross's most unchanged classic design.

It is also an unusual venue for a Ross course, set on very hilly terrain, strategically incorporating more elevation changes than at his Carolina parkland layouts. The very first hole tells this story, dropping down from a highly elevated tee box to the fairway below before climbing back up to a raised green. Like most Ross openers, it offers a forgiving tee shot to an ample, receptive fairway that will calm the nerves of the anxious golfer. It is also visually stunning: Lake George itself sits behind the green, providing a spectacular view for a spectacular opening hole.

The course sits on the mainland, not on the resort's island. It is carved from thick forest, and Ross used the setting to produce the broad shot variety he preferred. By incorporating sharp doglegs and angled approaches, he requires you to think twice before pulling the driver from your bag on the tee, and offers a par-5 best played with a midiron tee shot to the landing area, followed by a fairway wood down the length of the hole. This is uncommon in golf, but it fulfills Ross's goal of making you hit every shot in your bag. At the Sagamore you will also find his trademark green complexes, including several divided by hogback or "buried elephant" ridges. Thirteen is the most interesting hole, and very unusual for Ross, who strongly preferred sand to water. The long par-4 (427–446 yards) has not one but two strategically placed ponds and—astonishingly—not a single bunker.

Off the course you will find a cozy resort perfect for a weekend getaway, especially from New York City. The Sagamore is quite a departure from the heavily developed tourist region surrounding Lake George, full of souvenir shops and fast food. Connected to the mainland by a small bridge, the resort encompasses a ninety-three-acre private island upon which the hotel sits with its has spacious and modern rooms, casually furnished in Adirondack style. Visitors can choose between rooms in the main hotel building or surrounding lodges.

The hotel has several notable restaurants, especially Trillium, its excellent fine-dining eatery. Trillium has an extensive wine list and features wine-pairing dinners nightly. The Verandah is one of the best hotel cocktail lounges in the country, with indoor and outdoor seating, very authentic Spanish tapas served all day, and a raw and sushi bar during cocktail hour. A unique offering is a nightly dinner cruise on the hotel's boat. Besides golf, water is the recreational theme at the Sagamore, which offers boat rentals, swimming, fishing, and other Lake George activities. When the summer horse-racing season visits nearby Saratoga Springs, the Sagamore is a perfect home base for horse-loving golfers.

THE SAGAMORE AT A GLANCE

(800) 358-3585, www.thesagamore.com

Golf Course Info: Practice area; walking allowed.

$$$, 5,261–6,774 yards, three tees. *Slope rating* 122–137, *Course rating* 72.0–73.8.

Resort Info: $$$–$$$$. Rooms are available in the main hotel or in detached lodges nearby. Both are furnished in casual Adirondack style. Lodge rooms are larger and better suited for families. Amenities: spa, fishing, boat rentals, cruises, lawn games.

Getting There: The Sagamore is just north of Albany, the closest airport, about thirty minutes away. It's an easy three- to three-and-a-half-hour drive from New York City.

When to Go: Golf season runs from April through November. July and August are peak season, when the region usually has very good weather. In addition, convention business—on which the hotel depends—is low at this time. From the end of July through August, racing season at nearby Saratoga fills the hotel. Spring and fall offer better values and are less crowded, but large groups predominate.

Travel Deals: Very reasonable golf and lodging packages are offered in fall, which is also prime foliage-viewing time; the wooded hills around the course and lake offer stunning vistas.

Golf Travel by Design Courses Nearby: None.

THE BALSAMS, *Dixville Notch, New Hampshire*

New England's classic mountain resort is larger than Manhattan Island and full of outdoor activities, including great golf.

It takes an effort to get to the Balsams, but it's worth it. Dixville Notch is in remote northwestern New Hampshire, close to the Canadian border but not much else. Here you will find the Balsams, a resort that time seems to have passed over, offering friendly service in the style of the now defunct Catskills resorts. Like them, it draws repeat guests year after year.

The Balsams has vast grounds, more than 13,000 acres, which include miles and miles of hiking and biking trails, a large lake, and just about every possible outdoor pursuit. But despite its rugged and rural setting, it maintains a degree of classic formality, with jacket and tie required for dinner in the main dining room. Guests receive a table for the length of their stay, with the same uniformed waitstaff meal after meal, all of which are included on the Full American Plan.

The Balsams is home to Donald Ross's aptly named Panorama course, a mountainous layout that rises more than 2,000 feet above sea level and offers views of Vermont and Canada. It is as fun and challenging as it is scenic, with wide fairways and almost unnoticeable rough catering to resort play, but the domed and undulating greens Ross is famous for are pronounced and challenging. Another Ross trait, found mainly at his New England courses, can be seen here: Tee boxes are often angled to the right, pointing the player toward out-of-bounds and requiring compensation with aim. It is a long and hilly layout to walk, and unfortunately the routing has been changed several times, but the holes themselves are largely the same, with fifteen of them as Ross designed. The current course finishes dramatically with a long uphill hole playing back to the clubhouse.

Because of the distance involved in getting here, and the wealth of activities at the resort, many guests come for a week at a time. More than 80 percent of the guests are repeat customers, and after a visit you'll know why. It is also a top family destination, with scheduled activities daily for all ages and a never-ending summer-camp atmosphere.

Where Every Vote Counts

Politicians are famous for playing golf, and some of the nation's grand resorts have hosted innumerable presidents, governors, senators, and representatives. But few see as many dignitaries as the Balsams. The attraction in this case isn't golf—it's campaigning. The resort is so large that it's actually its own town, with its own power and phone companies; the few dozen full-time residents include the general manager of the hotel. These "locals" cast their votes in what is the first reported precinct in every presidential election, a bit of lore that brings Dixville Notch into the national spotlight every four years. When not in use, the ballot room is open to the public, and its walls are adorned with photos of famous campaigners, letters from politicians, and, of course, the handsome wooden ballot box.

THE BALSAMS AT A GLANCE

(800) 255-0600, www.thebalsams.com

Golf Course Info: Practice area, walking allowed.

Panorama: $$, 4,978–6,804 yards, three tees. *Slope rating* 115–136. *Course rating* 67.8–73.9.

Coashaukee: A nine-hole, par-33 executive course laid out in a flat field next to the hotel.

Resort Info: $$$. Four hundred rooms are available in the old or newer wings of the main hotel. Rooms are large and comfortable, and do not have televisions. The Balsams rates are all-inclusive (except liquor) and include three meals daily, plus all activities (including golf). Amenities: clay and hard tennis courts, 50 miles of hiking and mountain biking trails, organized nature tours, swimming, boating, fly fishing, lawn games, children's camp.

Getting There: The Balsams is four hours from Boston and seven from New York. The closest major airport is Portland, Maine, two and a half hours away.

When to Go: Golf season runs from May through October. July though Labor Day is Social Season, when groups are banned and only leisure guests are welcome. Rates at this time range $205–235 per person per night, all-inclusive. Discounts are available before and after this time, when corporate groups are common. There are discounted midweek golf specials in fall, when New England's acclaimed foliage is at its peak, from September until mid-October for around $175 per person.

Travel Deals: Since all rates include golf and meals, not many packages are offered.

Golf Travel by Design Courses Nearby: None.

MARRIOTT SEAVIEW, *Brigantine, New Jersey*

Before casino gambling, Seaview was *the* place to stay in Atlantic City. Today it offers a rare Donald Ross ocean course, the only resort course in the Northeast ever to host a major.

Before 2002's U.S. Open at Bethpage Black, there was only one place in the entire Northeast where the general public could play in the footsteps of a major champion, and they were big shoes to fill. The long-hitting Slammin' Sammy Snead won his very first major, the 1942 PGA Championship, on the Donald Ross–designed Bay course.

The layout is so named because its links hug the coastline of Reed's Bay. Ross is acclaimed for his inland parkland courses, so this is a rare coastal treat. The Bay course features his small, slightly elevated tabletop greens and a daunting array of more than one hundred large sand bunkers. The tricky greens are protected by water throughout the course, one of Ross's most penal designs. While the course is short by modern standards (6,263 yards from the back tees), Ross relied on sand, water, and wind to protect par. The wind whips in incessantly off the bay, causing club selection to vary by two or even three clubs from one minute to the next.

Besides being the sole regional resort to host a major, Seaview has several other distinguishing characteristics. While most of the Northeast's premier golf resort destinations are in the rural mountains, the Marriott is on the ocean in an Atlantic City suburb, close to Philadelphia and New York. And while most of its competitors rely on eighteen good holes, the Marriott has thirty-six. The second course was laid out by the respected duo of William Flynn and Howard Toomey, famous for the Country Club in Brookline and Shinnecock Hills, both U.S. Open venues. The Pines course is a fitting counterpart to Ross's oceanfront masterpiece. It is longer, more difficult, and more secluded, with narrow fairways cut through tall stands of mature trees. As a result of its superior golf, Seaview is host of the annual Shop Rite LPGA Classic.

With white-glove hotel service, the resort has attracted a steady stream of celebrities, VIPs, industrialists, and U.S. presidents since opening in 1912. It has a Gatsbyesque charm, decorated with valuable antiques and photographs of famous guests testifying to its long and illustrious history. In recent years the hotel undertook an extensive renovation and added such facilities as a new Elizabeth Arden Red Door Spa and a Nick Faldo Golf

Institute. Seaview also offers a wide range of nongolf amenities, including swimming pools, tennis courts, nature trails, and a jogging path through 700 pine-filled acres. Just minutes from the secluded resort lies the hustle and bustle of Atlantic City's casino hotels.

MARRIOTT SEAVIEW AT A GLANCE

(800) 932–8000, www.seaviewgolf.com

Golf Course Info: Practice area, walking allowed, forecaddies.

Bay: $$–$$$, 5,017–6,247 yards, three tees. *Slope rating* 114–122. *Course rating* 68.4–70.7.

Pines: $$–$$$, 5,276–6,731 yards, three tees. *Slope rating* 119–128. *Course rating* 69.8–71.7.

Resort Info: $$$. There are 270 rooms available in the main hotel, all recently renovated, as well as thirty new freestanding villas available for rent. Amenities: spa, tennis, jogging path, nature trails, golf academy.

Getting There: Seaview is an easy drive from Philadelphia or Baltimore and two and a half hours from New York.

When to Go: Golf season is year-round but the best weather is from April through November. Due to its oceanfront location, winter days can be surprisingly mild, and the off-season is heavily discounted.

Travel Deals: Internet special offers are occasionally available, and Marriott periodically runs chainwide specials.

Golf Travel by Design Courses Nearby: Pine Hill (sixty minutes).

THE BROADMOOR, *Colorado Springs, Colorado*

A Colorado mining magnate made it his mission to build no less than the finest resort hotel in the nation. As the longest-running recipient of the Mobil five-star award, he may well have succeeded.

f bigger is better, than the larger-than-life Broadmoor, more like a town than a resort, is better. The 3,000-acre complex holds three golf courses, a huge array of activities, so many restaurants it is difficult to count, and more than 700 guest rooms in three buildings. Personal service usually decreases as hotels grow in size, but the Broadmoor is a notable exception. It has held a Mobil five-star ranking for forty-one consecutive years, longer than anyplace else (it also gets five AAA diamonds). But rather than rest on these laurels, the resort just completed $180 million worth of renovations.

When it opened, the original Ross layout was the highest-altitude course ever built in the United States—more than a mile above sea level. It was expanded by Robert Trent Jones Sr., and the architects' combined work now includes two intertwined eighteens, East and West, with half the holes on each designed by Ross. The architectural dichotomy is obvious and interesting, a mix of Ross's straightforward resort holes highlighted by domed greens and Jones's trademark strategic designs, with downhill tee shots followed by uphill approaches to heavily bunkered greens. The mix works, since both are "classical" designs.

The courses are similar to Ross's famed *Pinehurst Number Two,* with resort golf that is fun for all abilities but challenges good players to score. Both are Carolina-style parkland courses carved from pine forests, raised 6,000 feet above sea level, with wide fairways, little water, and extremely tough greens. The East course, yet another Ross championship venue, has hosted the Women's U.S. Open but is actually the slightly easier eighteen from the two sets of men's tees. Like many classic Ross designs, this course plays relatively harder from the front tees. It has more water and elevation change, but is shorter. East is more balanced, but West has the resort's best nine. The latter's back side has a wide variety of length, bunkering, and approaches that require your mind to be fully involved in every shot. While longer, West has less trouble than East, with little water or woods; even high-handicappers can get around with one ball if all goes well. It is also an easier layout for high-handicap women players. They are a dead heat in terms of quality, both well worth playing.

The Broadmoor's third layout, the Mountain course, by Arnold Palmer and Ed Seay, was built on unstable land; after repeated rockslides the better back nine was closed indefinitely. Work is being done in the hope of someday

No Expense Spared

Turn-of-the-twentieth-century mining millionaire Spencer Penrose had a simple but grandiose dream: to build the grandest resort west of the Mississippi. To turn his fantasy into reality, no expense was spared, and he hired the greatest craftsmen of his time: Donald Ross laid out the course; Frederick Law Olmsted, father of landscape architecture, designed the grounds; and sharpshooter Annie Oakley opened a shooting school. The latter no longer exists, but nearly every other whim is catered to by a staff exuding unbridled enthusiasm. Throw in excellent food and a first-rate golf operation, and it is easy to see why the Broadmoor wins so many awards.

restoring the layout, but for the immediate future the Mountain is a nine-holer. It is much tighter and more penal than the two parkland layouts.

Although expansive, the resort is ideally laid out, with almost everything within walking distance of the guest rooms. The main compound is built around a small lake at the foot of Cheyenne Mountain. An attractive mix of buildings containing rooms, restaurants, and other facilities surrounds the lake. Accommodations are mostly in two buildings on either side of the lake, both of which house shops and restaurants. The very best rooms are twenty-one new lakeside suites, in their own small building. A large infinity pool and two water slides, plus posh poolside cabanas, were recently added at one end of the lake. On the opposite end of the oval lake sits the golf club and spa. For a sprawling property, the Broadmoor is surprisingly easy to navigate.

With ten restaurants, twenty-four-hour room service, and several bars, no one goes hungry here. Food is uniformly good, but the standout is the Penrose Room, the resort's most formal eatery. Service equals that of top French restaurants, with attentive staff, silver-domed plates, and beautiful china. The food is Colorado haute cuisine, with dishes such as venison chops and fresh trout, accompanied by sides like foie gras bread pudding. Dinner here is a must. Another unique offering is the Golden Bee, a pub that was brought over intact from England, with ornate pressed-tin ceilings and elaborate woodwork. It anchors the Broadmoor's nightlife with sing-along piano music and yards of beer.

As good as the golf and dining are, it is the spa that sets the Broadmoor apart. One of the nation's top facilities, it offers a huge range of treatments for men and women. Other amenities include horseback riding and a large tennis center. But the best activities are outside the resort in surrounding Colorado Springs, where you will find Pikes Peak, the quaint village of Manitou Springs, the Indian Cliff Dwelling museum, the U.S. Air Force Academy, and the Garden of the Gods, a park filled with redrock monoliths and hiking trails.

THE BROADMOOR AT A GLANCE

(800) 633-7711, www.broadmoor.com

Golf Course Info: Practice areas, walking allowed, caddies.

East: $$$, 5,921–7,119 yards, three tees. *Slope rating 122–139. Course rating 70.5–73.0.*

West: $$$, 5,573–7,190 yards, three tees. *Slope rating 127–132. Course rating 70.0–73.3.*

Mountain: $$$, 2,368–3,400 yards, four tees. *Slope rating 117–133. Course rating 67.3–72.1.*

Resort Info: $$$$. Seven hundred rooms are available in the two buildings of the main hotel, and all were recently renovated. There are also twenty-one new luxury lakeside suites in their own building. Amenities: spa, tennis, jogging path, horseback riding, scheduled area tours, kids' camp, live entertainment, wellness center, fly-fishing school, paddleboats.

Getting There: United is the major carrier to the Colorado Springs airport, and the hotel runs shuttles. The large Denver airport is less than two hours away.

When to Go: Surprisingly, they golf year-round here: Colorado Springs is much milder than most of the state. In the colder months a composite eighteen made from the front nines of East and West is kept open. Even in the middle of winter, temperatures can be in the fifties—but it can also snow. The best time for good weather and smaller crowds is October, but the courses are in good shape from May through November.

Travel Deals: The Broadmoor offers a number of theme-specific packages for golf, spa, and other activities that are updated winter and fall.

Golf Travel by Design Courses Nearby: None.

DONALD ROSS MEMORIAL COURSE AT BOYNE HIGHLANDS, *Harbor Springs, Michigan*

As the Father of American Golf Course Architecture, Ross was the first to be honored with a course meant as a tribute to his design genius.

Originally just a ski resort, Boyne Highlands has emerged as one of the Midwest's premier golf destinations. The resort now has four challenging courses, including one of the marquee works by Arthur Hills. But it also has one of the nation's most unique layouts, a Donald Ross course that was not designed by Ross.

The Donald Ross Memorial Course is a compilation of copies of the very best holes Ross designed, including many from top private courses he worked on, which most people do not have the opportunity to play. Of course, like most tribute or replica holes, these are rarely as good as the originals, since they have different settings, ambience, and even types of grasses. But Ross has a very recognizable design style, and the holes here epitomize that, making it both a fun course for the casual golfer and a historical experience for fans of golf course architecture.

Two holes at the Memorial course come from *Pinehurst Number Two*, and two each from his acclaimed private clubs Seminole, Oak Hills, and Oakland Hills, sites of important competitions including the Ryder Cup and U.S. Open. The rest of the holes are a compilation of some lesser-known private Ross courses, a few well-known ones such as Inverness and Scioto, and even a course from Scotland's *Royal Dornoch,* where Ross learned his trade and eventually did some renovations. The mix is a once-in-a-lifetime opportunity to see how the design elements Ross loved work on a variety of courses from a wide range of locales, and do it all under one roof.

The Sincerest Form of Flattery

Tribute and replica courses are currently one of the hottest trends in golf, with developers re-creating famous or exceptional holes from around the world in a variety of settings. Some courses take holes from private locales like Augusta and Pine Valley and re-create them in public settings. One course in Las Vegas re-created great holes from different British Open venues throughout Scotland and England. In recent years there have also been tribute courses geared around the work of particular architects, from Seth Raynor to Jack Nicklaus. But while this is a suddenly fashionable idea, the very first architect to be so honored was Ross himself, way back in 1989 when Boyne Highlands opened the Donald Ross Memorial Course, a collection of duplicates of the best holes Ross designed.

BOYNE HIGHLANDS RESORT AT A GLANCE

(800) GO-BOYNE, www.boynehighlands.com

Golf Course Info: Practice areas, walking allowed.

Donald Ross Memorial Course: $$$, 4,929–6,814 yards, five tees. *Slope rating* 119–132. *Course rating* 67.1–73.4.

Lodging Info: $$$$. Boyne USA resorts has several golf resorts in the region, including Boyne Highlands and Boyne Mountain.

Other Notable Donald Ross Courses You Can Play

- **Mt. Washington Hotel,** Bretton Woods, New Hampshire
- **Pine Needles,** Southern Pines, North Carolina
- **Southern Pines Elks Club,** Southern Pines, North Carolina
- **The Homestead (Old course),** Hot Springs, West Virginia
- **Bobby Jones Golf Complex,** Sarasota, Florida (thirty-six holes)

Harry Colt (1869–1951)
The Father of Parkland Golf

Willie Park is credited with bringing the game inland from the coast, but Harry Colt perfected the move, creating so many of the great early English parkland designs that it's harder to find ones he did not design than those he did. Colt's parkland courses have hosted every important tournament that can be held in England, from the Ryder Cup to the World Match Play Championships.

An Important Trendsetter

Although he was a scratch player, Colt was the first major designer who had not been a professional golfer, a trend that would continue for nearly a century. He also wrote the first-known treatise on design. He was widely admired (he was hired to consult on the world's number-one-ranked course, Pine Valley) and respected, and many of the qualities of parkland golf, which we take for granted, came from him. He also laid out the courses for the world's first two planned residential golf communities, Wentworth and St. George's Hill, paving the way for thousands of such developments worldwide.

He greatly influenced his sometimes partner Alister MacKenzie, who borrowed a Colt hole for Augusta, and was called upon to renovate many classic courses throughout the United Kingdom, including some Old Tom Morris designs. The British Open has been held no less than forty-seven times on courses designed or redesigned by Colt.

When you play one of Colt's parkland courses, you can expect:

- **Demanding tee shots.** While links courses often have surprisingly long holes, such as 450-yard par-4, these are often offset by the rock-hard fairways or prevailing wind at your back. Neither is the case on these parkland routings, and Colt intentionally demanded power off the tee. He also created forced carries from the land itself, in the form of water or expanses of the heather common to the Surrey region around London where he did his best work.

- **Hazards in the line of play.** While many designers relegate bunkers to the edges of fairways and around greens, Colt did not hesitate to require golfers to play over, around, or short of an imposing hazard in a straight line from tee to green. While these are notable exceptions at many early courses, for Colt they were more a rule.

- **Elevation changes.** Colt raised and lowered his tees and greens, requiring varied approaches to the putting surface itself.

- **Heather.** Since many of his best works are in a concise geographical region, a pilgrimage to the Colt courses will result in spending a considerable amount of time searching for your ball in this good-looking natural hazard. Colt frequently used this ground cover the way

THE BRITISH OPEN HAS BEEN HELD NO

LESS THAN FORTY-SEVEN TIMES ON COURSES

DESIGNED OR REDESIGNED BY COLT.

designers utilize waste area today—to separate tees from fairways and fairways from greens.

When most golf travelers think of a trip to the British Isles, they inevitably gravitate toward Scotland and Ireland, and not without reason. But Colt's parkland wonders, many within half an hour of London, are the easiest to reach. They present a formidable collection of courses that can be taken as a whole or incorporated piecemeal into pleasure or business trips to Great Britain's capital city.

WENTWORTH, *Virginia Water, England*

Birthplace of the Ryder Cup, Wentworth retains its ties with history while offering a fully modern golf experience.

Wentworth was nothing short of revolutionary, combining the ideals of the American country club experience with a planned residential community, only the second of its kind. Today Wentworth boasts three eighteen-hole courses, a world-class grass tennis facility, a modern spa and health club, and a host of other amenities, including a full practice range. The stately clubhouse is among the finest in the world, and its restaurant attracts golfers and nongolfers alike. It is, without a doubt, the most complete club of its kind in the United Kingdom.

Since its dramatic debut, Wentworth has come to be regarded as one of Britain's finest golf facilities. It has hosted the World Match Play Championships, a European PGA Tour event, and held the first "friendly" formal international competition, which later became the Ryder Cup. Stars throughout the ages, including Ben Hogan, Sam Snead, Gary Player, Arnold Palmer, and Seve Ballesteros have shone here. PGA players such as Ernie Els live in the stately homes on the premises. It's the two original layouts by Harry Colt that attract them all.

The West course hosts the championship events and is nicknamed the Burma Road for its length and difficulty, among the longest in Britain. Along with its sibling, the East, it enjoys a wonderful setting amid groves of fir and silver birch trees, and courses are full of flowering rhododendrons. The trees are thick enough that despite the parkland setting, you can rarely see one hole from another. In this lush region, the courses are among the best conditioned in Britain.

While the West gets the publicity as a true championship venue, it is the shorter par-68 East that most members prefer, and most first-time visitors will as well. The West is best reserved for low-handicappers seeking a challenge. The East was actually Colt's first course here and enjoys the sandier soil. It's a toned down version of the West with the same interesting multitiered and undulating greens. The two layouts make fitting companions, similar in style but with pronounced differences in terms of

Golf Travel by Design

difficulty. There is nothing wrong with the third course, the much newer Edinburgh layout by John Jacobs, but it is outclassed by Colt's work—and at these high suburban prices it's the classics that you should play.

WENTWORTH AT A GLANCE

+44 1344-842-201, www.wentworthclub.com

Golf Course Info: Practice area, caddies, walking allowed, nine-hole par-3 course.

West: $$$–$$$$, 6,094–7,047 yards, three tees.

East: $$$, 5,388–6,201 yards (par 68), three tees.

Edinburgh: $$$, 5,774–7,004 yards, three tees.

Lodging Info: The leading choice nearby is Great Fosters, a stately English country manor house hotel (+44 1784–433–822). The fabled Savoy hotel group in London has a corporate membership and long-standing relationship with the club, and can most easily arrange guest play and transportation. Its upscale city hotels include the Savoy, the Berkeley, Claridge's, and the Connaught (toll-free 011–800–63–SAVOY, www.savoy-group.co.uk). For a pure golfing trip, a good solution is to stay at Stoke Park, which has its own fine Colt course and can arrange play at nearby venues including Sunningdale, Wentworth, and St. George's Hill.

Getting There: Wentworth is thirty-five minutes from London, and taxis can be arranged.

When to Go: Golf is played year-round; summer is high season.

European Travel Tips: Like many top courses in the British Isles, Wentworth is technically a private club and has limited tee times daily for visitors. It can be quite arduous to arrange your own itinerary: The time difference and international calling can make it difficult to contact many European courses, each has certain days reserved for competitive member play, and some have days reserved for women members. For this reason, many travelers make all their tee time, lodging, and transportation arrangements in the U.K. through specialized golf tour companies, of which the best are Perry Golf (800–344–5257, www.perrygolf.com) and Wide World of Golf (800–214–GOLF, www.wideworld ofgolf.com).

Golf Travel by Design Courses Nearby: Sunningdale (fifteen minutes); St. George's Hill (twenty minutes); Stoke Park (thirty-five minutes).

SUNNINGDALE NEW COURSE, *Sunningdale, England*

At Sunningdale, home to many important championships, golf legend Bobby Jones played what many believe to be the most perfect round of golf of all time.

A fierce rivalry exists between Wentworth and Sunningdale for bragging rights as the finest private club in the London area, and both sides cite their Harry Colt masterpieces as evidence. Off the course they are as different as night and day, and Sunningdale enjoys a very low-key clubhouse and old-school pro shop. But like Wentworth, it has hosted important events, including the Dunlop Masters, European Open, the first Walker Cup and the British Women's Open in 1997 and 2001. And like Wentworth it has two equally fine layouts: the Old by Willie Park and the New by Harry Colt, who served as club secretary here for many years.

The Old course is easier, with all four of its par-5s reachable in two shots, and three short par-4s. It is tree lined and sheltered from the wind. It is a living definition of a parkland layout. Colt's New, on the other hand, is open and windswept, built on sandier soil and crawling with treacherous heather, a pure heathland design. It has fast, well-built greens that maintain their pace throughout the winter, making it one of the best year-round layouts in England. The New is the more difficult because of its longer holes—not to mention the heather, the wind, deep fairway bunkers, and a pond in play on fifteen.

SUNNINGDALE AT A GLANCE

+44 1344–621–681, www.sunningdalegolf.co.uk

Golf Course Info: Practice area, caddies, walking allowed.

Old: $$$, 5,825–6,619 yards, four tees.

New: $$$, 6,083–6,617 yards (par 71), three tees.

Lodging Info: The leading choice nearby is Great Fosters, a stately English country manor house hotel (+44 1784–433–822). For a pure golfing trip, a good solution is to stay at Stoke Park, which has its own fine Colt course and can arrange play at nearby venues including Sunningdale, Wentworth, and St. George's Hill. It is also possible to stay in London and commute.

Travel Deals: Sunningdale offers a discounted price for those wishing to play both courses in a single day, at a considerable savings.

Getting There: Sunningdale is forty-five minutes from London, and taxis can be arranged.

When to Go: Golf is played year-round; summer is high season.

European Travel Tips: See Wentworth.

The Perfect Round

Sunningdale's place in golf history was secured in 1926 during a qualifying round for the British Open when Bobby Jones played a round with what many consider the best ball striking ever seen, Tiger Woods notwithstanding. Jones hit seventeen greens in regulation, mostly with long irons and fairway woods, and took an unfortunate 33 putts en route to his 66, meaning he used less than 2 strokes per hole to reach the greens, shooting nothing but 3s and 4s the entire round, before heading to Royal Lytham to win the Open.

Golf Travel by Design Courses Nearby: Wentworth (fifteen minutes); St. George's Hill (twenty minutes); Stoke Park (thirty-five minutes).

STOKE PARK, *Slough, England*

As Agent 007, Sean Connery, a real-life golf fanatic, played his fictional match against nemesis Goldfinger at this classic resort.

For the traveling golfer visiting the London area, Stoke Park, formerly known as the Stoke Poges golf club, is a must-visit. It is the only one of the Colt courses in the region that is truly a golf resort, sporting its own hotel with charming rooms set in the main club building, a startling edifice that bears more resemblance to the U.S. Capitol than a clubhouse. In fact, members claim that its dome inspired the home of the U.S. Congress. The twenty upscale guest rooms and fine restaurant led to Stoke Park's being the first private club ever admitted into the prestigious Leading Hotels of the World group. It recently added a brand-new modern spa and health club facility.

Just 7 miles from Heathrow airport, Stoke Park occupies a long-standing country estate whose grounds are so beautiful they were used to film the recent *Bridget Jones's Diary*. But Stoke's real celluloid claim to fame is as the site of spy James Bond's fictional golf match with the nefarious Goldfinger, who owned the club in the film. Bond visited again in the more recent *Tomorrow Never Dies*, also filmed here. As a result, the former Harry

Colt bar downstairs was renamed the James Bond bar, and is decorated with souvenirs from the films.

A recent nine was added to Colt's original eighteen, allowing the resort to cater to more golfers. The Colt layout offers a taste of resort golf, English style, and is much more forgiving than his nearby courses. The main reason for this is the total absence of heather, which flourishes in the region and adorns Colt's other layouts. The course is also flat for Colt, although water does come into play. It is a user-friendly design that would make a good introduction to Colt's work on a tour of his London-area parkland and heathland routings. Stoke's highlight is the par-3 seventh hole, with its long, thin green angled away from the line of play, fronted by a creek and backed by large bunkers with no bailout area in any direction. If this hole, regarded as one of the world's great par-3s, sounds familiar, it probably is. A copy by Colt's sometime partner Alister MacKenzie was used as the twelfth at Augusta National, home of the Masters, where it anchors the famed Amen Corner.

For Queen and Country

James Bond, fictional Agent 007 of Her Majesty's Secret Service, is so revered for his gentlemanly ways and code of honor that he has been entrusted by his government with the discretionary "license to kill." Bond, as much as anyone, knows the rules of good behavior and is aware that for a professional player, there is no worse sin in life than to cheat at golf. While the amateur frequently succumbs to the urge to move a ball away from a tree root or out of a divot, this convenience is simply unacceptable at the tournament level or even among friends—when money is involved. Money, in the form of a huge gold ingot, was exactly the issue when no one less noble than Bond cheated his opponent, Ernst Blofeld, aka Goldfinger, out of a large check by switching balls on Blofeld and accusing him of having violated the rules. At least Bond had a good reason—the economic survival of the free world.

(877) HOTEL–UK, www.stokeparkclub.com

Golf Course Info: Practice area, walking allowed.

Colt/Alison 18: $$, 6,377–6,744 yards, two tees.

Lane Jackson 9: $$, 2,864–3,060 yards, two tees.

Resort Info: Stoke Park has twenty well-appointed guest rooms with oversized tubs, balconies, and golf course views, plus two pubs, a fine-dining restaurant, and an assortment of recreation including billiards, tennis, a spa, a health club, and walking trails. The concierge can arrange play at nearby venues including Sunningdale, Wentworth, and St. George's Hill.

Getting There: Stoke Park is 7 miles from London's Heathrow airport.

When to Go: Golf is played year-round; summer is high season.

Golf Travel by Design Courses Nearby: Wentworth (fifteen minutes); St. George's Hill (twenty minutes); Sunningdale (thirty-five minutes).

ST. GEORGE'S HILL, *Weybridge, England*

Known best as the first planned residential golf community, this hidden gem may also be Harry Colt's preeminent design.

This London-area layout is Colt's least known, but—in the eyes of many fans—also his best work. Its unique location combines the trademark heather and trees of the Surrey region with a very hilly, almost mountainous setting. This provides dramatic elevation changes, starting with the very first hole, which plays from an elevated tee down into a valley and back up to an elevated green, a good taste of what is to come.

Since Colt was among the first to build inland courses, he was among the first to truly build greens, complete with subsurface drainage, which allowed him to contour undulations and tiers and increase putting speed. St. George's is the pinnacle of this effort, with fast, tricky, and convoluted putting surfaces.

At the same time, Colt not only uses the hilly setting for elevation change but also has several fairways that slope dramatically, demanding well-placed or even-shaped tee shots to hold. In true Colt style, he uses some quite long par-4s, demanding power off the tee. The result is not penal, but rather a strategic challenge that will engage the best players while still providing a fun round to the less talented. For some, the real challenge will come from simply walking the rolling layout.

There are twenty-seven holes at St. George's Hill, with the Red and Blue nines comprising the standard layout, and the optional Green nine being shorter but tighter. This club was the very first planned residential golf community, followed shortly thereafter by nearby Wentworth.

ST. GEORGE'S HILL AT A GLANCE

+44 1932-847758, www.stgeorgeshillgolfclub.co.uk

Golf Course Info: Practice area, walking only, caddies with advance request.

Red/Blue 18: $$, 6,243–6,496 yards, two tees.

Green 9: $$, 2,680–2,897 yards, two tees.

Lodging Info: The leading choice nearby is Great Fosters, a stately English country manor house hotel (+44 1784–433–822). For a pure golfing trip, a good solution is to stay at Stoke Park, which has its own fine Colt course and can arrange play at nearby venues including Sunningdale and Wentworth. It is also possible to stay in London and commute.

European Travel Tips: See Wentworth.

Travel Deals: There is a substantial discount for playing thirty-six holes per day.

Getting There: St. George's Hill is less than forty-five minutes from London.

When to Go: Golf is played year-round; summer is high season.

Golf Travel by Design Courses Nearby: Wentworth (fifteen minutes); Stoke Park (twenty minutes); Sunningdale (thirty-five minutes).

EDEN COURSE, *St. Andrews, Scotland*

There is more than one course at the birthplace of golf, and while it's often overlooked by tourists, locals know the Eden is St. Andrews's hidden gem.

So many visitors come to St. Andrews only to play the Old course—the birthplace of the game—that constant promotion is needed to get visitors out on the other fine courses. This is a shame, because although the Old course is certainly magical, it is so different from any other golf course that it confounds, frustrates, and often disappoints American visitors. While the Old course is an acquired taste, Harry Colt's Eden is instantly likable.

The courses of St. Andrews are public in the truest sense. Local residents do get some preferred tee times, but layouts are open to all—and kept that way through an act of Parliament guaranteeing their democratic nature. The body that oversees the operations is known as the St. Andrews Links Trust, a nonprofit group that operates a total of six courses, all

The Pond on the Other Side of the Pond

Perhaps it was his parkland roots, but Colt added a pond to Eden that comes into play on both the fourteenth and fifteenth holes. This would not cause a second glance in the States, but it is the subject of much discussion in St. Andrews, where it remains the sole inland water hazard on these ninety-nine legendary links holes.

adjacent to one another: the full-size Old, New, Jubilee, and Eden; the shorter Strathtyrum; and the nine-hole Balgove for juniors.

Tee times on the Old course are very much in demand, probably more so than any other course on earth, and they are difficult to obtain. Likewise, the New course was financed by a contribution from the Royal and Ancient golf club, and as a result, its members retain fully half the tee times. For this reason, the Eden remains the most popular with locals, a well-kept secret that is helped by the fact that it starts from its own clubhouse at the opposite end of the property from the Old, New, and Jubilee. The Eden is a superior course to the Jubilee (which is constantly being tinkered with to improve playability) and warrants a round from any visitor to St. Andrews.

The Eden makes a fun and inviting round and is a bit of a departure for Colt, since it is a true links, sitting on the game's most hallowed grounds. It actually has more dramatic seaside terrain than the Old course, with the third green reaching the estuary of St. Andrews Bay and the fourth, seventh, thirteenth, and fourteenth playing along it. It is immediately adjacent to the Old; sliced tee shots on the first three holes will put you on the back nine of the more fabled links. The most interesting facet of the course is its "crossover" par-3s, five and eight, which play from two adjacent tees to two adjacent greens, crossing each other in an X pattern. This is unique, and it allows players to examine the eighth hole well before playing it.

St. Andrews is a wonderful town off the golf courses, with numerous shops, restaurants, and a fine university, as well as its famous castle and cathedral ruins. It is pedestrian friendly and well worth a stroll. It becomes extremely crowded with tourists in summer. Still, unlike the Old and New, reservations for tee times on the Eden are easy to come by—and are a bargain at about $40, a quarter of the price of the Old.

+44 1334–466–666, www.standrews.org.uk
For Eden course tee times: www.golfagent.com

Golf Course Info: Practice area, walking only, caddies.

Eden: $, 5,485–6,146 yards (par 70), three tees.

Old: $$$, 6,063–6,930 yards, two tees for visitors.

New: $$, 6,027–6,642 yards (par 71), three tees.

Jubilee: $$, 6,077–6,840 yards, three tees.

Strathtyrum: $, 5,094 yards (par 69), a beginner course designed for high-handicappers.

Balgove: $, 1,530 yards (par 30), a nine-hole course for juniors.

Lodging Info: There are dozens of small hotels and bed-and-breakfasts within walking distance of the courses, which are all located in the center of town. The leading choice in St. Andrews is the Old Course Hotel, overlooking the seventeenth fairway of the Old course. It is a modern full-service luxury hotel, with a spa, several restaurants, a wing of lavish luxury suites, and what is reputed to be the largest collection of single-malt whiskeys in Scotland. The hotel has its own eighteen-hole course, the Duke's, located outside of town (+44 1334–474–371, www.oldcoursehotel.co.uk). A newer choice is the St. Andrews Bay resort, a full-blown American-style golf resort with two excellent courses, a spa, and modern facilities located 3 miles outside of town (+44 1334–837–000, www.standrewsbay.com).

Travel Deals: There are three- and seven-day tickets available, which allow play on all courses except the Old. These are a great value, especially on the pricier New and Jubilee layouts, where the savings are almost 50 percent.

Old Course Info: There are several ways to obtain Old course tee times. One is to write the Links Trust well in advance requesting specific dates. Golf tour operators such as Perry Golf (800–344–5257, www.perrygolf.com) and Wide World of Golf (800–214–GOLF, www.wideworldofgolf.com) purchase some guaranteed tee times, which they resell to clients. This is the easiest—and most expensive—way to ensure playing the Old course. Each day, half of all the available tee times go into a lottery. You enter the lottery for the next day; winning names are drawn and posted in the late afternoon. In summer the chances are reputed to be around 30 percent of obtaining a tee time via the lottery. For complete information, visit the Links Trust Web site.

Getting There: St. Andrews is less than two hours from the Edinburgh airport.

When to Go: Golf is played year-round; summer is high season, but spring offers the best weather and smallest crowds.

Golf Travel by Design Courses Nearby: Muirfield (forty-five minutes); Prestwick (two hours).

The epic seaside dunes help make Royal Portrush one of the most beautiful–and challenging–links courses in the British Isles.   LARRY OLMSTED

ROYAL PORTRUSH, *Portrush, Northern Ireland*

Two rare coastal links layouts from the parkland master—including the only course in Ireland to host the British Open.

While Harry Colt is known primarily for his many great inland courses, Royal Portrush is his links triumph and widely considered one of the most beautiful courses in the world. When describing links courses, *dunes* is a much-used word, from the grass-covered hillocks at St. Andrews to the much larger dunes creating blind shots at **Lahinch** and **Royal County Down.** Still, no course on earth has the staggering, towering dunes found at Portrush. Totally defined by these huge mountains of sand, the course plays through the valleys between them, reducing golfers to insects in a land of giants. This is fitting, because the course lies along the coast near the Giant's Causeway, Northern Ireland's premier natural wonder.

Colt designed two courses here. The premier is the Dunluce, the only course in all of Ireland ever to host the British Open. While it is quite difficult to score well on, it is fun for all abilities, and as a result, although it does not have the same precise shotmaking values as Royal County Down, we regard it as the best all around course in Northern Ireland. Unlike many championship links venues, however, the second course here—the Valley—should not be skipped. It's a fine layout that would headline most golf resorts.

While Portrush is unmistakably a links, Colt employs many of his familiar parkland devices: devious pot bunkers to be avoided at all costs, plateau greens, and, most of all, narrow fairways that also curve, creating one of the most demanding tests of driving to be found. Every hole save the first and last dog-legs left or right. Still, there are few surprises, and blind shots are rare, adding to the fun. There are also tremendous views of the Giant's Causeway, the white rocks offshore, the isle of Islay, and even Scotland on a clear day. Any list of the greatest views in golf includes the fifth tee at Portrush.

The most famous hole here is Calamity Corner, a 200-plus-yard par-3 whose green is perched atop an 80-foot-deep crater. Ace this one and you can celebrate at Ireland's famous Bushmills distillery just up the road.

The Valley course is set among the smaller dunes between Dunluce and the sea, and has many excellent holes that use natural shelves on the dunes as green sites, playing in the valleys between them. It is much too beautiful a setting to stop after just eighteen holes, so you might as well play both courses when you visit, which you should. Soon.

ROYAL PORTRUSH AT A GLANCE

+44 1265-822-311

Golf Course Info: Practice area, walking only, caddies.

Dunluce: $$$, 6,161–6,751 yards, three tees.

Valley: $, 5,495–6,146 yards (par 70), three tees.

Lodging Info: The modest Royal Court hotel overlooks the links here and has a decent pub and restaurant (+44 2870–822–236). There are also numerous small hotels and bed-and-breakfasts in the heart of the town, a summer resort laid out around Portrush harbor.

Getting There: Flying into Belfast (via London or Dublin) is the most convenient, but the majority of visitors fly into Dublin or Shannon and drive north.

European Travel Tips: See Wentworth.

When to Go: The best conditions can be found from mid-March through the end of October; in March and April the course is quite empty.

Golf Travel by Design Courses Nearby: Royal County Down (two hours).

Other Notable Harry Colt Courses You Can Play

- **Royal Belfast,** Belfast, Northern Ireland
- **Blackmoor,** Whitehill, England
- **County Sligo,** Rosses Point, Ireland
- **Swinley Forest,** Berkshire, England
- **Walton Heath,** Walton on the Hill, England

Dr. Alister MacKenzie
(1870–1934)

The Father of International Golf

While his contemporaries would occasionally cross the ocean or the Canadian border to create a course, Alister MacKenzie roamed the world. He was the first architect whose impact was felt on a global scale, from South America to Australia, North America to his English birthplace. A Cambridge-trained physician, MacKenzie, like Harry Colt before him, did not come to golf from a professional background—he came from a military one. A surgeon in the Boer War, MacKenzie became an expert on earth battlements and trenches, which he designed for Britain in World War I. Golfers often speak of attacking a course or the course's defenses. In MacKenzie's case, this is accurate, and his military training is evident today in his famous irregular, curvaceous bunkering.

"A Complete Absence of Annoyance"

While most architects have a style, MacKenzie had more of a code, outlined in his memoirs as his thirteen rules of golf design. He strongly believed that "there should be a complete absence of the annoyance and irritation caused by the necessity of searching for lost balls." This did not mean you could not lose them, as in the ocean. It just meant you wouldn't look for them. Toward this end, he was against rough in all forms, blind shots, and anything else that might hide a ball. The traveling golfer will be thrilled to learn that his most important rule was "a hole should, as far as possible, be ideal for both scratch and long-handicap players." To achieve this, he used:

- **Surprisingly few hazards.** Although famous for his shapely bunkers, MacKenzie employed very few of them. Same with rough, which he used little or none of. He fiercely believed courses should be playable by anyone, and stated, "No hole can be considered perfect unless it can be played with a putter." He did not like forced carries and believed there should be a dry, hazard-free route from tee to green on every hole, even if it meant taking the long way. Even his most famous hole, the epic par-3 over the ocean at Cypress Point, has a long way around. A pure strategic designer, this suited his risk-reward beliefs.

- **Hazards in the line of play.** While he used few hazards, their purpose was to make players decide what to do. He first studied with Harry Colt, who also felt strongly about this. Many early designers used bunkers at the edges of fairways, but not MacKenzie, who emphatically stated, "No bunker is unfair wherever it is placed."

- **Large, undulating greens.** He did this in part because these were easier to drain, but mainly because he wanted subtleties and difficulties on his courses. While his courses were very playable for all abilities, he

HIS MOST IMPORTANT RULE WAS

"A HOLE SHOULD, AS FAR AS POSSIBLE,

BE IDEAL FOR BOTH SCRATCH

AND LONG-HANDICAP PLAYERS."

challenged players to putt well. Nowhere is this as evident as at the Masters each year, where the best players in the world overpower the midlength course only to chip poorly, pitch poorly, and 3-putt their way into big numbers.

- **Two loops of nine holes.** While this the first of his thirteen principles, MacKenzie was adamant that it should not be employed if it meant sacrificing good natural hole locations, and so at his Cypress masterpiece, he broke his own rule.

- **Few hills.** He did not think mountains were places for golf courses and abhorred hill climbing. He did, however, think that even on flat sites fairways and greens should have substantial rolling undulations, such as at the Old course, his favorite.

- **Hazards next to the green.** Before MacKenzie, true greenside bunkers were uncommon. More likely, a player hit over a huge bunker en route to the green. But MacKenzie wanted to reward accuracy, and he felt that there should be a big difference between hitting the green and just missing it. As the same time, he felt that being in the greenside hazard was often better than being just outside it and having to hit a short pitch over it, so he rewarded the player who missed the green by less.

- **Subtleties.** A student of the Old course and the first to really map and diagram each hole, MacKenzie believed that a player should learn from the course. If a hole could be better played by bouncing a shot off a hill next to the green, he found this wonderful. He built courses for members, not travelers, and his expectation was that people would play the course over and over—and it should reveal secrets.

Sadly, MacKenzie's two most renowned works, Cypress Point and Augusta National, both contenders for the coveted "best course on earth" title, are very private. But there are still some fine examples you can play, especially if you are willing to get on a plane. If you look at any major golf magazine's Top One Hundred courses list, you will find three by MacKenzie in the Top Ten, including Cypress, Augusta, and the much more accessible Royal Melbourne in Australia. It may be a long trip, but it is worth it, especially since there are so many other fine courses next to it. If you undertake a pilgrimage to a MacKenzie course, here or abroad, you will quickly realize it was worth it.

ROYAL MELBOURNE, *Melbourne, Australia*

Surprising Melbourne has more great golf courses than any city in the world, and Royal Melbourne is the best of the best.

f you visit Australia, you will find dozens of so-called MacKenzie courses. He did visit the country a single time, and toured it, designing several of its best courses. But at the same time, existing courses or new designs would ask him for advice; if he suggested they move a bunker, the MacKenzie

The Seven Sisters of the Sandbelt

Why does Melbourne, of all places, have the world's best urban golf? A 25-square-mile swath of sandy soil perfect for golf inspired the nation's top club, Royal Melbourne, to move here, and this was quickly followed by many fantastic layouts, including several courses frequently ranked in the world's Top One Hundred, such as Huntingdale, Metropolitan, and Kingston Heath, another bona fide MacKenzie design. These courses literally are adjacent to one another, so that an errant shot at one can land in a fairway at its neighbor. For this reason, they have come to be called the Seven Sisters of the Sandbelt. Perhaps the planet's greatest concentration of excellent urban courses, they make for a fine week of golf. There is not one course among them that should be skipped.

name was slapped on the layout. Whether it was love of the man who revolutionized golf Down Under or simple marketing savvy, he is associated with far more work than he ever could have done in his one visit.

What we do know is that MacKenzie did design the first course at the new home of Royal Melbourne, Australia's oldest club. Known as the West, it is always the highest-ranked course on the continent and among the top in the world. MacKenzie was assisted by Alex Russell, the premier Australian player of the day, who went on to design the East course, giving the club thirty-six holes. MacKenzie's West is the premier course, but the East is very, very good, and should not be missed.

The very first hole shows MacKenzie's love for St. Andrews. It is straightaway, with the green at the end, slightly elevated, and a fairway so wide it is almost incomprehensible. It would take a good player trying hard to miss it. The green is a similarly huge target, and if you could just 2-putt it would be easy to walk off with an opening par. Of course, in MacKenzie style, this is easier said than done, because the green pitches and falls in all directions. Once you get on the putting surface, you will see why the greens are sometimes compared to MacKenzie's Augusta—except these are faster. This is how you are welcomed into the round.

MacKenzie's big, beautiful, and erratically contoured bunkers are found here, more of them than on any of his other layouts, but almost all are greenside. The opening hole sports just a small solitary hazard to get the flow going, but every green after that is flanked by three, four, five, or even six sand traps, which—as he preferred—often run right up the edge of the putting surface.

From a design perspective, the key holes are six and eight, two perfect examples of the strategic school. Six is a par-4 that plays from an elevated tee and doglegs at almost a right angle, with the corner guarded by a Pine Valley–style waste area of natural sand and low shrubs. It is tempting to try to cut the corner, but requires a very good shot. Fail to do so and, while you can get out of the hazard easily enough, you cannot reach the green from it. Clear the corner, and you are rewarded with a much shorter approach to the trickiest green complex on the course, an elevated putting surface guarded by a very deep bunker. Eight is the ultimate short par-4, a 305-yard hole that doglegs slightly left, with a very long and rather deep bunker beginning at the elbow and running almost to the green, all of which must be carried to earn an eagle putt. Even the safe player must use judgment on this hole: A drive to the layup area cannot be hit too far.

For many avid golfers, life is not complete without a pilgrimage to Scotland and Ireland to play the great links courses. Add the heathland wonders of Melbourne to your list.

ROYAL MELBOURNE AT A GLANCE

+61 3-9598-6755, www.royalmelbourne.com.au

Golf Course Info: Practice area, caddies with advance reservation, walking only.

West: $$$, 5,848–6,589 yards, two tees.

East: $$$, 5,846–6,598 yards, two tees.

Lodging Info: There is a wide range of lodging choices in Australia's second largest city. The premier hotel is the Park Hyatt Melbourne (800–55–HYATT, www.hyatt.com).

Getting There: The sandbelt courses are about thirty minutes from downtown Melbourne and can reached by car, taxi, or public transportation. Qantas now offers direct daily service from Los Angeles to Melbourne. All other flights connect through Sydney.

When to Go: It does not get very cold in Melbourne, rarely dropping below fifty degrees, and golf is played year-round. Still, it does get quite hot in their summer December through February. Spring (November) and fall (March) are the best times.

Australian Travel Tips: Australia seems like it is very far away, but from the West Coast, especially Los Angeles, it is closer than Europe, certainly Scotland. It also offers world-class lodging and dining far superior to any you will find in the British Isles. Because of the weak Australian dollar, it is even less expensive for

Melbourne's sandbelt features the same soil and flora that makes Pine Valley the top course in the States, and here in Australia MacKenzie built his greatest course the public can play, Royal Melbourne. LARRY OLMSTED

U.S. golfers than Canada, and the best golf courses are bargains. Couple this with good weather, friendly and sophisticated residents, and a welcoming attitude toward North Americans, and you can understand why we think it is a great golf destination. Like many top courses abroad, Royal Melbourne and the other sandbelt courses are private clubs and have limited tee times for visitors. They are slightly more formal than their Scottish counterparts; if you're attempting to make reservations on your own, many require a letter from your home club. Still, whether you belong to a club or not, you may find it much easier to arrange a trip through a golf tour operator specializing in the region, which can make tee times and arrange transportation and, if you need it, lodging as well. The best choices are Koala Golfday (+61 3–92–598–2574) and Wide World of Golf (800–214–GOLF, www.wideworldofgolf.com).

Golf Travel by Design Courses Nearby: Kingston Heath (two minutes); Royal Adelaide (one-hour flight); Moonah course (seventy minutes).

KINGSTON HEATH, *Melbourne, Australia*

On just 125 acres of flat land, Dr. MacKenzie carved out a course routinely ranked in the world's Top Thirty.

The land where Royal Melbourne sits was too good for just one MacKenzie course, so he followed up with a neighbor at Kingston Heath. While the Royal Melbourne site invited the wide fairways, huge greens, and grand scale he loved, however, the much smaller plot at Kingston Heath demanded a totally different design, yet one that would benefit from the perfect heathland terrain. The result is a very intricate routing, with holes doubling back in all directions, fit into the land like a jigsaw puzzle—albeit a very good one. MacKenzie firmly believed that as you played a course, no hole should be like the one before it, and here, even more than at Royal Melbourne, he achieved that.

The fairways are narrow by MacKenzie standards, and there are more trees, since adjacent holes needed to be separated and screened from one another. There is still little rough, however, and although you cannot wander as much with the driver, it is quite playable and enjoyable for all abilities. The greens are smaller, but not small, and still have the trademark contours that make every putt an adventure. But what really makes Kingston Heath stand out is its exceptional bunkering, mostly greenside, with all the flamboyant scalloped edges and deep faces MacKenzie could muster.

Kingston Heath is consistently ranked the second best course in Australia. As with any close margin, there are those who think it is actually superior to Royal Melbourne. There is only one way to find out: Go play them both.

KINGSTON HEATH AT A GLANCE

+61 3-9551-1955, www.kingstonheath.com

Golf Course Info: Practice area, walking only.

$$, 6,049–6,969 yards, two tees.

Lodging Info: There is a wide range of lodging choices in Australia's second largest city. The premier hotel is the Park Hyatt Melbourne (800–55–HYATT, www.hyatt.com).

Getting There: The sandbelt courses are about thirty minutes from downtown Melbourne and can reached by car, taxi, or public transportation. Qantas now offers direct daily service from Los Angeles to Melbourne. All other flights connect through Sydney.

When to Go: It does not get very cold in Melbourne, rarely dropping below fifty degrees, and golf is played year-round. Still, it does get quite hot in their summer December through February. Spring (November) and fall (March) are the best times.

Australian Travel Tips: See Royal Melbourne.

Golf Travel by Design Courses Nearby: Royal Melbourne (two minutes); Royal Adelaide (one-hour flight); Moonah course (seventy minutes).

ROYAL ADELAIDE, *Adelaide, Australia*

By trying his hand at a links course Down Under, MacKenzie earned yet another spot on the world's Top One Hundred.

A delaide, in South Australia, is not on the itinerary of most first-time visitors Down Under, but it should be. A beautiful small city with a quaint downtown pedestrian area, it combines the cosmopolitan charms of Melbourne and Sydney with the laid-back rural life that typifies much of the continent. It is also the gateway to the fertile Barossa Valley, where some of the best wines on earth are produced, making it a perfect destination for the golf-loving oenophile.

Twenty-five miles outside of town lies an area where the receding sea left traditional linksland, the closest thing in Australia to the Scottish coast. It was here that Royal Adelaide was built first in a hodgepodge style by several successive expatriate Scots, and finally by Dr. MacKenzie, who unified, modified, and expanded the existing routing. Unlike traditional links courses, however, it is not adjacent to the sea but slightly inland, with a few stands of trees. The routing is very much a traditional parkland one—a crude square with the clubhouse dead center—rather than an out-and-back series of parallel nines. The result is a unique links-parkland-heathland hybrid that, like many MacKenzie designs, consistently lands on the world's Top One Hundred rankings. Those who appreciate the humble origins of the game, reflected in many Scottish links, will be glad to discover it even has train tracks running along it.

The course has more rough than MacKenzie would have liked, but in most places he was able to substitute exposed sandy waste area for tall grass. It features the sandy dunes native to links golf, but the land's main topographic feature is the huge crater lined with sand behind which he built the eleventh green—now the course's signature hole. It is quite a flat course, open to the winds, and has relatively few bunkers, mostly reserved for the greenside areas. It presents much different challenges than his sandbelt courses in Melbourne, with the wind requiring lower ball flight; the course is more geared to a bump-and-run game, with no elevated greens. The course is quite long, stretching over 7,200 yards, and has just three 1-shotters, earning it the unusual par of 73.

+61 38-8356-5828, www.royaladelaidegolf.com.au

Golf Course Info: Practice area, walking only.

$$, 6,124–7,236 yards, three tees.

Lodging Info: There are numerous hotels in Adelaide, premier among them the Hilton Adelaide in the center of town (800–774–1500, www.hilton.com).

Getting There: Adelaide is an easy flight from Sydney or Melbourne. The course is 25 miles from downtown.

When to Go: It does not get very cold in Adelaide, rarely dropping below fifty degrees, and golf is played year-round. Still, it does get quite hot in their summer (December through February). Spring (November) and fall (March) are the best times.

Australian Travel Tips: See Royal Melbourne.

Golf Travel by Design Courses Nearby: Royal Melbourne (one-hour flight); Kingston Heath (one-hour flight).

PASATIEMPO, *Santa Cruz, California*

MacKenzie loved this course—a pet project of his—so much that he chose to live here, building a house on the sixth fairway.

Despite his far-flung adventures, you need not cross any oceans to play a legendary MacKenzie layout. If you live on the West Coast, you do not even have to cross the country. Santa Cruz, California, is home to the highest-ranked public MacKenzie layout in the United States, a course with an almost fanatical following that thinks it should be ranked much, much higher. Of all the places he built courses and traveled to, it was here, far from his English roots, that he chose to build a home and live, along the sixth fairway.

There are several factors that set the course apart from other MacKenzie designs. It is heavily treed, and the overall piece of land is quite small, resulting in a midlength course that has narrower fairways than he usually laid out. The two nines are quite distinct, with the front opening gently, as he preferred, with an unusual short par-5. The front continues with very straightforward holes, few bunkers, and scarcely a dogleg along the way. This simple design actually reflects the way many links courses play and meets his standards of no blind shots, but seems odd in the wooded setting where doglegs are more common. He did fulfill his goal of building two distinct loops; the front nine runs south from the clubhouse in an almost mini links routing, while the back mirrors this to the north. But the back is much more fraught with hazard, incorporating the numerous rugged ravines on the site, which can be found both in the fairways and guarding the front of the greens. The front nine is a good warm-up—as it should be, because the back is much tougher, and woe to the golfer who steps to the tee of the dogleg- and ravine-studded par-5 tenth without playing the front. The course finishes with a long par-3, a very rare closer that is even more rarely used successfully, a design we have found pleasing on so few courses in the world that they can be counted on one hand. Pasatiempo makes that list.

It is said that the fearsome sixteenth hole here was MacKenzie's favorite of all he designed—though oddly it violates many of his rules, with no safe "putting" route to the green and a blind tee shot over a ridge. The fairway is guarded on the left by a ravine, on the right by out-of-bounds, and no matter how far you strike your tee shot, all approaches are played from a downhill lie over a ravine and stream in front of an elevated, three-tiered green guarded on the sides by deep bunkers.

Since Pasatiempo was originally built with club members in mind, the clubhouse, maintenance, and facilities are all of the highest standards, making this one of the most pleasant public golf experiences you will experience.

The Woman Who Changed Golf

It was when he was laying out Cypress Point that MacKenzie met Marion Hollins, the 1921 U.S. Women's Amateur Champion, who was athletic director for Samuel Morse, the telegraph magnate who built both Cypress Point and the entire Pebble Beach resort. Hollins was the driving force behind the creation of Cypress Point, widely regarded as one of the handful of top private courses in the world and perhaps MacKenzie's best work. It was Hollins who found another fantastic piece of land overlooking the ocean, became obsessed with putting a golf course on it, rounded up the investors, and brought in MacKenzie. The result was Pasatiempo, her labor of love, and the traveling golfer owes her a huge debt to this day.

(831) 459–9169, www.pasatiempo.com

Golf Course Info: Practice area, walking allowed.

$$$, 5,629–6,445 yards, three tees. *Slope rating* 135–141. *Course rating* 71.1–74.1.

Lodging Info: The charming Inn at Pasatiempo sits adjacent to the course, an upscale country inn with well-equipped rooms. Suites feature fireplaces and Jacuzzi tubs (800–834–246, www.innatpasatiempo.com).

Getting There: The course is forty-five minutes from the San Jose airport and about two hours from San Francisco.

When to Go: The area has mild weather all year long, although heavy rains can and do occur in winter months.

Golf Travel by Design Courses Nearby: Links at Spanish Bay (forty-five minutes); Spyglass Hill (forty-five minutes); Half Moon Bay (forty-five minutes); Wente Vineyards (two hours).

NORTHWOOD, *Monte Rio, California*

A MacKenzie course so obscure that it cannot be found in most guidebooks, Northwood has three things going for it: location, location, and location.

Many golfers cannot bring themselves to accept that a lone nine-holer can be a "real" golf course, and as a result Northwood is the least known MacKenzie design in the United States. Nonetheless, its setting and unusual history make it worth a visit.

Jack Neville, a successful real estate developer, was a member of the then powerful Bohemian Club based in San Francisco, and he found this seventy-acre wooded tract along the Russian River in the wine country north of the city. Neville figured it would make an ideal spot for his club to build its own course, and Neville knew a thing or two about golf, having designed the world-famous Pebble Beach Golf Links on the Monterey Peninsula, America's most famous course. Yet he elected to employ MacKenzie to lay out Northwood, which has since passed from the club's hands and is now a public course.

There is nothing wrong with the parkland design, which still features the MacKenzie touches, most notably his contoured greens, and it meets his ideals as a fun, welcoming course with few onerous hazards. Yet its intrinsic appeal comes more from its rarity, since he designed so few public courses in this country, and from its setting, near both Napa and Sonoma, the twin pinnacles of the American wine industry. The two valleys are among the nation's finest tourist destinations, and packed with excellent restaurants, lodging, shopping, and, of course, dozens of public wineries, all in a gorgeous natural setting. It can be hard to pull yourself away from these surroundings to play golf, and nine holes fits the bill perfectly. This is made even more relevant by the surprising dearth of quality public courses in the region. Considering that south of San Francisco is the best concentration of golf courses in the country, and the land to the north is so beautiful, there is hardly anywhere to play; the major public venues, such as Silverado, are overpriced and overrated. All of which makes it more tempting to drop in between wine tastings for a quick ninety-minute round on this hidden MacKenzie design.

NORTHWOOD AT A GLANCE

(800) 330-1167, www.northwoodgolf.com

Golf Course Info: Practice area, walking allowed.

$, 2,780–2,858 yards, two tees.

Lodging Info: For lodging in wine country, it is worth splurging, if you can, on these two unparalleled boutique hotels: Meadowood (707–963–3646), with a nine-hole course, or Auberge du Soleil (707–963–1211). Both have great rooms and fine restaurants, and are among the nation's best small hotels. There are plenty of less expensive options, and many hotels to choose from in San Francisco itself.

Getting There: The course is forty-five minutes from San Francisco.

When to Go: Wine country has mild weather all year long, although heavy rains can and do occur in winter months.

Golf Travel by Design Courses Nearby: Wente Vineyards (ninety minutes).

THE JOCKEY CLUB, *Buenos Aires, Argentina*

**The richest club in the world asked
Dr. MacKenzie to design its courses, and he brought
a touch of Scotland to South America.**

Playing the Old course at St. Andrews is something many golf fans want to do once in their lifetimes, but actually getting a tee time can take longer: There is only one St. Andrews. Still, there are some close substitutes, the best of which can be found in Buenos Aires.

At one time the polo-oriented Jockey Club was said to the world's wealthiest private club, and its multimillionaire tycoon members saw golf as a fitting diversion to add to their horse racing and polo. MacKenzie was thus brought in and no expense was spared, resulting in what is widely considered the finest course on the continent. But because the members knew little about golf—unlike so many who insert opinions into the design process—MacKenzie was given free rein and created a course remarkably similar to his one true love, the Old course. As he stated in his memoir, "We made the ground extremely undulating by constructing a series of irregular swales . . . They give the place such a natural appearance that the undulations appear to have been created by the effects of wind and water thousands of years ago. The course has a greater resemblance—not only in appearance but in the character of its golf—to the Old course at St. Andrews than any inland course I know."

It was the *Shadow Creek* of its day, transformed through money and effort from a dead-flat field with just 3 feet of elevation change to a superbly rolling course, complete with the most modern automated irrigation system of its time. As a result of this, and the city's moderate year-round climate, it is always in fantastic shape.

The Red course, the premier layout, has among the fewest bunkers of any MacKenzie design, relying instead on the tricky bounces and off-kilter lies of the undulating fairway and hillocks to protect par. The few bunkers are used strategically, as at Royal Melbourne, to create risk-reward options, especially on short par-4s, the hardest holes on which to accomplish such a feat. Yet MacKenzie was a master of this. An example is the 340-yard fifth, with a cross bunker in the fairway at 220 yards, forcing the decision between a short layup or a long drive to set up a chip to the green. Throughout the Red course he meets his goal of varied hole designs, with long, short, and medium examples of every par. The greens are typically fast, undulating, and as reliable as any you will see.

The Blue course is very similar in both spirit and layout, but notably shorter, playing to just 6,229 yards from the tips. This makes it a fantastic experience for shorter hitters, since few foreign courses offer the tee selection common in the States; in many cases there is only one choice of tees for men or women.

A trip to the Jockey Club is also rich in culture, because the lavish club is a Buenos Aires institution. This; the city itself, known as "the Paris of South America"; and the large number of quality courses being built in the country in modern years all make it one of the more interesting and exotic golf destinations you will find.

JOCKEY CLUB AT A GLANCE

www.jockeyclub.com.ar

Golf Course Info: Practice area, walking allowed.

Red: $$, 5,440–6,628 yards, two tees.

Blue: $$, 5,034–6,229 yards, two tees.

Lodging Info: Buenos Aires is a large city with a wealth of lodging choices, but the cream of the crop is the Park Hyatt (800–55–HYATT, www.hyatt.com).

Argentina Travel Tips: Even more so than in the United Kingdom, arranging golf and other details of your trip can be a real challenge, because most Web sites and people you will reach on the phone use Spanish. We recommend using a tour operator familiar with golf in the area, many of which combine golf in Buenos Aires with excursions to other parts of Argentina to see its natural wonders or wine country. We recommend Patagonia Golf (+54 291–641–4361, 800–359–7200, www.patagoniagolf.com).

Getting There: The course is twenty-five minutes from downtown.

When to Go: Golf is played year-round. Their summer (November through March) is quite warm; it's also peak tourist season.

Golf Travel by Design Courses Nearby: None.

Other Notable Alister Mackenzie Courses You Can Play

- **Moortown,** Yorkshire, England
- **The Alwoodley** (with Harry Colt), Yorkshire, England
- **University of Michigan,** Ann Arbor (students and alumni only)
- **Ohio State University,** Columbus (thirty-six holes, students and alumni only)
- **Blairgowrie (Rosemount course),** Perthshire, England
- **New South Wales Golf Club,** La Perouse, Australia

Stanley Thompson (1894–1952)
The Father of Canadian Golf

Like Alister MacKenzie and Donald Ross, who did their best work far from the British Isles, Stanley Thompson was born in Scotland. After he received the opportunity to build a course outside Toronto, though, he never looked back, making Canada's largest city his home and proceeding to build wonderful courses throughout the country. He designed more than 200 in all, but the vast majority are private. While Ross, MacKenzie, and others ventured north on occasion, Thompson dominated the development of the game in Canada; a frequent matter of debate is not which course is the nation's best, but which Thompson design holds that title. Various critics make arguments for his works at Jasper Park, Banff Springs, Capilano, and Cape Breton Highlands, all with good reason.

As Much Artist as Architect

Canada and Thompson's ideals fit together perfectly. In love with nature, he was as much an artist as an architect. This was reflected in his unusual tactic of venturing into the woods with a bottle of gin and returning only when the tee, green, and fairway sites had been revealed to him in the wilderness. Beautiful physical settings are plentiful in the golf world, but it is no hyperbole to say that Thompson got the most incredible golf course locations in a nation with some of the most incredible scenery on earth. Playing a course like Banff Springs, it is very easy to overlook design entirely—which in fact was Thompson's goal: He thought the course should blend into the surroundings, not the other way around. If this meant putting in walks of several hundred yards between holes to utilize the best land, so be it. The result is courses that seem to have built themselves, when in fact the level of design detail and innovation to create this effect was enormous. To achieve it, Thompson would often:

- **Frame the scenery.** His routing would be laid out to locate the most prominent natural features behind the green, creating one breathtaking vista after another. This is especially true at his mountain masterpieces in northwestern Canada, where he framed the high peaks with the fairways and greens. Likewise, he often used elevated tees to reward golfers with glorious views.

- **Create flamboyant par-3s.** As if the 1-shot hole gave him the chance to compress nature into one swing, Thompson used forced carries and dramatic elevation changes to create often penal, but undeniably memorable short holes. Players' hands may shake even on his shortest 1-shotters, but the emotional reward of conquering such holes is high. Always the artist, he chose colorful names such as Bad Baby, Wishing Well, and the Devil's Cauldron.

- **Work on scale with nature.** It was not enough for his courses to blend in;

THOMPSON DOMINATED THE DEVELOPMENT

OF THE GAME IN CANADA; A FREQUENT

MATTER OF DEBATE IS NOT WHICH COURSE IS

THE NATION'S BEST, BUT WHICH THOMPSON

they had to complement the natural setting. At his mountain courses, Thompson was the first to contour the lips of the bunkers to mirror the shapes of the mountain ranges behind them—a beautiful subtlety that does not have to be recognized to be enjoyed, and one that other architects have used with abandon. In his larger-than-life setting at Vancouver's Capilano, Thompson created a larger-than-life course, with oversized bunkers, mounds, and fairways to suit the scale of the surroundings.

- **Make it fun.** While his courses are always demanding, Thompson followed the Donald Ross ethic of using wide fairways and ample playing areas so the layouts could be enjoyed by all. Rather than long, tight holes, he used tricky green complexes, frequent elevation changes, illusions to distort depth perception, and hazard-strewn par-3s to provide resistance to scoring.

Thompson does not enjoy the name recognition in the United States that many of his peers do, but his role in the development of golf course architecture is undeniable. His protégé Robert Trent Jones Sr. went on to become the most prolific designer in the game. Thompson not only laid out some of the most beautiful golf courses ever built, but also inspired future generations of designers to do the same.

BANFF SPRINGS, *Banff, Alberta*

Home to the Devil's Cauldron, considered by many the finest par-3 in the world, this is one of the most wonderful golf settings imaginable.

Banff is Stanley Thompson's best-known work, and his most breath-taking. The course is located at the castlelike Banff Springs Hotel, a grand mountain fantasy resort with hundreds of rooms and towering spires, like something out of a fairy tale. The entire resort resides at Canada's oldest national park, set in a pine forest among the towering mountain peaks of the Rockies.

When the course was built in 1927, it was reputed to be the first on the continent costing more than $1 million. The result dazzles golfers, with snowcapped vistas in every direction and herds of elk—plus the occasional grizzly bear—roaming the course. Thompson's ragged-edge bunkers, contoured to mirror the mountain ranges behind them, add to the drama. Of course, they serve another purpose as well, toughening up the course, and there are a staggering 144 of them.

The course may be in the mountains and woods, but Thompson used a very traditional out-and-back links routing along the banks of the Bow River, except that the front nine runs on the interior side then back along the water, the reverse of the normal design. The benefit of this is that the player gets to the famous Devil's Cauldron faster. The fourth hole is like no other hole on earth. Once you play it, you will never, ever forget it.

Jasper Park shows Stanley Thompson's love for nature with its use of lakes, trees, and expansive views. FAIRMONT HOTELS & RESORTS

The tee box is on a clifflike setting more than 65 vertical feet above the green. Far below sits the green, less than 25 feet in diameter, ringed with bunkers and fronted by a boulder-strewn glacial pond filled with milky white water, a daunting shot under any circumstances. But what makes the hole so special is that the green sits at the bottom of a massive granite rock face, more than 3,000 feet high, soaring vertically from the back of the complex. Down this face run cataracts of melting snow, which in turn feed the lake. It is a hole on the scale of Thompson's artistic vision.

Perhaps Thompson routed the return along the river knowing that anything following the Devil's Cauldron could easily be anticlimactic. He avoids this with a succession of beautifully set and varied holes playing back to the stunning hotel. The hotel has an additional, newer nine holes, but it is hard to imagine skipping another go at this masterpiece to play them.

Golf Travel by Design

BANFF SPRINGS HOTEL AT A GLANCE

(800) 441–1414, www.fairmont.com

Golf Course Info: Practice area, walking allowed.

Thompson Course: $$, 5,607–7,083 yards, four tees. *Slope rating* 139–142. *Course rating* 72.5–74.4.

Tunnel: $, 2,806–3,357 yards (par 36), three tees. *Slope rating* 121–134. *Course rating* 67.0–73.8.

Resort Info: The hotel has nearly 800 rooms and an assortment of facilities to match, including a spa, bowling alley, tennis center, and a dozen restaurants, one Scottish themed in the spirit of Thompson. The castle motif is fully developed inside the hotel as well, right down to the suits of armor decorating the halls. You can walk into the town of Banff Springs, filled with shops and restaurants; outdoor activities of every description, from rafting to hiking, can be found in the national park.

Getting There: Banff is ninety minutes from Calgary.

When to Go: A lot of snow in the area means a short golf season—May through September, but June, July, and August are ideal.

Travel Deals: The weak Canadian dollar and frequent golf package offers from owner Fairmont hotels can make this upscale resort more affordable than its American peers.

Golf Travel by Design Courses Nearby: Jasper Park Lodge (three hours).

JASPER PARK LODGE, *Jasper, Alberta*

A recent historical renovation makes this the least-changed Stanley Thompson course in the world.

Jasper Park is essentially a sister hotel to Banff Springs, located three hours north at the other end of the scenic Ice Fields Parkway, in Jasper National Park. While it's slightly less dramatic than the imposing Banff course, many critics feel the course is better from a strategic point of view. In any case, both the course and the hotel are much different in character than Banff, yet equally charming.

The Jasper Park layout is carved through much thicker woods and built around a lake—its key geographical feature—while slightly farther removed from the surrounding mountains. To bring the mountain views more into play, Thompson used many elevated tee boxes to offer vistas above the tree line and framed the larger peaks in the distance at the ends of fairways and behind greens, bringing the mountains, in essence, closer to the course.

History Repeats Itself

It is often difficult for the modern player to assess the work of classic designers because so few of their courses remain the way they designed them. Even vaunted Augusta National retains few of its original MacKenzie touches. But once in a while, golf history rewards players with a blast of the past. This is the case at Jasper Park, where a 1994 renovation returned the course to the original Thompson design using his blueprints and focusing on restoring the elaborate jagged-edge bunkers that silhouette the mountain ranges behind them.

The fairways are characteristically wide, allowing players of all ability to get off the tee, but they tend to narrow as they approach the green, challenging second and third shots. His par-3s are, as always, challenging, with the difficulty here from elevated and heavily contoured green complexes rather than water. But the highlight of Jasper Park is the lake, so clear that it reflects the surrounding mountains like a jigsaw puzzle image. Thompson took advantage of the pristine setting by building three dramatic holes on a peninsula jutting into the water.

The resort itself takes equal advantage of the lake. While nearby Banff evokes a medieval castle, Jasper is pure Wild West, with a large log-cabin-style main building overlooking the lake, complete with outdoor barbecue restaurant. The guest quarters are found in a variety of log lodges and individual cottages laid out along the water's edge. The resort sits on more than 1,000 pristine acres within the park. While Banff is in a bustling tourist town, Jasper is in remote wilderness, and you feel it both on and off the course.

JASPER PARK LODGE AT A GLANCE

(800) 441–1414, www.fairmont.com

Golf Course Info: Practice area, walking allowed.

$$, 5,935–6,663 yards, three tees. *Slope rating* 121–122. *Course rating* 70.5–73.5.

Resort Info: The hotel has 450 rooms spread among log chalets, lodges, and cabins along a large, pristine mountain lake. Despite its rugged character, it is a true luxury resort, with food, service, and facilities to match, including a large equestrian center and guided outdoor activities of every description.

Getting There: Jasper is four hours from Calgary.

When to Go: A lot of snow in the area means a short golf season—May through September—but June, July, and August are ideal.

Travel Deals: The weak Canadian dollar and frequent golf package offers from owner Fairmont hotels can make this upscale resort more affordable than its American peers.

Golf Travel by Design Courses Nearby: Banff Springs (three hours).

CAPE BRETON HIGHLANDS GOLF LINKS,
Ingonish, Nova Scotia

Often ranked Canada's number one course, this design is so good that it gets more than 20,000 rounds each summer—and it's five hours from the nearest city.

The excesses of the 1990s and the private jet mentality that came with it spawned a worldwide scramble to find the best coastal settings for new golf courses, no matter how remote, resulting in wonderful recent creations in hard-to-reach places such as **Bandon**, Oregon; Manzanillo, Mexico, and Kauri Cliffs, New Zealand. But long before these there was the Highland Links in Cape Breton National Park, at the southeast tip of Nova Scotia, the end of the huge province farthest from the mainland—and thus from American roads.

The land Thompson found was beautiful, but it's not traditional linksland. It has quite a variety of terrain, with gentle rolling bluffs above the sea, holes running right down to the beach, inland hills, and even riverfront property. Built in part on a peninsula, the course offers stunning ocean views at every turn. To utilize the best hole locations in each area, and to avoid the unusable steep slopes along the way, he left spaces—often huge—between holes. The effect is wonderful: The course truly fits its park setting, with the holes scattered. The long walks offer rewarding views of the Cabot Strait, but those used to riding in carts may object to the extra distance—as much as several hundred yards between some holes. In recent years, the cart option has been added to the formerly walking-only layout.

Besides the enormous variety of hole shapes and terrain, golfers can look forward to small, undulating greens and, of course, Thompson's challenging par-3s, such as the twelfth, which stretches to 227 yards from the tips and drops off to the river left of the green. The setting is beautiful, and the oddly spaced routing makes it one of the more unusual coastal courses you will encounter anywhere. Fine lodging and the Acadian cuisine built around local lobster and other shellfish help make up for the arduous journey required to reach it.

Call for Tee Times

Stanley Thompson's course is in the remotest part of Nova Scotia, but he was not the first person to be lured by the area's beauty. Cape Breton's most famous resident was Alexander Graham Bell, inventor of the telephone and the inspiration behind the region's second most famous golf course, Bell Bay.

CAPE BRETON HIGHLANDS GOLF LINKS AT A GLANCE

(800) 441–1118, www.highlandlinksgolf.com

Golf Course Info: Walking allowed.

$$, 5,664–6,596 yards, three tees. *Slope rating* 131–141. *Course rating* 73.3–73.9.

Lodging Info: The Keltic Lodge is a fine hotel located at the course, and it offers golf packages. The resort includes a main lodge with thirty rooms, a larger inn, and several two- to four-bedroom freestanding cottages, many of which have fireplaces. It sits high on a cliff overlooking the sea, and emphasizes the regional cuisine and decor of northeastern Canada with two restaurants and a bar. The lodge operates only during golf season (877–375–6343, www.signature resorts.com).

Getting There: Cape Breton is five hours from Halifax, or two hours from the small airport at Sydney.

When to Go: The short golf season runs from late May through late October.

Golf Travel by Design Courses Nearby: Bell Bay (ninety minutes).

LE CHATEAU MONTEBELLO, *Montebello, Quebec*

On a 65,000-acre estate lies this rare treat, a once private Stanley Thompson design that is now open to the public.

This is the rare instance in which a Stanley Thompson course is almost overshadowed by its resort. While Banff Springs and Jasper Park are both beautiful and unusual, Le Chateau Montebello is truly unique.

In 1930 a Swiss immigrant decided to build an homage to the alpine chateaus of his own country, except out of logs. A camp had to be built to accommodate 3,500 laborers; 1,200 boxcars full of timber later, including the 10,000 giant cedar logs used for the exterior, the largest log structure in the world was ready. For four decades the building and the estate it sits on were privately owned by a club whose members included Prince Rainier and Princess Grace of Monaco. It was sold in 1970 to Fairmont hotels, which now operates it. Of course, along the way the club members had commissioned Stanley Thompson to build them a private course, now part of the resort.

No expense was spared in building the course, and Thompson carved much of site out of the granite slopes of Mount Westcott. The result is a rolling, hilly layout, and, as might be expected, Thompson used every rise to present stunning views of the surrounding area. This is the best of all his courses to play during fall foliage season, when the Quebec countryside comes to life with yellows, reds, oranges, and purples. The rest of the year you will have to settle for another fun Thompson routing that pleases all abilities. But because this was built as a private challenge, not a resort course, the greens are quite demanding, small, fast, and undulating. Because of the limited play and lavish budget, it is also one of the best-maintained Thompson routings available.

LE CHATEAU MONTEBELLO AT A GLANCE

(800) 441-1414, www.fairmont.com

Golf Course Info: Walking allowed, practice facilities.

$$, 4,998–6,235 yards, three tees. *Slope rating* 128–129. *Course rating* 70–72.

Resort Info: Le Chateau Montebello is a full-feature luxury resort with numerous sporting options, including indoor and outdoor tennis and a wide variety of guided outdoor pursuits on the vast property. The French Canadian cuisine reflects the culture of this unique part of Canada.

Getting There: Montebello is 60 miles from Montreal.

When to Go: The golf season runs from May through October. Summer is high season, but fall foliage, in late September, is especially lovely.

Golf Travel by Design Courses Nearby: Le Geant (forty minutes).

GREEN GABLES GOLF COURSE,
Cavendish, Prince Edward Island

Anne of Green Gables may not have played golf, but her home is visible from the eleventh hole of this Stanley Thompson design.

Perhaps no designer built as many courses in parks as Thompson, who seemed to be in the favor of Canadian national park officials. His layouts at Jasper, Banff, and Cape Breton Highlands are all within such parks, and so is the Green Gables Golf Course in Cavendish.

Vintage, no-nonsense Thompson, this course was designed to be walked, and should be, since it is not especially long. As usual, Thompson provides generous fairways and makes the most of an already scenic setting: The course runs along Cavendish Beach, overlooking the sea. Water comes into play on six holes, more than on the typical Thompson layout, and the small greens make tricky targets.

Prince Edward Island National Park is home to the legendary "Anne of the Green Gables" house, which is visible from, and gives its name to, the par-4 eleventh hole. It is here that the story of the red-haired orphan was set in the novel, and all of the holes on Thompson's design are named for places or events in the book, such as the Haunted Woods.

The size of Delaware, Prince Edward Island is quickly becoming a hotbed of golf, with more high-profile courses in a concentrated area than anyplace else in Canada. The new Confederation Bridge, among the longest in the world, links the island with New Brunswick and makes it much easier to play courses on both sides of the Northumberland Strait.

GREEN GABLES GOLF COURSE AT A GLANCE

(902) 963-2488

Golf Course Info: Walking allowed, practice facilities.

$$, 5,589–6,459 yards, three tees. *Slope rating* 120–124. *Course rating* 70.5–72.0.

Lodging Info: Prince Edward Island is small enough that you can drive almost anywhere in the main tourism district in forty-five minutes or less. Green Gables is close enough to Charlottetown, the island's main city, that you can easily stay downtown. The top hotels are the Delta (800–268–1133, www.deltahotels.com) and the Rodd (800–565–RODD, www. Rodd-hotels.ca), both full-service urban branches of Canadian chains. Rodd also has a new golf resort property at the Links at Crowbush Cove, the island's top-ranked layout and not too far from Green Gables—a good choice for those on a golf vacation. For more information on the island, try (888) PEI–PLAY, www.peiplay.com.

Getting There: Drivers can take the Confederation Bridge from New Brunswick, while those flying can come right into Charlottetown on Air Canada.

When to Go: The golf season runs from late May through early October, but June, July, and August are the best months.

Golf Travel by Design Courses Nearby: The Links at Crowbush Cove (fifteen minutes); The Algonquin (three hours).

Other Notable Stanley Thompson Courses You Can Play

- **Whirlpool Golf Course,** Niagara Falls, Ontario
- **Sleepy Hollow,** Cleveland, Ohio
- **Big Met Golf Club,** Cleveland, Ohio
- **Clear Lake,** Onanole, Manitoba
- **The Pines,** Digby, Nova Scotia

Robert Trent Jones Sr.
(1906–1999)
The Father of Modern Golf

Even by the prolific standards of Donald Ross, Robert Trent Jones was a busy man, designing or renovating more than 500 courses in three dozen countries. Like Ross, MacKenzie, and Thompson before him, he emigrated from Great Britain to become an institution on this side of the Atlantic. He became the first person to study golf course design in an academic setting when he combined courses in engineering, hydraulics, and agronomy into a degree program at Cornell University. After graduation, he joined mentor Stanley Thompson and cut his teeth on the beautiful design at Canada's *Banff Springs*.

A New Era in Golf Course Design

Jones's big break came when he redesigned the South course at Oakland Hills, a famed Ross design, for the 1951 U.S. Open. In what has now become common renovation practice, he moved all the fairway bunkers farther from the tee to ensnare big hitters, earning the course the moniker "The Monster." His expertise soon made him the master of preparing U.S. Open courses, a role his younger son Rees would inherit.

Once out on his own, Jones joined the modern era and the mechanized earthmoving equipment that came with it. Coupled with his academic knowledge, this allowed him to do things no one else had ever done and build courses out of beach sand, granite, even volcanic rock, bringing quality golf to the Caribbean and Hawaii in the process. It allowed the easy creation of artificial ponds and lakes, hazards that Jones embraced. It also marked the beginning of a new era in which the land would no longer dictate the course. Natural settings were still important for aesthetics, but a flat course could be made hilly, a tree-lined course cleared, a dry course filled of lakes.

This consequently changed the way the game was played. Building water hazards in front of greens demanded high shots and eliminated the ground game and bump-and-run shots to the green. As American-style play became more power and less finesse oriented, Jones kept making his courses tougher and more penal. A good player himself, who started by redesigning courses to challenge the world's best, he tended to design courses suited to low-handicap play—unlike his predecessors, who emphasized fun for all. In many cases he took the strategic decision out of the players' hands and instead demanded the execution of particular shots.

Equally important was Jones's skill as a slick marketer, which made him a household name and created demand for his work. He was the first to employ a slew of trained "design associates" to help him juggle his many projects. His contributions both to the science and art of design, and to the overall health of the game, are vast, and he created many stunning masterpieces. When you visit one you will find:

ROBERT TRENT JONES II, LLC

NOT ONE TO GIVE GOLFERS AN

EXCUSE NOT TO PLAY FOR PAR, JONES

- **Signature holes.** Before Jones there were famous holes aplenty, but he mastered the marketing idea of designing a stunning hole that could serve as the mouthpiece for a course. He even advertised the slogan "Give your course a signature" for his design business. One of the first courses he created, the Dunes in Myrtle Beach, South Carolina, is recognized as being the birthplace of the signature hole. Today nearly every golf course built has one or more so-called signature holes.

- **Water hazards.** In early golf course design, water hazards were rare and tended to exist only where they were naturally occurring. On the ninety-nine holes at St. Andrews there is but one body of water, a small pond. Jones embraced the water hazard, whether naturally occurring or human-made, and especially used it on the flat courses of the South, where digging out a pond was an alternative to building up artificial mounds in order to create interest. Human-made water hazards are an accepted and intrinsic part of golf course design today.

- **Very elevated greens.** As part of his respect for the power game, Jones built quite a few holes that had steep climbs to the green complexes, far more than ended downhill. This would add between one and two clubs to every such approach. He especially employed this technique when the tee shot played downhill from an elevated tee and increased the length of the drive. Indeed, the prototypical Jones par-4 plays down and up again, often higher than it began.

- **Forced carries.** Not one to give golfers an excuse not to play for par, Jones demanded performance and was not afraid of requiring a penal hazard be carried to reach the green or fairway. He built island-hole par-3s long before Pete Dye's TPC Sawgrass popularized them, put ponds in front of greens routinely, and put lakes in front of the tee boxes.

- **Runway tees.** These very long rectangular tee boxes could sometimes stretch 40 yards, enabling courses to greatly change their length by sliding the tee markers back and forth. They get their name from a resemblance to airport runways.

- **Large, visible fairway bunkers.** Here Jones was not seeking to penalize players so much as to define the boundaries of play and give spatial perspective. In fact, he often put in far-off aiming bunkers that served as targets rather than spots to be avoided.

Jones's venues usually prove exciting places for tournaments, because the drama of missed shots is amplified by penal hazards. But unlike some designers, he was not penal for the sake of it, and in a sense he bridged the two main schools of design philosophy. The shots he required were not superhuman, but they had to be executed, even if it was just a 130-yard 9-iron over a pond to a par-3. And on his par-5s, he did tend to create alternate strategic routes to the green, often with a heroic design choice. His courses tend to be visually dramatic as well, incorporating water hazards, ocean, and sand or rock outcroppings. More than a few of them should be on any golf traveler's must-play list.

ABOVE *Situated on a private island in New York's Lake George, the Sagamore resort and its well-preserved Donald Ross course make a great weekend escape.*
PHOTO COURTESY OF THE SAGAMORE

BELOW *Mother Nature and Harry Colt have made Royal Portrush one of the most beautiful links courses on earth, with epic sand dunes running along the coast and sea views throughout.*
PHOTO LARRY OLMSTED

ABOVE *One of the most classic Robert Trent Jones Sr. designs, the Gold course in Williamsburg has fast firm greens and plenty of bunkers.*
PHOTO ©MIKE KLEMME/GOLFOTO

OPPOSITE PAGE ABOVE *Alister MacKenzie's trademark greenside bunkering is on display at Royal Melbourne, one of the top ten courses in the world.*
PHOTO LARRY OLMSTED

OPPOSITE PAGE BELOW *With an incredible setting in Canada's oldest National Park, the Banff Springs resort offers everything for the traveling golfer, from a castle-like luxury hotel to one of the most breathtaking courses in the world.*
PHOTO FAIRMONT HOTELS & RESORTS

BELOW *Robert Trent Jones Sr. used long narrow fairways in a beautiful natural setting to make Spyglass Hill one of the most difficult courses on the PGA Tour.*
PHOTO ©MIKE KLEMME/GOLFOTO

ABOVE *Stanley Thompson purposely picked his green sites to frame natural features, such as the snowcapped Canadian Rockies at the Jasper Park Lodge.*

BELOW *One of Thompson's best designs, Jasper Park has a little bit of everything, including three holes on a peninsula that juts into a cobalt blue lake.*

ABOVE *Once an exclusive private club, Le Chateau Montebello now offers the traveling golfer the most beautiful Stanley Thompson course to play during fall foliage season.*

BELOW *The Chateau Montebello course is a classic parkland design routed around Mount Wescott on the 65,000-acre resort grounds.*

ABOVE *The most memorable of the many great holes at the Straits course, the seventh, named Shipwreck, will test the nerve of the world's best players in the 2004 PGA Championship, playing more than 230 yards from the back tees.*
PHOTO COURTESY OF KOHLER CO.

OPPOSITE PAGE ABOVE *Built on the sandy shoreline of Lake Michigan, Pete Dye's Straits course at Whistling Straits was the first great modern links built in this country.*
PHOTO COURTESY OF KOHLER CO.

OPPOSITE PAGE BELOW *The Straits has everything you would find in Ireland, including pot bunkers, fescue grasses, sheep, and caddies, which come in handy since carts are not permitted.*
PHOTO COURTESY OF KOHLER CO.

ABOVE *The windswept Ocean Course on Kiawah Island, which has hosted the Ryder Cup matches, features raw, primal nature at its best.*

PHOTO KIAWAH ISLAND RESORTS

RIGHT *Jack Nicklaus's Reflection Bay outside Las Vegas combines the best of a desert setting with a huge manmade lake to offer drama and beauty on every hole.*

PHOTO COURTESY
OF REFLECTION BAY

Golf's first "signature hole" revolutionized the way water hazards were used—and golf courses were marketed.

n 1948, when Robert Trent Jones Sr. designed the Dunes, there were only two courses in Myrtle Beach. Today America's golf capital has more than a hundred layouts, but the Dunes is still among the best. It captures the essence of Jones's designs and demonstrates his earliest use of many features he reused all over the world.

The Dunes' claim to fame is the thirteenth, a 575-yard par-5 that is alternatively described as a boomerang, U-turn, or horseshoe. It is more accurately thought of as a V or wedge, with water in the middle. When you stand on the tee, facing the fairway, the green is off to your right, almost at a right angle. The line of play would be right at the green, but the lake is too wide to carry here, so you play down the fairway, away from the green. The options are to hit your tee shot down the right, as close to the water's edge as possible, then play across the narrower end of the lake to get within 100 yards of the green, or to play safely to the center, then around

To Go or Not to Go?

The short par-5, a hole that can be reached in regulation in 2 rather than 3 shots, has been around since the very first golf course in St. Andrews. But Jones added a wrinkle. Most reachable 5s featured the risk on the second shot, with a small green that was often flanked by hazards. In this case you can hit your drive, then decide whether to go for the green based on the result of your tee shot. But Jones's signature hole at the Dunes, and many after it, takes a different tack. If you want to go for it in 2, you must decide before you hit your tee shot, then play for the ideal landing area as close to the water's edge as possible off the tee. This further accentuates the risk-reward dilemma, because it brings the water into play on the tee shot, and also makes reaching in 3 much more difficult if your tee shot is less than ideal and you change your mind.

Always the pioneer, Robert Trent Jones Sr. built the very first island green at Williamsburg's Gold course. © MIKE KLEMME/GOLFOTO

the bend on the second shot to face a much longer approach with the water along the right. An amazing hole, it broke new ground for the use of water hazards and instantly became golf's first signature hole.

But the Dunes is more than just the thirteenth. It features Jones's long runway tees, many elevated greens, and prominent fairway bunkering. There are short forced carries over water on two holes, a heroic risk-reward carry choice on another, and a pond in front of the green on the par-5 eighteenth. Favoring the long hitter, the course stretches more than 7,000 yards. The second hole doglegs so severely and so close to the tee that to have a decent chance of reaching in 2, you must play your tee shot over the tall trees of the corner—a shot rarely demanded in golf. It also has one other novelty: The routing includes nineteen holes, allowing the club to take one out of play for maintenance at any time, ensuring that high standards are always met.

Today's golfer will not find some of Jones's holes as radical as they were in the designer's day, but will still enjoy the fine layout and the variety of different shots required. Of course, your round will be even more memorable if you par the thirteenth.

(843) 449-5914, www.dunesgolfandbeachclub.com

Golf Course Info: Practice area, walking allowed.

$$, 5,390–7,165 yards, four tees. *Slope rating* 121–141. *Course rating* 69.7–75.4.

Lodging Info: Myrtle Beach has more than one hundred public golf courses and even more hotels, motels, and resorts. Almost all offer packages combining lodging and golf at lower prices than arranging them separately. Myrtle also has the best visitor bureau of any golf destination, with a detailed printed catalog of options, helpful live operators, and a very good Web site. Book your trip here and you will be able to stay and play for $40–100 per day (800-845-4653, www.golfholiday.com).

Getting There: The Myrtle Beach airport is thirty minutes from the Dunes.

When to Go: Golf is played year-round, but spring is high season. Summer is hot and humid; winter temperatures can dip into the thirties.

Golf Travel by Design Courses Nearby: Legends Heathland (fifteen minutes); Caledonia and True Blue (forty-five minutes); Ocean course at Kiawah Island (two hours); Wild Dunes (two hours).

The Unanswerable Question

There are few topics as hotly debated by golf writers as what the correct order of quality at Pebble Beach is; and six different experts will defend all six possible permutations. The Pebble Beach Golf Links is always the most highly ranked in magazines, but these polls weight on the basis of tradition, and Pebble Beach moves up because it is a frequent U.S. Open venue. Hosting that prestigious championship notwithstanding, an equally good argument can be made that the Links at Spanish Bay or Spyglass Hill is the best. Many repeat visitors to the resort think that Spyglass is the best of the bunch, and while we place it ahead of Pebble, we cannot make up our minds about Spanish Bay. In any case, it is one of the must-play wonders of the golfing world, and the very best Jones course.

SPYGLASS HILL, *Pebble Beach, California*

The most difficult course on the Monterey Peninsula invites golfers to frolic where pros fear to tread.

Despite its five-star ranking from *Golf Digest*, awarded to just sixteen courses in this country, Spyglass Hill gets little respect. Part of the great triumvirate of courses that anchor the famed Pebble Beach resort, it usually trails its siblings, the Pebble Beach Golf Links and the Links at Spanish Bay, in name recognition, and it is often visitors' third choice.

It is also among Jones's most difficult when played from the back tees, and that is saying something. The course is part of the AT&T Pro-Am, and three holes here have been rated among the most difficult eighteen of all the courses on the PGA Tour. The 465-yard par-4 sixteenth must feel like a chip and a putt to Tour players coming two holes after a 555-yard *par-4!* But this is from the back tees, where Spyglass's formidable reputation is much deserved. Played from the middle tees, it is still quite challenging, yet great fun. It is also the very best course Robert Trent Jones Sr. ever designed.

The main criticism leveled at Spyglass is also its strength: It seems unable to make up its mind whether it is an oceanfront, wooded, mountainous, or heathland course. The more generous among us describe this as variety, the best of all worlds. Few courses have more than a handful of holes on the ocean, and with five Spyglass has roughly as many as its neighbors. But they are the first five holes—the most electrifying start in golf—rather than spaced sparingly. Most courses build to a crescendo finish while Spyglass sprints out of the gate. Jones's secret weapon is that the inland holes are also very good, and there are far fewer distracting homes than on the other two layouts.

The opener is a par-5 that plays downhill to the sea and immediately lets the player know something special is going on—few other opening holes plunge to the coast. The first five play along the coast on sandy soil, with stunning, stark waste areas of bright white sand and coastal shrubs enhancing the view. As it turns up from the coast and begins to rise and fall in the hilly setting, the layout enters thicker pine forest; as at Augusta, mature trees frame the fairways. It is an indisputably beautiful course, with a wide variety of hole types and challenges, made more interesting by Jones's frequent use of small lakes and ponds and many different green complexes, some large and undulating, others small and severely sloped. For a golf course, Spyglass Hill defines the term *roller-coaster ride.*

SPYGLASS HILL AT A GLANCE

(800) 654–3900, www.pebblebeach.com

Golf Course Info: Practice area, walking allowed, caddies available.

Spyglass Hill: $$$$, 5,618–6,855 yards, three tees. *Slope rating* 133–148. *Course rating* 72.8–75.3.

Links at Spanish Bay: $$$$, 5,309–6,820 yards, three tees. *Slope rating* 129–146. *Course rating* 70.6–74.8.

Pebble Beach Golf Links: $$$$+, 5,197–6,840 yards, three tees. *Slope rating* 130–142. *Course rating* 71.9–74.4.

Del Monte: $$, 6,069–6,339 yards. *Slope rating* 120–125. *Course rating* 70.3–71.6. This eighteen-hole short course is rarely full, and popular with local residents trying to beat the crowds on the other three layouts.

Resort Info: Pebble Beach has three hotels, the Lodge at Spanish Bay, the Inn at Pebble Beach, and Casa Palmero, a small boutique hotel that is the most luxurious of all. All three are high-end, and in summer months every weekend sells out. Technically you do not have to be a guest to play, but only guests can reserve an advance tee time, a virtual prerequisite for Pebble and almost as important for Spyglass and Spanish Bay. Singles can walk on the morning of play, but may have to wait several hours. The resort sits on the famed 17-mile drive along the coast and has a full range of amenities, including a large equestrian center, spa, and several restaurants. It's near the charming town of Carmel.

Getting There: Pebble Beach is two and a half hours from San Francisco. The Monterey airport, served by a few major carriers, is thirty minutes away.

When to Go: The area has mild weather all year long, although heavy rains can and do occur in winter months.

Golf Travel by Design Courses Nearby: Spanish Bay (five minutes); Pasatiempo (forty-five minutes); Half Moon Bay (forty-five minutes); Wente Vineyards (two and a half hours).

VALDERRAMA AND SOTOGRANDE, *Cadiz, Spain*

Ask an American to name any course in Continental Europe, and odds are good you will get Valderrama, its number-one-ranked course and home to two Ryder Cups.

The words *beautiful* and *gorgeous* are used often when describing the world's best golf courses, but at Valderrama beauty is more than a feature; it is the lifeblood. Industrialist Jaime Ortiz-Patino and a group of friends purchased an existing course here and set out to build nothing less than the "Augusta of Europe." This meant planting and tending beautiful flowers and incorporating the compelling native cork trees that have made the course famous. It means limiting outside play to two hours a day, all but banning carts, and courting members who play little but spend lavishly on upkeep. It means closing the course for the entire month of June each year for routine maintenance. The results are stunning.

But Valderrama is more than mere eye candy. Here Jones achieved one of his best works, blending his penal instincts and requirement for power with a large dose of strategic design. Like Pinehurst Number Two, he gives you plenty of fairway to work with, but requires you to hit specific parts of it to obtain the correct angle of approach. The cork trees, while beautiful, are natural shot blockers, and he carefully locates stands of them to frustrate the recovery from ill-placed tee shots—one of the most inventive uses of trees in golf. On top of all this, Jones has assembled four spectacular 1-shot holes, a feat limited to a few great courses.

Ironically, the course has far less water and is less penal than many of his designs, but it is best known for the pond fronting the seventeenth green, one of only two in direct play on the course. It is here in the Ryder Cup matches that Tiger Woods and other top players routinely backspin their approaches off the superslick green and down the steep slope into the pond. Bunkers in the steep face behind the green prohibit bailing out long, which would result in a downhill bunker shot toward the pond.

We expect a signature hole from Jones, and despite the televised hoopla at seventeen, here it comes much earlier at the fourth. This par-5 plays less than 520 yards from the white tees, and the green is extremely elevated, atop a high hill. If this doesn't dissuade you from going for it in 2, the greenside pond on the right might, because it flows into a waterfall and fills a succession of staggered pools down the side of the hill's front, both beautiful and deadly. A deep bunker awaits those missing left, but the real success of the hole is that any shot left even a foot short of the putting surface on the uphill approach will roll all the way back down the fairway, up to 40 yards from the green. This challenges even those who go for it in 3.

Next door lies Sotogrande, Valderrama's much older sister course, also designed by Jones. It is the yin to Valderrama's yang. A classic parkland course, with much taller mature cork trees framing fairways, it is flatter—except for the elevated greens on the long par-3s—more traditional, with Jones's aiming bunkers and runway tees; and surrounded by stately villas instead of isolated in a lush garden. But it is a wonderful course, considered the best in Spain before its precocious sibling came along, and no trip to Cadiz is complete without playing both courses.

Sotogrande is a stately course, one that gives you room to play but requires power off the tee. Next door, impeccably tended and rolling through the hilly Spanish countryside, Valderrama is a dream come true for members and visitors alike.

VALDERRAMA AND SOTOGRANDE AT A GLANCE

Valderrama: +34 956-791-200, www.valderrama.com; Sotogrande: +34 956-795-050

Golf Course Info: Practice area, walking only, caddies.

Valderrama: $$$, 5,349–6,883 yards, six tees.

Valderrama Par-3 Short Course: 857–885 yards.

Sotogrande: $$$, 5,584–6,846 yards, three tees.

Lodging Info: The Ryder Cup players stay at the San Roque Club a few miles away, and so should you. Club guests also get preferential tee times at Valderrama—very important, since so few are available—and access to Sotogrande. The premier lodging choice in the region, the club features rooms in individual casitas and full resort services including an interesting eighteen-hole Dave Thomas design of its own (+34 956–613–030, www.sanroqueclub.com). A less expensive but high-quality choice is the Almenara Golf Hotel, on the very impressive and mountainous Almenara course, the third best in the region (+34 956–582–000). Both are just minutes from the courses.

Spanish Travel Tips: These courses are easier to arrange play on than many foreign clubs: Valderrama has a high-tech tee time system and good Web site. Still, there are only a handful of tee times each day. Sotogrande has more times, less demand, and is easier to get on. If you don't want to make arrangements yourself, you can stay at the San Roque Club and have the concierge book everything, but have him do this well in advance. Tour operators Perry Golf (800–344–5257, www.perrygolf.com) and Wide World of Golf (800–214–GOLF, www.wideworldofgolf.com) both serve this region.

Getting There: Most people fly to Malaga, an hour and a quarter away, or arrive in Malaga by high-speed train from Madrid. A better bet is to fly to Gibraltar via daily service from London on British Airways. Although it is over the border, it is just fifteen minutes away.

When to Go: The area is at the end of the Costa del Sol (Coast of the Sun), which has more than 320 sunny days each year. Golf is played year-round, but summer gets hot and humid—and Valderrama closes for all of June.

Golf Travel by Design Courses Nearby: None.

CRUMPIN-FOX, *Bernardston, Massachusetts*

Always the pioneer, Jones led the charge to better public golf in Massachusetts, firing a shot that would be heard around the world.

Once upon a time, not so long ago, there were just three kinds of golf courses in America: private, resort, and bad. Okay, so this is a bit of an exaggeration. There have always been some standout municipal courses, such as Bethpage Black and Torrey Pines, but these were exceptions. The average muni was run-down and uninspired, and so were many public courses.

Today we have an endless number of what are called "high-end daily fee" or "member for a day" courses, which try to give average golfers a country club experience, both on and off the course, usually for quite a bit more than they're used to paying. The concept is popular, and today we take them for granted. Some designers, such as Mike Stranz, do nothing else.

It is unclear whose idea the high-end daily fee was, but many give credit to the Crumpin-Fox course. It was one of the first such layouts, and one of the first to get a lot of attention, with high rankings in the magazines and its selection as a regional qualifier for the U.S. Open. It remains one of the most popular public layouts in Massachusetts, and is a relative bargain as well.

Jones built courses in every kind of terrain all over the world and in forty different states, and always managed to adapt to the local surroundings. It is no different here, where he has laid out a true New England parkland masterpiece. The trees, a mix of hardwoods and pines, are dense enough that you rarely see another hole, and the bubbling brooks and small ponds fit the landscape perfectly. The back nine is chiseled from sections of rocky ledge, allowing ingenious use of the hillside, such as the green sitting in a pocket on the hillside for the short par-3 eleventh. Under the shade of mature trees, you find undulating greens surrounded with plenty of bunkers. While one par-3 characteristically plays over a pond, sand and length are the major defenses at Crumpin-Fox, one of Jones's subtler designs.

CRUMPIN-FOX AT A GLANCE

(800) 943-1901, www.sandri.com

Golf Course Info: Practice area, walking allowed.

$$, 5,432–7,007 yards, four tees. *Slope rating* 131–141. *Course rating* 71.5–73.8.

Lodging Info: There is not much near the course besides the Fox Inn, which offers packages combining golf and lodging (800–436–9466, www.sandri.com). The course is half an hour from Springfield, Massachussettes, which has several large chain hotels.

Getting There: Crumpin-Fox is 30 miles from Springfield, Massachussetts, and just over an hour from Bradley International Airport in Hartford, Connecticut.

When to Go: Golf is played from April through November, but June through October are the best months.

Golf Travel by Design Courses Nearby: None.

GOLDEN HORSESHOE GOLD COURSE,
Williamsburg, Virginia

Colonial Williamsburg is a living museum full of American history, and this Robert Trent Jones Sr. classic fits right in.

Robert Trent Jones Sr. is rightfully described as introducing the modern era, but for most Americans, many of his designs are classics. The runway tee boxes, straightaway fairways with gleaming bunkers on either side, and steady parkland designs with the occasional pond fronting the green are what we grew up thinking of as the quintessential golf course. Nowhere is this more evident than in Virginia, fittingly at Colonial Williamsburg.

The course opens with a classic hole, a par-4 with a slight dogleg right and a lone greenside bunker. While the course gets more difficult from here on in, the first captures the spirit and sets the mood. The second is a short par-5 with a pond in front of the green, a real risk-reward decision to go for in 2. The third is a midlength downhill par-3 over water to a redanlike green complex. By the fourth hole you have seen as much variety as you will find on some courses, and it keeps getting better. The course continues in this fashion with varied, fun holes carved from the Virginia forest.

It closes in typical Jones fashion with a difficult long hole, and by the end of the round you have experienced the elements that made Jones great. The runway tees allow the course to vary the way holes play daily, and the fast undulating greens are superbly conditioned. There are several approaches over water and surprisingly frequent elevation changes, with his trademark downhill tee shots followed by uphill approaches. Built in 1963, the Gold course even claims to have the first island green. All four par-3s play over water, but none is long, and these somewhat repetitive 1-shotters are the weak link that keep this very good course from being great.

The Gold is part of the Golden Horseshoe complex, which recently added a second course, the Green. It is adjacent to the Gold but starts from a new clubhouse. It was designed by Jones's son Rees, who also renovated his father's layout in 1998. The Green is a good course but much different, with mounds and hillocks lining most fairways and a more secluded feel. Both are part of the Colonial Williamsburg resort, a sort of historical Disney World that includes a re-created colonial village, period shops, and numerous hotels. With the Busch Gardens amusement park just minutes away, and the three courses at Kingsmill, home of the PGA's Michelob Championship, just down the road, it is a perfect place to mix golf with a fun—and educational—family vacation.

GOLDEN HORSESHOE AT A GLANCE

(800) 447-8679, www.cwf.org

Golf Course Info: Practice area, walking allowed.

$$$, 5,168–6,817 yards, four tees. *Slope rating* 124–144. *Course rating* 65.6–76.7.

Lodging Info: Colonial Williamsburg has lodging options at every price point, from motels to the very luxurious Williamsburg Inn, the impeccably decorated jewel in the resort's crown. The latter is a few steps from the golf club (800–447–8679, www.cwf.org). You'll also find a full selection of chain motels and hotels throughout greater Williamsburg, a popular tourist destination.

Getting There: Williamsburg is midway between the Norfolk and Richmond airports, just over an hour to either.

When to Go: Early spring to late fall. For the best weather after the crowds, try October or early November.

Golf Travel by Design Courses Nearby: Royal New Kent (twenty-five minutes).

ROBERT TRENT JONES GOLF TRAIL, *Alabama*

Robert Trent Jones Sr. designed or renovated more than 500 courses worldwide, but nowhere was he more prolific than in Alabama where he laid out 18 entire courses in a single blow.

Robert Trent Jones always thought big. From his first signature hole at the Dunes to the heroic par-3 over the Pacific at Mauna Kea to Texas's fifty-four hardest holes at Horseshoe Bay, many of Jones's golf designs were on a grand scale. So when the largest golf course project the world has ever seen was undertaken, it was fitting that he should be involved.

The state of Alabama wanted to accomplish three important goals: increase tourism, attract new residents, and get a return on the funds stashed in the state employees' retirement fund. After careful research, officials decided that the way to do this was to build golf courses. But not just any golf courses. They had to be high-quality daily fees, with first-rate maintenance, clubhouses, and facilities. They had to be inexpensive and located near major highways. And to encourage tourism, there had to be a lot of them. Alabama's bold solution was to build a golf trail, a series of complexes along the state's two major interstate highways, with no more than a two-hour drive between courses. Robert Trent Jones Sr, would design them all.

To be honest, by the time Alabama approached him, Jones had quit working, and although he technically came out of retirement, his right-hand man Roger Rulewich did most of the work. Rulewich is an accomplished architect in his own right who worked on many of Jones's highest-profile courses and has been very successful recently on his own. In fact, even Jones's death has not stopped the state from expanding the trail and building three more of "his" designs. There are now eight complexes with twenty-one courses.

What Alabama ended up with is sort of an homage to Jones, complete with his forced carries and penal hazards, tough-finishing holes, flashy

The Biggest Golf Construction Project in History

It took Pinehurst, the nation's largest golf resort, a full hundred years to build eight courses. Alabama officials decided to build 324 holes, or the equivalent of eighteen full-sized courses, simultaneously. They built seven different complexes, and each facility had either three full-sized nines plus a nine-hole par-3 course (thirty-six holes) or two full-sized eighteens plus an eighteen-hole par-3 course (fifty-four holes). More facilities have been built since.

fairway bunkers, and, most of all, elevated greens. It seems like more than 300 of the 378 finish uphill. But while the courses are vintage Jones, they are also quite modern, with excellent drainage and a plethora of tee boxes suited to all abilities. For the public, this is a huge addition to the nation's supply of inexpensive high-quality golf. Prices have gone up slightly, but when the trail opened, it was possible to play every hole on it for less than the cost of a single round at Pebble Beach. These are courses that have hosted the Nike Tour Championship and other serious events.

If there is one knock against the trail, it is the cookie-cutter nature of the operation. It appears that a set of "Jones holes" was designed, and then reused over and over, creating a sense of déjà vu on courses hundreds of miles apart. Even the clubhouse floor plans are identical. But there are few, if any, golf bargains like this in the United States, and whether he meant to or not, Jones left a gift to the golfing public that will be enjoyed for years to come.

ROBERT TRENT JONES GOLF TRAIL AT A GLANCE

(800) 949–4444, www.rtjgolf.com

Golf Course Info: Practice area, walking allowed.

$–$$. There are twenty-one courses of varied length. All details are available in the trail guide or on the trail Web site.

Lodging Info: Near every stop along the trail, there are several inexpensive chain motels and hotels. Two companies, SunBelt Golf (800–949–4444, www.rtjgolf), which administers the trail, and Fairways Golf (800–647–2447, www.fairwaysgolftravel.com), offer a multitude of packages combining golf and lodging that are hard to beat.

Travel Deals: The trail sells multiday passes that allow play at different facilities at a discount. In addition, all the individual facilities offer unlimited daily play or heavily discounted replay options depending on the time of year.

Getting There: No place in Alabama is more than two hours from a facility. The courses are also accessible from New Orleans, Biloxi, Memphis, Nashville, Columbus, the Florida panhandle, and the border areas of Ohio, Tennessee, and Mississippi.

When to Go: Golf is played all year, but summer is hot and humid; spring and fall are ideal.

Golf Travel by Design Courses Nearby: None.

BALLYBUNION NEW (CASHEN) COURSE,
Ballybunion, Ireland

The chance to craft a final masterpiece on some of golf's most hallowed ground completed a life well lived for Robert Trent Jones Sr.

The Old course at Ballybunion elicits stronger reactions than almost any other set of holes on earth. Everyone from repeat British Open Champion Tom Watson to outspoken architecture critic Tom Doak to the most famous golf writer of all, Herbert Warren Wind, has proclaimed it the world's best. It is more than just the highest-ranked course in the Republic of Ireland; it is a source of national pride. Built in 1893, its mystique is furthered by the mystery of an unknown designer.

So when the good people of Ballybunion decided to add a second course, it was with no small trepidation. Such situations rarely work out for the best; with expectations so high, loyalists would inevitably proclaim any effort inferior, even if surpassed the original. While most architects would covet such an assignment, they would also fear the derision almost sure to follow. Not Robert Trent Jones Sr. After all, he had been through this once before, when he built the follow-up to the Pebble Beach Golf Links. At the tender age of seventy-four, he did not merely accept the commission, he threw himself into it, inspired to craft one last masterpiece.

A minority believe Jones succeeded in creating at least an equal; even his critics admit that they could hardly accept it if he dethroned the legend. He did not. If you can play only one course at Ballybunion, make it the Old, and experience a bit of pure links golf. But instead of choosing, play them both, because Jones did not fail at all. Rather than try to out-Ballybunion Ballybunion, he built a much different course, and it is worth a visit.

What Jones did was combine his talents for manipulating nature and

The Old Country

The British Isles are where it all began for golf, and they are so full of the sport's traditions that many residents are still suspicious of the U.S. version of the game. Nonetheless, American designers have begun to make their mark in the Old Country: Jack Nicklaus, Tom Weiskopf, Robert Trent Jones Jr., and even newcomer Kyle Phillips have crafted well-received courses in Ireland, England, Wales, and Scotland. But all of these were either new projects or—in the case of Nicklaus's Gleneagles and Mount Juliet designs—resort layouts. Robert Trent Jones Sr. is the only American designer to crack the inner sanctum and design a course for one of the Old Country's most revered and historic "private" clubs, Ballybunion. The fact that club members chose him is a testament to the body of Jones's work and the respect he has commanded in the industry.

his flair for do-or-die shotmaking with a traditional links routing on a near-perfect piece of linksland. But whereas most links courses are content to let the land dictate the greatness of the holes, Jones wanted drama on every single one. This tract had not been utilized before because of the steep, rugged contours of its terrain, which made construction extremely difficult, but someone who invented machinery to pulverize volcanic rock would not flinch from this challenge.

The result is sort of a links course on steroids—everything is bigger, brasher, and more penal. The landscape has gigantic scale, with huge dunes and trenchlike valleys; the best holes are laid out through, over, and around this otherworldly geography. A few play above this setting with expansive views, creating the feeling of being at the top of the world. But in some places Jones tinkered with the linksland too much, such as when he built a tee atop a giant dune and a green atop an even higher dune 233 yards away. So difficult was this 1-shotter that it was almost immediately designated a par-4, perhaps the world's shortest, with players pitching to the fairway in the valley below. The design fared so poorly with the locals that they replaced it with a par-3 of their own. In addition, Jones could not resist forcing players to fly balls to the greens, and the penalty for missing them is severe. This is anathema to links tradition, which emphasized chipping, pitching, and recovery. The most unusual criticism, in a land where golf carts are considered traitorous, is that the course is too hard to walk.

Still, it appears that Jones had the last laugh. Just as his early ideas were revolutionary and often shocking before becoming mainstream, his nouveau links seems to be catching on. The very unusual routing, with five par-5s and five par-3s, seems prescient given the fantastic acclaim for Tom Doak's new **Pacific Dunes,** lauded (rightfully) as the second coming of links golf, which features five par-3s and four par-5s, three of them on the back. His fantastically and diabolically undulating greens, which were roundly abhorred, are no less extreme than those at Scotland's new Kingsbarns links, which is touted in the press as Fife's finest course, although Fife is home to St. Andrews. Greg Norman's new and hotly anticipated **Doonbeg,** a links intended to be raw, primal, and old-fashioned, is set in the same type of vertical dunescape and even has a par-3 played from one dune to another, although much shorter than Jones's. In the nearly two decades since it opened, critics have warmed to his design, which now gets high marks. But don't play it for them, play it for yourself. Play it to experience Robert Trent Jones's last great effort, a course that truly is larger than life.

NEW (CASHEN) COURSE AT A GLANCE

+353 682-7146, www.ballybuniongolfclub.ie

Golf Course Info: Practice area, walking only, caddies.

New (Cashen): $$, 5,676–6,413 yards, three tees.

Old: $$$, 5,504–6,865 yards, three tees.

Lodging Info: The Teach de Broc Guest House was built a few years ago specifically for golfers, and sits just steps from the first tee and the practice range (+353 682–7581, www.ballybuniongolf.com). There are several other choices in the seaside town that can be booked through the visitor bureau (www.ballybunion.org).

Travel Deals: There is a combined fee for playing both courses in a day that is quite a discount.

Irish Travel Tips: Like many top courses in the British Isles, Ballybunion is technically a private club and has limited tee times daily for visitors. It can be quite arduous to arrange your own itinerary: The time difference and international calling can make it difficult to contact many European courses, each has certain days reserved for competitive member play, and some have days reserved for women members. For this reason, many travelers make all their tee time, lodging, and transportation arrangements in the British Isles through specialized golf tour companies, of which the best are Perry Golf (800–344–5257, www.perrygolf.com) and Wide World of Golf (800–214–GOLF, www.wideworldofgolf.com).

Getting There: Ballybunion is less than an hour from the Shannon airport.

When to Go: Golf season is year-round but the best weather is from April through November; renovations are often undertaken in early spring.

Golf Travel by Design Courses Nearby: Ballybunion New course (sixty minutes); Doonbeg (thirty minutes).

Other Notable Robert Trent Jones Sr. Courses You Can Play

- **Turnberry Isle,** Aventura, Florida (thirty-six holes)
- **Wigwam Resort,** Phoenix, Arizona (thirty-six holes)
- **Horseshoe Bay Resort,** Horseshoe Bay, Texas (fifty-four holes)
- **Montauk Downs,** Montauk, New York
- **Mauna Kea Resort,** Kohala, Hawaii
- **Boyne Highlands (Heather course),** Boyne, Michigan
- **Treetops Resort (Masterpiece course),** Gaylord, Michigan
- **Woodstock Inn,** Woodstock, Vermont
- **Dorado/Cerromar Beach,** Puerto Rico (seventy-two holes)
- **Celtic Manor,** Newport, Wales
- **Adare Manor,** Adare, Ireland
- **Madeira Golf Club,** Madeira, Portugal

The Modern Masters

B efore 1920 it was largely accurate to say that God was the codesigner of virtually every golf course. Architects embraced, but were also constrained by, natural features, and occasionally their routings were made less than ideal by the need to go around, over, or under obstacles.

In the 1920s and 1930s, technology began to have an impact. Powerful earthmoving equipment appeared on the scene, enabling architects to move more dirt and stone, and move it faster, than they could with horses, plows, and shovels. Thus flat and previously uninteresting sites could be built up, first with rolling mounds, and later with actual hills. It also allowed the proliferation of human-made water hazards, pioneered by Robert Trent Jones Sr. as the classical era came to a close. This merger of technology with the art of golf course design also changed the nature of the designers themselves. Originally populated by professional golfers and those involved with golf courses, such as superintendents, the field began to attract more trained architects. Among the modern masters, only Jack Nicklaus first gained prominence as a player.

Some designers got carried away with their new mechanical toys; during this period, golf courses were built longer, with daunting features piled one on top of another. Whereas early designers embraced shot values and often offered numerous strategies for attacking golf holes, modern-era designers, mostly American, changed the way the game was played by emphasizing long tee shots and accurate long-iron approaches. The game became as vertical as it was horizontal, with holes requiring high lofted shots that landed on the green, a change from the running ground game popularized on the links courses of the British Isles.

Another effect of the modern era was greatly improved maintenance and conditioning. The introduction of bulldozers allowed designers to build courses in layers, from the ground up, scraping away undesirable grasses and soil types and replacing them with clay, sand, or whatever best suited the terrain and drainage needs. This allowed for the installation of elaborate irrigation systems as well. Whereas in the classical era, brown was a common color in the game, golfers in the mid–twentieth century came to expect lusher and lusher greens, raising a bar that would prove hard to lower.

The following courses are the highlights of the modern era. Some have taken their place alongside the classics in the pantheon of great golf courses, while others remain controversial. All, however, have had a dramatic impact on the game, our perception of it, and the way it is played.

Honorable Mention

Some other notable designers who have shone in the modern era include:

Jay Morrish. Nowhere is the modern trend of using machinery to convert any terrain to golf courses more evident than in the desert, and no one has had as much success at this uniquely American style as Morrish. His *Troon North Monument* course in Scottsdale is still the gold standard for target-style desert golf, and his thirty-six-hole efforts at the city's posh Boulders resort and *TPC Scottsdale* reinforced his reputation.

Robin Nelson. Hawaii is a ripe landscape for the modern designer, with everything from dramatic coastal cliffs to rain forest and rugged mountains in a condensed area. Many of the most stunning Hawaiian courses had to be carved from lava fields, and almost all combine coastal and inland sections. No designer has laid out more courses in the state than the little-known Nelson, whose pinnacle work is the thirty-six-hole Mauna Lani complex on the Big Island.

Roger Rulewich. Only after a long and respected career in golf course design is Rulewich stepping into the spotlight on his own. The head designer on Robert Trent Jones Sr.'s team, he worked alongside the master on many of the courses that typify the modern era, including *Valderrama.* Since Jones's death, Rulewich has continued on his own, winning awards and accolades with his more recent successes, including Ballyowen and Wild Turkey in New Jersey, and the stunning new Grande Dunes in Myrtle Beach.

Bob Cupp. The bulk of Cupp's best work has been in the burgeoning golf region of the Pacific Northwest, and he stands alongside Ted Robinson as one of the architects mixing first-rate designs with environmentally sound practices. Two of his marquee courses, the award-winning Crosswater at Sunriver, Oregon, and Newcastle, built on a former coal mine outside Seattle, elevated the natural setting beyond the golf course. Cupp is also the game's preeminent pioneer in the use of computer software to assist with design.

Tom Fazio (1945–)
Building Great Courses Anywhere

Fazio has dominated his craft since he entered his uncle's family design business at age nineteen. He has more courses on the Top One Hundred rankings than any other architect and has been referred to by many critics as the greatest living architect. Yet his work is hard to put a finger on, because it is so diverse. Fazio has not concentrated on one region or one style of course. In fact, if he has one outstanding trait, it is his belief that modern equipment and design transcend the land itself.

Diamonds in the Rough

Such an attitude is anathema to most designers and many in the golf trade, but Fazio stands firm. In his book *Golf Course Design*, he flatly states that there are "a million excellent potential golf course sites in the continental U.S. today." Perhaps it is because he has rarely been given the stunning natural settings to work in, the Pebble Beaches or Bandon Dunes of the world, that Fazio takes this tack. In fact, his most acclaimed courses are on some of the worst sites in the traditional sense. Shadow Creek, his pièce de rèsistance, was built on a flat, empty desert lot in Las Vegas. World Woods was an equally unattractive flat site in central Florida. His acclaimed courses in Primm, Nevada, also had nondescript desert settings. He is unafraid to use technology to achieve his desire, and in Tucson, at Ventana Canyon, he built a green with both subsurface heating and cooling systems to combat the drastic desert temperature fluctuations.

Fazio's strength is confidence in his own vision: He visualizes the course and he builds it, letting nothing come between him and his final product. Perhaps he is so adored by the public because he crafts masterpieces in such unlikely settings. Or perhaps it is because unlike many designers, his courses embrace the average player rather than tournament participants. Fazio designs are generally playable and beautiful, two things traveling golfers admire. His other traits include:

- **Beautiful and elaborate bunkering.** Often used more for visual effect than strategic purposes, his bunkers are almost always oriented so they can clearly be seen off the tee, with higher back slopes than fronts. He also frequently places bunkers on uphill slopes to reduce the feeling of ascent.

- **No blind shots.** Fazio has never liked them, and he'll remove boulders and smooth hills so players can see the greens.

- **Trouble left.** As part of his user-friendly playability, Fazio tends to put serious trouble, such as water hazards, on the left sides of holes, since the vast majority of players slice and miss right.

- **Massive earthmoving.** Fazio can build a parkland course in the desert or vice versa, and while his skills hide the effect from the player to make

FAZIO'S STRENGTH IS CONFIDENCE IN HIS

OWN VISION: HE VISUALIZES THE COURSE

AND HE BUILDS IT, LETTING NOTHING COME

them look natural, they are often out of context with the regional environment. He creates dunes where there are no dunes and hills on flat sites.

- **The Pine Valley look.** Fazio's uncle George was the pro at Pine Valley, and Fazio is a member. He also built the club's private replica course and two Pine Valley homages, one next door and one in Florida. As a result, he has embraced the dune-and-waste-area look; vast sandy waste areas edged with natural vegetation and high grasses have increasingly become a part of his design style.

While Fazio has worked in every type of terrain the United States offers, from Carolina barrier islands to deserts and mountains, he has done little work abroad. He has also done a large number of resort and daily fee courses, making him one of the most accessible of the great architects for the traveling golfer.

SHADOW CREEK GOLF CLUB, *Las Vegas, Nevada*

Reputed at the time to be the most expensive course ever built, Shadow Creek taught the golf world that, indeed, anything is possible.

To say that no expense was spared in the construction of Shadow Creek is a gross understatement. It is more accurate to say every expense was embraced. The numbers are daunting. Fazio and casino hotel tycoon Steve Wynn started with an empty desert lot, so flat that the entire 320-acre site had less than 6 feet of pitch. It would have been difficult enough to build a good desert course on the land. But Wynn did not want the difficult, he wanted the impossible: to re-create a traditional Carolina parkland course, like Pinehurst, with wooded forests so thick that no hole could be seen from another.

How did Fazio accomplish this? He transplanted more than 21,000 fully mature trees, mostly pines and cottonwoods, many over 30 feet high. He moved so much dirt that the elevation change on the site went from less than 6 feet to more than 213 feet. He installed boulder-lined streams to form strategic water hazards; to avoid the uphill battle of growing grass from seed in the desert, he sodded every inch of the course with pregrown grass, an unheard-of expense. As a result, Shadow Creek is rumored to have cost about $40 million to build in the early 1980s. You can build a very good golf course today for $5 million.

An aerial photo of the land before Fazio arrived shows basically a parking lot made of sand, without hills, ravines, or even bushes. In stunning contrast today is the fifth hole, the only one you can see from the winding entrance road. A gorgeous par-3 nicknamed "The Quarry," it plays from an elevated tee over a tree-filled crater to an even higher elevated green with a false front. To appreciate the extent of Fazio's work, consider

The Nation's Most Expensive Course: To Build or to Play!

Shadow Creek resides just barely within the limits of what can fairly be described as *public golf*. A marketing tool for MGM Mirage Casinos, which owns it, the course's play is largely limited to invited casino guests, high rollers who gamble enough to wrangle a free tee time. The other alternative is exclusively for guests of one of the company's hotels, who can play the course from Monday through Thursday for $500, the highest green fee in the nation. The price tag is daunting, but the reality is that because of less expensive lodging and dining, a round at Shadow Creek typically ends up costing less than a visit to Pebble Beach or Pinehurst Number Two—and it is a first-rate private club experience.

that you are hitting over the tops of trees four stories high that sit *below* the level of both tee and green—on land that was once completely flat.

Shadow Creek is more than just one of the world's greatest courses. It is proof that a great course can be built anywhere with sufficient resources. This course, possibly more than any before it, has changed the way architects work. For better or worse, Fazio created a new standard that others are already trying to outdo.

SHADOW CREEK GOLF CLUB AT A GLANCE

(877) 209-9897, www.shadowcreek.com

Golf Course Info: Practice area, caddies included with green fees, walking only.

$$$$+, 6,701–7,239 yards, two tees.

Lodging Info: MGM Mirage resorts operates several major Las Vegas casino hotels, including the Mirage, Bellagio, Treasure Island, MGM Grand, and Golden Nugget. You must be a guest of one to play the course (877–880–0880, www.mgmgrand.com).

Getting There: Las Vegas has one of the largest, most easily reached airports in the world, with direct flights from many cities. The hotels are all within a ten-minute cab ride of the airport; green fees include round-trip limo transfers from the hotel to and from the golf club.

When to Go: Golf is played year-round, but temperatures climb above one hundred degrees in summer, and can be uncomfortably cold in winter. In fall overseeding takes place, and the course may close for maintenance. Early spring is ideal.

Golf Travel by Design Courses Nearby: Rio Secco (twenty minutes); Cascata (thirty minutes); Las Vegas Paiute Resort (twenty minutes); Primm Valley (sixty minutes); Reflection Bay (thirty minutes); Bear's Best (twenty minutes).

PINEHURST NUMBER EIGHT,
Pinehurst, North Carolina

On the seventh try, America's largest resort got a course that rivals—or even surpasses— its famed Number Two in quality.

In many ways Pinehurst Number Eight was a breakthrough course for Fazio. Built to honor the resort's hundredth birthday, it is also named the Centennial; the very fact that Pinehurst, whose portfolio includes the work of many top designers, chose Fazio for this project, was a recognition of his stature: Pinehurst wanted the most respected architect of the time to build its new marquee course.

Fazio made a statement as well, marking the beginning of his "Pine Valley" style that would be seen again on future courses, but has never been better executed than at Pinehurst. Despite Fazio's belief that anything can be accomplished anywhere, the fact is that Pinehurst is situated in the North Carolina sandhills, on terrain remarkably similar to that of Pine Valley. As a result, the setting lends itself to the vast expanses of open waste area that are both beautiful and daunting, though in reality they are far

Four Is Half of Eight

Following the success of Fazio's Pinehurst Number Eight, the resort asked him to remodel Number Four, one of the least-touched courses at the resort since it was built. More than a renovation, Fazio substantially changed the course, which reopened in 2001. Members speak very highly of the new Number Four, which is now yet another reason to visit the nation's largest golf resort.

from penal. In fact, the choice of waste area over woods, water, or even deep rough is symbolic of Fazio's playable courses, because recovery is almost always possible. These ample waste areas immediately set the layout apart from the seven previous traditional parkland routings at the resort.

On the other hand, Fazio made a bit of an homage to Number Two with his greens, which are very fast, firm, and large. Some players find them even more difficult than Ross's. While they have less undulation, they are larger—meaning longer putts—and almost always faster.

From start to finish the course is packed with Fazio's trademark visual drama, as different as night and day from the flat, open Number Two. It incorporates not just the waste areas but also rolling mounds producing off-kilter lies, an old sand mine, even marshes. If you can play only one course in Pinehurst, you should probably choose Number Two for its history and its greens, but the Centennial is equally a must-play that you should make time for.

PINEHURST RESORT & GOLF CLUB AT A GLANCE

Golf Course Info: See Pinehurst Number Two.

PINEHURST NUMBER EIGHT AT A GLANCE

Golf Course Info: See Pinehurst Number Two.

Travel Deals: Pinehurst offers a wide range of golf packages, most of which include a Modified American Plan. Less expensive packages include golf on courses One, Three, Five, and Six, with various additional surcharges for courses Two, Four, Seven, and Eight. If playing the four most desirable courses is your goal, more expensive packages that waive the surcharges are a better deal. Due to the popularity of Number Two, most packages limit guests to one round on this course per visit.

PRIMM VALLEY GOLF CLUB, *Primm, Nevada*

Only a handful of golf facilities in the nation get more than one course on the coveted *Golf Magazine* Top One Hundred Courses You Can Play list, and even fewer have more than one selected by the same architect. Fazio's dazzling pair in Primm meets this challenge.

Shadow Creek proved Fazio could work in the desert as well as, or better than, any other designer, but it wasn't a desert course. Fazio filled the void in his résumé with two courses in Primm, a small town with three casino hotels about an hour from Las Vegas on the Nevada-California border. Virtually every local who plays golf will tell you that these layouts are more than worth the drive, a better value than any of the other Las Vegas venues.

The two courses are quite different, but both reflect what we expect from Fazio. The Lakes layout puts wide, lush, rolling, carpetlike fairways in the flat desert setting, a la Shadow Creek, but employs much more water in the form of large human-made lakes, ponds, meandering creeks, even waterfalls. It is visually enticing, as most Fazio layouts are, and he uses the water to create numerous risk-reward options and heroic carries. While taking the long way and using the wide fairways will enable even high-handicappers to enjoy the course, better players will have many chances to cut corners, such as on the downhill over-water 347-yard par-4 tenth.

The Desert course is longer and uses more of its natural surroundings but still features wall-to-wall grass, unlike the limited-turf target-style designs of Scottsdale. Again, this makes it more enjoyable for less skilled players. But those seeking challenge will appreciate the longer layout, which showcases Fazio's penchant for elaborate sculpted bunkering. These hazards are often built into the rolling ridges alongside the fairways, making them more visually prominent. The fairways, while wide, wind irregularly between clumps of bunkers, giving the desert course a suitable snakelike quality. The routing was designed to intentionally showcase surrounding views of the deserts and mountains, and like its partner, it's gorgeous.

PRIMM VALLEY GOLF CLUB AT A GLANCE

(800) 386-7867, www.primmvalleyresorts.com

Golf Course Info: Practice area.

Desert: $$V, 5,397–7,191 yards, four tees.

Lakes: $$V, 6,019–6,945 yards, four tees.

Lodging Info: $$. There are three casino hotels in Primm, all of which are jointly owned and associated with the courses: Buffalo Bill's, the Primm Valley Resort, and Whisky Pete's.

Getting There: Primm is a one-hour drive from Las Vegas.

When to Go: Golf is played year-round, but temperatures climb above one hundred degrees in summer and can be uncomfortably cold in winter. In fall, over-seeding takes place, and the course may close for maintenance. Early spring is ideal.

Travel Deals: The three major casino hotels in Primm are all owned by the MGM Grand/Mirage Group, which also owns the two Fazio courses. These hotels are significantly less expensive than their Las Vegas counterparts and offer very reasonable lodging/golf packages.

Golf Travel by Design Courses Nearby: Rio Secco (fifty minutes); Cascata (ninety minutes); Las Vegas Paiute Resort (seventy minutes); Shadow Creek (sixty minutes); Reflection Bay (sixty minutes); Bear's Best (seventy minutes).

At Pinehurst Number Eight, Tom Fazio paid homage to Donald Ross with crowned greens dropping off to grass and sand bunkers. PINEHURST INC.

WILD DUNES, *Isle of Palms, South Carolina*

On a barrier island outside Charleston, Fazio created one of the country's greatest coastal courses— along with a radically different sibling.

uilt in 1980, the two courses at Wild Dunes were Fazio's highest-profile works since going solo from his uncle George. They immediately put him on the map and helped build the demand for his work that continues today. Fazio did not have to employ as much of his beloved heavy machinery, since the land was already perfect for golf. One of the few islands in the region that had not been cleared to grow valuable Sea Island cotton, the Isle of Palms boasted old-growth oaks dating back centuries, tidal marshes, ocean exposure, and most important, sandy dunes, some 50 feet high. It was his first high-profile chance to work amid the sandy waste areas that characterize his home course, Pine Valley (which is inland), and also to do a coastal routing.

The mix of oak, palm, cedar, and magnolia trees along with the dunes and marsh grasses made it virtually impossible to create a less-than-beautiful course, but Fazio accentuated the natural beauty with a set of stunning par-3s, the holes those who play the Links course will remember best. One borders a lagoon, another a lake, and a third the Atlantic. Unlike more recent Fazio designs, the bulk of the trouble is penal and lies to the right. The course is also exposed to wind, and when it blows, the Links—although short by today's standards—is a very difficult course.

The second layout at Wild Dunes, the Harbor course, gets little attention in light of the high rankings its neighbor receives. Many think this is a mistake, and the Harbor course has equally adamant groups of fans and detractors. The former love the back nine, which is unusually narrow for Fazio and emphasizes accuracy over length. Naysayers think the earthmoving is too contrived. Indeed, while it lacks the oceanfront drama of the Links, marshes and the Intracoastal Waterway bring water into play on all but one hole, creating a long day for errant players. Both courses are very well maintained, with first-rate greens and fairways.

WILD DUNES RESORT AT A GLANCE

(800) 845–8880, www.wilddunes.com

Golf Course Info: Practice area, walking (Links course only).

Links: $$$, 4,849–6,722 yards, four tees.

Harbor: $$, 4,774–6,446 yards, four tees.

Lodging Info: $$–$$$. The Wild Dunes Resort includes a variety of private homes, villas, and condos, and recently added the upscale ninety-three-room Boardwalk Inn (888–845–8926). It is just 12 miles from Charleston, which also hosts some fantastic hotels including the deluxe Charleston Place and Planters Inn. The Kiawah Island golf resort is also close by.

Getting There: Isle of Palms is 12 miles from Charleston, which has an airport.

When to Go: Golf is played year-round, but summer through late fall is hurricane season, and the barrier islands can be hit hard. Spring is the best time.

Golf Travel by Design Courses Nearby: Ocean course at Kiawah Island (thirty minutes); Caledonia and True Blue (two hours); Legends Heathland (two hours); The Dunes (two hours).

WORLD WOODS, *Brooksville, Florida*

A taste of two of the world's top private courses, Pine Valley and Augusta National, at bargain prices in central Florida.

Before the recent spate of "build it and they will come" courses in remote destinations such as Bandon, Oregon, Manzanillo, Mexico, and Kauri Cliffs, New Zealand, there was World Woods. Japanese developers were convinced that if they built two fabulous courses and a world-class practice facility in the middle of otherwise desolate central Florida, golfers would make the trip. They were right.

World Woods opened in 1993, at the pinnacle of Fazio's "I can build anything, anywhere," success, and he once again proved himself. The two courses were intended to be homages to the two most highly acclaimed private clubs in this country—courses that sit in locations very different from each other and very different from Florida. Pine Barrens is his first tribute to Pine Valley, not just borrowing elements but in fact seeking to re-create the experience for the public golfer. It uses ample waste areas fringed with knee-high rough, and while it's the shorter of the layouts here, it's considerably more difficult. Waste areas cut entirely across the fairways, breaking them into target-style landing areas. The exposed sand is very impressive to the eye. Fazio got creative, too, using two greens that alternate on one hole, and a split fairway on another.

Rolling Oaks seeks to re-create the manicured beauty of Georgia's oak-lined Augusta National, home of the Masters. Fazio imported mature oaks, many dripping with atmospheric Spanish moss, installed well-tended flower beds, and—to further capture the feel of Augusta—built rock-lined creeks and small cascades. Like Augusta, the course is very user friendly with wide fairways, but the greens are nowhere near as fast as the slick Georgia versions.

Neither layout is a copy of the real thing; instead Fazio sought to capture the ambience of the two originals. He succeeded, but the drama is not as high as might be expected. It is better to look at them as two well-laid-out, well-maintained public courses that offer bargain golf in often expensive Florida. In this light, they are worth the road trip from Tampa, especially to take advantage of thirty-six-hole special rates.

The World's Best Warm-Up?

The real standout at World Woods is its practice facility, also designed by Fazio, which simply has no equal in golf. It includes a twenty-acre driving range with natural grass tee areas that alternate on all four sides, an undulating two-acre putting green, several smaller practice greens, plus bunker and chipping areas, along with three full-sized practice holes, a par-3, a par-4, and a par-5. There is even a nine-hole short course. At World Woods there is no excuse for not being warmed up on the first tee.

(352) 796–5500, www.worldwoods.com

Golf Course Info: Extensive practice area, walking.

Pine Barrens: $–$$V, 5,301–6,902 yards, four tees.

Rolling Oaks: $–$$V, 5,245–6,985 yards, four tees.

Lodging Info: $–$$. The area immediately around Brooksville is full of inexpensive chain motels. Several offer packages in conjunction with the golf facility, which has no lodging of its own.

Getting There: World Woods is a ninety-minute drive northeast of Tampa.

When to Go: Golf season is year-round, but summer can be quite hot and humid, while winter can bring frost delays. Spring and fall are ideal.

Travel Deals: World Woods is widely considered one of the nation's top values, but the most extreme savings are in the summer off-season and for playing both courses—thirty-six holes—in a single day. These two-round fees start at well under $100.

Golf Travel by Design Courses Nearby: None.

PINE HILL, *Pine Hill, New Jersey*

Fazio's lifelong love affair with the world's top-ranked private course yielded a public gem.

Fazio, a longtime Pine Valley member, has tried on various occasions to re-create the course's charms in the North Carolina sandhills, South Carolina's coastal islands, even flat central Florida. But he finally got the chance to give it his best shot on the terrain best suited for the challenge: right next door to the real thing.

Pine Hill is the result, and while it's less than two years old, it has been snapping up accolades, including the top public rating in the state from New Jersey's regional golf magazine. It shares many things with its private neighbor besides identical topography. Like Pine Valley, each hole is screened from every other by thick stands of oaks, walnuts, maples, and, of course, pines. It employs wild sandy waste areas to create both visual charm and intimidation. It has superb bent grass greens that roll true and challenge with undulation. Most of all, like Pine Valley, which has one of the nation's highest slope ratings, it is a beast from the tips, clocking in at just under 7,000 yards for a par-70 layout.

Pine Hill is simply a superb example of high-end daily fee golf. It is well worth a visit to experience the aura of Pine Valley—as well as one of Fazio's best designs.

The World's Number One Course!

The golf world is full of divergent opinions, but one thing remains constant: Pine Valley, an ultra-exclusive private course in the New Jersey pine barrens, has long dominated the Top One Hundred lists, garnering first-place positions from *Golf Magazine*, *Golf Digest*, *Golfweek*, and just about anyone else keeping score. It routinely beats out renowned gems such as Cypress Point and Augusta. For most fanatics of the game, there is nowhere they would rather tee it up . . . if only they could.

PINE HILL AT A GLANCE

(877) 450–8866, www.golfpinehill.com

Golf Course Info: Practice area, walking.

$$–$$$, 4,922–6,969 yards, five tees.

Lodging Info: Pine Hill is in the suburbs of Philadelphia, which offers an ample array of lodging options.

Getting There: Pine Hill is less than 15 miles southeast of Philadelphia.

When to Go: Golf season is year-round, but winter can be chilly with periodic snow. Spring through fall is ideal.

Golf Travel by Design Courses Nearby: Marriott Seaview (one hour).

Other Notable Tom Fazio Courses You Can Play

- **Dancing Rabbit,** Philadelphia, Missouri (thirty-six holes)
- **PGA at the Reserve,** Port St. Lucie, Florida (thirty-six holes)
- **Osprey course,** Walt Disney World, Florida
- **Raptor course, Grayhawk,** Scottsdale, Arizona
- **Pelican Hill,** Newport Beach, California (thirty-six holes)
- **White Columns,** Alpharetta, Georgia
- **Fazio course, Treetops,** Sylvan, Michigan
- **Barton Creek,** Austin, Texas (thirty-six holes)

Pete Dye (1925–)

The Fine Line Between Pleasure and Pain

Pete Dye's designs have been called "architorture," and are so "Dyeabolical" that the term has been incorporated by Dye himself on many courses to describe his toughest hole. When golfers think of Dye, they tend to think of hard courses and lost balls. But there is far more to Dye's design work than terror. No architect's portfolio is as varied, and no one has had as much impact on the modern era. In the 1960s, when Dye was coming into his own as a designer, the "power game" was emerging and courses were being built longer than ever. As a result of the modern-era changes introduced by Robert Trent Jones Sr., they incorporated uphill approaches and required ever-more-lofted and solidly struck shots. After a tour of Scotland's classic courses, however, Dye turned his back on the trend, dealing the golf design fraternity a shocking blow in 1969 when he built Hilton Head's Harbour Town. It was only one in a long string of revolutionary impacts Dye had on the game.

A Return to Golf's Roots

With his Scottish experience in mind, Dye—along with his apprentice Jack Nicklaus—built a course that was very short by the standards of the day, playing about 6,500 yards (it has been lengthened since). Rather than elevating greens and installing ponds, he built mounds and swales around the greens, shrank the putting surfaces, exposed the layout to ocean winds, and put the shot values and ground game back into golf. The effect on the golf community was twofold: It showed that a course did not have to be long and could rely on finesse to make it tournament worthy, as Donald Ross had done at Pinehurst Number Two; and it reintroduced the admiration of the Scottish and Irish courses among designers. Just as Seth Raynor and C. B. Macdonald had toured Scotland to learn the trade, such pilgrimages would again become de rigueur among contemporary designers. Elements of this region would be used, more often wrongly than with grace, in thousands of golf courses built since.

Dye pioneered so many things in golf course design that it is easy to overlook their individual importance. Dye was a very good golfer, Indiana Amateur Champion, and like Nicklaus saw things from the point of view of someone who could execute the most demanding shots. His wife, Alice, was his design partner from early on, and the two-time USGA Women's Senior Amateur Champion played an important role in Dye's evolution—as well as the industry's. She was the first female member of the American Society of Golf Course Architects and championed female-friendly courses. As a result, no one has done as much to change tee design as the Dyes. Early tees were simply huge runway boxes or spots of ground. Later, architects broke them into separate areas of differing yardages. But it was the Dyes who incorporated numerous small, irregular tee boxes, and—rather than just separate them by length—the two located them so hazards played much

DYE WAS A VERY GOOD GOLFER . . . AND LIKE

NICKLAUS SAW THINGS FROM THE POINT

OF VIEW OF SOMEONE WHO COULD EXECUTE

THE MOST DEMANDING SHOTS

differently from each box. Even Dye's toughest courses usually have a tee box with little or no forced carry. Choose the right box and you can usually enjoy your round. Choose the wrong one and pay the price.

Another Dye breakthrough was the stadium or Tournament Players course. The idea of building courses specifically to host tournaments and accommodate spectators was the PGA's, and the group turned first to Dye at Sawgrass, where he flanked fairways with massive slopes to seat viewers and built amphitheaters around greens. The TPC concept has become very popular. There are now nearly twenty courses in the network, and every well-known designer has followed in Dye's footsteps.

Is There Anything He Didn't Invent?

Yes, there are two things that Dye did not in fact create—but he's so famous, most people think he did. One was the island green, which had been done before. Dye, however, popularized it by showcasing it on national television as the seventeenth hole of the TPC Sawgrass, and subsequently at many other courses. The second is the extensive use of railroad ties to bulkhead first bunkers and then lakes. On his original trip to Scotland in the 1960s, he visited Prestwick and saw bunkers so large and steep that their walls needed to be shorn up to keep from collapsing. He also saw pot bunkers so small and deep, grass grew from their sides. He would incorporate both features in many courses. Dye extended the railroad tie concept to water hazards, which allowed him to build artificial lakes lower than the level of the fairway, a style that has been widely copied.

While Dye's original breakthrough at Harbour Town was minimalist, he has never hesitated to move vast quantities of earth, and has in fact become well known for this: Many consider him more a builder than an architect. Dye has experience operating every type of heavy machinery and has done much of his own grading and shaping from the seat of huge bulldozers. He has repeatedly experimented with revolutionary ideas, and has never been afraid to thrust new designs into the limelight. As a result no architect has flown so high with renowned courses such as Whistling Straits, Casa de Campo, and the Ocean course at Kiawah Island—and at the same time borne the brunt of so much criticism over unplayable layouts like the Stadium course at PGA West.

There is no single Pete Dye style. Still, at his courses you may find:

- **Severe mounding.** Mounds, hills, slopes, and elevated fairways are regular tools of the trade to Dye, who does everything but leave flat expanses on the golf course.

- **Bulkheaded water hazards.** Before Dye, modern golf course design introduced the human-made pond. By shoring up its walls, Dye was able to lower a pond below the fairway. This could hide it from view—but also prevented flooding and helped with maintenance while adding visual drama.

- **Island and peninsula greens.** Although he has replicated his pure island green from Sawgrass at other locales, he also tends to jut peninsula greens into the water, with lakes either behind or—more ominously—in front.

- **Pot bunkers.** Few modern designers use these as extensively as Dye.

- **Varied and multiple tees.** Numerous tee boxes, including a short set taking almost every forced hazard out of play, is typical Dye. The shorter tees are also oriented to minimize the impact of hazards farther down the hole. In most cases Dye succeeds at giving every golfer a chance. Nowhere is this more evident than at the Ocean course at Kiawah—one of the most difficult layouts in the world from the tips yet perfectly pleasant from the shorter tees.

- **Difficulty.** Dye has built some of the game's most testing playing grounds, with holes that some object to as unfair, because they fail to reward good shots.

As an architect Pete Dye is especially appealing to the traveling golfer, because his courses are so easy to visit. One of the few designers to monopolize major resorts, he has four courses at the American Club, three at Casa de Campo, two at Sawgrass, three at the Las Vegas Paiute Resort, and three at La Quinta/PGA West. He holds five of the top twelve spots in *Golf Magazine*'s Top One Hundred Courses You Can Play list, but at the same time he has designed a handful you should never play.

THE AMERICAN CLUB, *Kohler, Wisconsin*

The American Club, while less famous than Pebble Beach, Pinehurst, or St. Andrews, stands right alongside them as a place all serious golfers must visit in their lifetimes.

The American Club is arguably this nation's best golf resort. It certainly stands even with its only peers, Pinehurst and Pebble Beach. But the American Club has better lodging and dining than either, and unlike Pinehurst, all of its courses are exceptional. While the Pebble Beach resort features the work of three designers, and Pinehurst five, all the courses at the American Club are the handiwork of Pete Dye.

If the name isn't familiar to you, don't worry. The American Club has just one weakness: name recognition. Originally the resort had two courses, River and Meadow Valleys, comprising a facility called Blackwolf Run—a name that was used interchangeably with *American Club*, the resort's main hotel. Blackwolf Run hosted the Women's U.S. Open on a combination of nine holes from each course. When the third course, Whistling Straits, opened at its own clubhouse 12 miles from the resort, it was sometimes called Whistling Straits at the American Club. Then when the fourth course, the Irish, opened, the third was renamed the Straits course and—along with the Irish—comprised the Whistling Straits facility. If that's not confusing enough, the entire complex is often just called Kohler, the name of both the town and the giant company that owns the resort.

Whatever you call it, go there. The four courses are very different, and very good, showcasing Dye's design talents and ability to work in a variety of styles. The highlight is surely the Straits course, currently ranked fourth among the nation's public layouts. Built on the shores of Lake Michigan, a spot that is geographically and climatically a fairly good rendition of the Scottish coast, this was the first great modern links course built in this country, spurring the creation of the two courses at Bandon Dunes. Hundreds of attempts to re-create Scotland have failed on our shores since early successes at Shinnecock Hills and the National, but Dye pulled it off. The use of imported fescue grasses and letting sheep loose on the course are gimmicks, but the layout is not. It is stunningly beautiful and appears natural. The dunes, rough, bunkering, and fairways could have been airlifted whole from the other side of the Atlantic. The holes along Lake Michigan are especially dramatic, with a par-3 called Shipwreck that features three tiers of beautiful bunkers cut into the side of the cliff below the green—a recovery so difficult, golfers may wish they'd just put the ball in the lake. The PGA has chosen the course as the site of its major, the PGA Championship. From the back tees, the pros will have their hands full, hitting par-3s more than 200 yards long with the carry entirely over Lake Michigan.

For the total golf experience, with amazing ambience, memorable holes, and mandatory but first-rate caddies, the Straits course is the star. But the River course at Blackwolf Run is the most strategic, and while it's as different from the Straits as a course can be, it is another must-play, this ranking eighth in the nation. The best holes are along the namesake river, which Dye uses to force carries on approaches. Trees, an often overlooked

Built for Champions

Spurred on by the success of the Women's U.S. Open played at Blackwolf Run, owner Herb Kohler set out to build not just a great course, but also one that would quickly attract a men's major—no small challenge amid growing competition. No one was better suited to the task than Dye, who purposely built the Straits to land such a tournament. You would have to be among the world's best players to tackle this course from the 7,288-yard back tees, which bring into play long forced carries over water that average players don't contend with. Nine and eighteen are stunning holes playing back to the clubhouse and the crowds. Dye and Kohler succeeded: Tiger Woods and company will be here for the 2004 PGA Championship.

architectural element, are a very important part of the designs at Blackwolf Run; you must decide whether to go around or over them. While the River is harder to score on than Meadow Valleys, it is also more forgiving, with wide fairways and ample mounding rather than harsh rough. At Meadow Valleys, Dye uses high, penal rough to create a much different feel on adjacent land. The latter course is less well protected but harder to recover on. Both, like the Straits, use a Dye trademark and play vastly differently from the assorted tee boxes, which are ranked by handicap. Check your ego at the door, take the starter's advice, and err on the side of shorter.

The latest course is the Irish, Dye's homage to the great links of southwestern Ireland, which don't get as much press as their Scottish counterparts. It is built just inland of the Straits and sits on higher land, commanding lake views without having waterfront holes. Once again Dye built towering dunes, but the fairways between them are much narrower, the greens larger, and bunkers and pot bunkers are installed everywhere. There is even a blind par-3 with a crater green surrounded by bunkers, a la Old Tom Morris's **Lahinch**.

Off the course the American Club earns high marks as well. The luxurious main hotel showcases its owner's fine plumbing fixtures, with some of the best bathrooms in the nation, as well as first-rate restaurants and dining. A more moderately priced hotel, a shopping mall, a new spa, a hunting preserve, and an elaborate fitness center are also part of the resort.

THE AMERICAN CLUB RESORT AT A GLANCE

(800) 344-2838, www.americanclub.com

Golf Course Info: Practice area, walking allowed, caddies available (Straits course is walking only).

Straits: $$$$V, 5,381–7,288 yards, five tees.

Irish: $$$$, 5,109–7,201 yards, five tees.

River: $$$–$$$$, 5,115–6,991 yards, four tees.

Meadow Valleys: $$$–$$$$, 5,065–7,142 yards, four tees.

Lodging Info: All four courses are truly public, with no discounts for resort guests. Still, guests do get advance tee times, and these courses are extremely popular in Wisconsin's brief golf season. The American Club is the very high-end choice, but the resort also offers the more modest Inn at Woodlake.

Getting There: Kohler is less than an hour from Milwaukee, and shuttle service is available. It is a two-and-a-half-hour drive from Chicago.

When to Go: The season is April through October, but May through September are the most reliable months. Some early- and late-season discounts are available.

Golf Travel by Design Courses Nearby: None.

OCEAN COURSE, *Kiawah Island, South Carolina*

After the Ryder Cup here, several pros complained that the course was too hard and vowed never to return. Their loss is your gain.

Anyone can build a hard golf course, even someone who knows nothing about golf. The more difficult challenge is to build a course that challenges great players and pleases high-handicappers. Pete Dye has stepped up to this challenge more than just about any architect, but nowhere is it as evident as at the famed Ocean course.

Every time you move back a tee on this layout, you bring more marsh, wind, and forced carry into the equation. In the Ryder Cup the world's top pros played from the back tees, which hold the nation's fourth highest slope rating, and walked off shell-shocked at the punishment they took. Part of the course's mystique is hidden tee boxes beyond even the back ones for such tournament play, stretching the layout to an unmeasured distance longer than the 7,296 yards indicated. Yet from the first or second set of tees, the average resort guest will love the course. Even from the blues, the set most low-handicappers will tackle, there are no unusually long forced carries. In all, there are a rare six sets to choose from, although only four appear on the scorecard.

So much attention is given to the difficulty that the beauty of the course often gets overshadowed. There are many good courses on the Carolina coast and coastal islands carved from tidal marsh, but none is as inspiring as this. Dye's manufactured mounding provides relief from the flat setting, and his elevated greens surrounded by swales—Pinehurst Number Two on steroids—raise these targets from the marsh surroundings and make them more prominent. Waste areas define the playing corridors and keep errant shots out of the marsh, while elaborate scenic boardwalks carry players through the sensitive areas. Views sweep across the marsh to the Atlantic. Indeed, the course enjoys a setting so wild and primal, you almost expect to see dinosaurs emerge from the swamp grasses.

The Kiawah Island resort occupies the entire island and includes four other courses by Tom Fazio, Jack Nicklaus, Gary Player, and Clyde Johnston, as well as a hotel and a wide assortment of condos, rental homes, restaurants, and other facilities. It's one of the nation's largest and most complete golf resorts.

KIAWAH ISLAND RESORT AT A GLANCE

(800) 654–2924, www.kiawahresort.com

Golf Course Info: Practice areas, walking allowed, forecaddies (Ocean course only).

Ocean: $$$$, 5,327–7,296 yards, six tees.

At Whistling Straits, Pete Dye used native sand and imported fescue grasses to recreate links golf on the shore of Lake Michigan. COURTESY OF KOHLER CO.

Turtle Point: $$$, 5,205–6,925 yards, four tees.

Cougar Point: $$$, 4,776–6,887 yards, four tees.

Osprey Point: $$$, 5,023–6,871 yards, four tees.

Oak Point: $$$, 4,956–6,759 yards, four tees.

Lodging Info: $$$–$$$$. The Kiawah Island Inn is the resort's main hotel. In addition, there are fifteen different complexes of various villas and more than sixty one-of-a-kind private homes—including some palatial beachfront mansions—offering an array of lodging for every budget. All resort guests get preferred tee times, golf discounts, and free transportation around the island.

Getting There: Kiawah is thirty minutes from the Charleston airport; no car is necessary at the resort.

When to Go: Golf is played year-round, but winter months can be quite chilly, and late summer through fall brings hurricane season. March through June are the best months.

Golf Travel by Design Courses Nearby: Wild Dunes (thirty minutes); Caledonia and True Blue (two hours); Legends Heathland (two hours).

TPC SAWGRASS, *Ponte Vedra Beach, Florida*

The televised Players Championship and Pete Dye's design flamboyance combine to make the seventeenth at Sawgrass the most famous hole in golf.

When the PGA Tour decided it needed a home course at its Ponte Vedra Beach headquarters to host its own large tournament, it turned to Pete Dye. The result was extraordinary, since at the time there was no such thing as a "stadium" course. The unusual design was highly controversial, but Pete Dye makes no bones about his work: His priority was providing a venue for the spectators. His attention to the golf course may have been secondary, but he still turned out quite a product.

On the course his goal was equally simple: to challenge the best players in the world when they teed it up each year. While not quite as daunting as his Ocean course from the tips, and far more manageable than his later effort at duplicating the course in Palm Springs, it is still a test—especially the last two holes, where scores can swing by four or more strokes.

Known as Tournament Players Courses, the TPC network (of which the two layouts at Sawgrass were the first) are courses built specifically to host tournaments and accommodate spectators. So famous is the Stadium course at Sawgrass that many golfers do not even realize there is a second TPC at the same facility, the Valley course.

In order to accommodate viewers, many fairways are flanked by very high, banked slopes, meant to be out of play for the Tour pros, upon which crowds can sit. For the average player visiting Sawgrass, this gives a huge, forgiving amount of room for errant shots. There are also bowl-shaped natural grass amphitheaters around many greens for the spectators. The Stadium course does have water on every hole, but the vast majority is off to the sides. Besides the famous island hole, there are no forced carries at all, except from the back tees. Dye uses a lot of waste bunkers to penalize errant shots, but the course is surprisingly short and, like many Dye designs, can be navigated handily from the right tees. It is one of the few fearsome championship venues that can be enjoyed as a resort course.

The famous island-green par-3 seventeenth is among the holes that Tour pros most hate, which goes to show what pressure can do them, since it is not a difficult hole. Even from the tips, it is short, and top players are hitting wedges into a large green that, even with the occasional winds, seems impossible for them to miss. Yet miss it they do, piling up penalty strokes aplenty. There are much harder par-3s on many courses both pros and amateurs contend with, but the do-or-die penal tee shot and the stark, Dye bulkheaded green rising from the lake must affect the nerves. Eighteen is a much more difficult hole, statistically among the hardest on the Tour, a very long par-4 playing around curving coastline with a lake that swallows shots and little room for conservative bailout.

The TPC Valley course, while overshadowed, also offers up a very pleasant golf experience—in fact, it starts out stronger than its famous sibling. It too has water on every hole, but even wider fairways make it easier. The Valley has its own trademark par-3, a short one over a watery inlet that is just as strong as the island hole. The downside of the Valley course is that it is lined with unattractive homes.

MARRIOTT SAWGRASS RESORT AT A GLANCE

(800) 457-GOLF, www.marriotthotels.com/jaxsw

Golf Course Info: Practice areas, no walking.

TPC Stadium: $$$$, 5,000–6,954 yards, four tees.

TPC Valley: $$$$, 5,126–6,864 yards, four tees.

Lodging Info: $$$–$$$$. The courses are technically private, open only to members, members of other TPC courses, and Marriott guests through a special arrangement with the hotel. You must stay at the hotel to play. Marriott guests also get special privileges at three other nearby clubs, but none is worth playing.

Getting There: Sawgrass is 40 miles from Jacksonville.

When to Go: Peak season is winter, but Sawgrass is far north of most Florida resorts and can be quite cool. Prices drop in the hotter summer, and spring and fall are ideal.

Golf Travel by Design Courses Nearby: None.

CASA DE CAMPO, *La Romana, Dominican Republic*

Built almost entirely by hand, the stunning Teeth of the Dog course is the Caribbean's finest, showcasing Pete Dye at his very best.

Like most architects, Dye won't play favorites. He has said that like children, he loves all his courses and can't choose one above the rest. But those who know him suggest he has a soft spot for Teeth of the Dog at Casa de Campo. Long before the Straits course, it was a crowning accomplishment that could not be overlooked, and while critics complained that the Ocean course was too hard or Sawgrass too artificial, it was impossible to knock this seaside stunner. In addition, Dye has always loved the building-and-shaping part of the business, and here he had a virtual army of laborers at his disposal to do the work by hand—in Dye's opinion the best way possible.

Casa de Campo, winner of many awards and accolades, has a near-mythical aura, but if you haven't been there it is confusing. Casa de Campo is the resort, and Teeth of the Dog is just one of four Dye-designed golf courses there, although it's the only one you hear about. It has eight holes along the ocean, or—as many observers have noted—in the ocean, since the holes jut out from the land at near sea level. While most oceanfront courses like Pebble Beach play along high cliffs, several holes at Teeth of the Dog are at the ocean's edge; waves crash against the side of the greens as you putt. The namesake sixteenth is a par-3 that drops off on the right to sharp coral formations that resemble teeth. The course is treacherous, with water, rough, and Dye's favorite hazard, bunkers, at every turn. But in prototypical style he has a vast array of tees that greatly influence how these hazards come into play, allowing golfers of all abilities to enjoy the course.

Dye's Links course is terribly misnamed, but it's still a fun and well-thought-out course that deserves more attention than it gets in the shadow of its famous sibling. With no holes on the ocean, Dye made a layout very different in character, with the defining element high rough of a native grass so thick that it's like playing through the jungle. Greens are much smaller than at Teeth of the Dog, and the Links is quite a bit shorter, but wind is a factor at both courses, and Dye puts a premium on shot values, forcing players to hit specific shots.

The La Romana Country Club is a private course for residents, also designed by Dye and hailed as another of the Caribbean's best, although it is not open to resort guests unless accompanied by a member. Dye is finishing up a third public course at the resort, on a site a bit removed from the other two layouts, overlooking the sea and playing along a river. A pet project that has been under way for years, it should open very soon and looks to be another strong addition to the Caribbean's best golf resort.

The resort itself is vast, consisting of hotel rooms, villas and homes on 7,000 acres. All-inclusive packages cover green fees and meals at Casa de Campo's twelve bars and restaurants. The grounds are so vast that villa guests are issued golf carts for their stays to get around the property, which includes an equestrian center, tennis, and a wide array of water sports.

Golf at the Edge of the Sea

Many of the world's top golf courses are along the coast, and the bulk of these overlook the sea from clifftop perches. But Casa de Campo's Teeth of the Dog goes one better, with its marquee holes laid out at beach level, right along the sea. The result is simply one of the best, most beautiful golf courses on earth.

CASA DE CAMPO AT A GLANCE

(800) 877-3643, www.casadcampo.com

Golf Course Info: Practice area, walking, caddies.

Teeth of the Dog: $$$V, 4,779–6,989 yards, five tees.

Links: $$-$$$V, 4,410–6,602 yards, four tees.

Third Course: Under construction.

Lodging Info: $$$–$$$$. Choices include hotel rooms, villas, or rental homes. All-inclusive rates make this a bargain compared to other world-class golf resorts, with meals, golf, and other sporting activities included in room rates.

Getting There: Casa de Campo has its own airport at the resort, with scheduled service on American Airlines. It is about an hour from the airport at Punta Cana, and three hours from the island's main airport in Santo Domingo.

When to Go: Golf is played year-round, but Caribbean hurricane season extends from summer through fall.

Travel Deals: One of the world's premier golf resorts, Casa de Campo is also one of the best buys, in both low- and high-season. The resort is all-inclusive, but in an upscale fashion, as it includes alcoholic drinks and all meals at a choice of more than a dozen bars and restaurants. Some packages even include room service. Lodging is in hotel rooms, villas, or deluxe villas. Packages that include unlimited golf, all food and drink, accommodations, and other sports (tennis, etc.) range from around $275 in summer to around $350 in winter, per person per night.

Golf Travel by Design Courses Nearby: None.

LAS VEGAS PAIUTE RESORT, *Las Vegas, Nevada*

The first major big-name designer to cast his sights on the Nevada desert, Pete Dye helped transform Las Vegas into a major golf travel destination.

The number of golf courses in Las Vegas has been growing by leaps and bounds, with more and more new courses opening each year. But the recent onslaught of high-end daily fee courses began with the thirty-six-hole Dye-designed Las Vegas Paiute facility. Without any theme or other Las Vegas gimmicks, Dye and the Paiute Nation built what they thought the city needed: high-quality desert golf courses at a reasonable price, at least by Vegas standards. They were right, and despite a rush of competition, these remain among the city's most popular courses. In fact, they're so popular that Dye just built a third course alongside the originals, and the Paiute resort is moving ahead with plans to build lodging, gambling, and convention facilities on the site.

The first two layouts, Snow Mountain and Sun Mountain, both feature his exaggerated tee separation and placement, with five sets to choose from, offering radically different levels of challenge. Dye uses the raw desert for his waste areas and includes many severe doglegs around the natural hazards, emphasizing the beauty of the desert environment while constantly asking the golfer to choose between risk-reward routes that involve cutting the corners. While these are clearly not Scottish-style layouts, Dye uses many of the traits picked up on his visit to the Old Country: Pot bunkers abound, larger bunkers are shored up with his trademark railroad ties, and most of the approaches to the very firm greens are left open, which encourages bump-and-run shots. The courses are very similar, but Snow Mountain is intentionally designed as a kinder, gentler Dye experience, with an astonishingly low 125 slope rating from the 7,146-yard back tees. Very wide fairways and landing areas and unobstructed approaches are a Dye rarity. Sun Mountain is tightened up a notch, with more use of the human-made water hazards.

The new layout, Wolf, is priced as the resort's premier tract, and it's much more Dye-like. It has a Sawgrass-clone island green, puts more water in play, and stretches a truly daunting 7,604 yards from the tips, far longer than Dye's most feared torture tracts. But what makes the Wolf special is its site: While it's next to the other two courses, it's also on higher and more rugged desert terrain. It features vastly more elevation change and exposed rock, playing in and out of desert canyons. All three courses benefit from a lavish maintenance budget and are among the region's most impeccable, with bent grass greens lovingly tended to in the harsh desert setting.

LAS VEGAS PAIUTE GOLF RESORT AT A GLANCE

(800) 711-2833, www.lvpaiutegolf.com

Golf Course Info: Practice area, no walking.

Snow Mountain: $$$–$$$$, 5,341–7,146 yards, five tees.

Sun Mountain: $$$–$$$$, 5,465–7,112 yards, five tees.

Wolf: $$$$, 5,483–7,604 yards, five tees.

Lodging Info: $$–$$$$. There is a wide range of lodging at every level of style and price in the Las Vegas area. The course is located north of Summerlin, about thirty minutes from the city. The major resort in Summerlin is the J. W. Marriott, one of the city's most opulent. The Marriott also has special tee time, discount, and golf shuttle arrangements with the Paiute courses. If you want to stay in Summerlin, this is the best choice; otherwise, there are ample options in the city.

Getting There: The Paiute courses are thirty-five minutes from the Las Vegas Strip or airport.

When to Go: Golf is played year-round, but temperatures climb above one hundred degrees in summer and can be uncomfortably cold in winter. In fall overseeding takes place, and the course may close for maintenance. Early spring is ideal.

Golf Travel by Design Courses Nearby: Rio Secco (forty minutes); Cascata (twenty minutes); Bear's Best (fifteen minutes); Primm Valley courses (sixty minutes); Reflection Bay (forty minutes); Shadow Creek (twenty minutes).

LA QUINTA/PGA WEST, *Palm Springs, California*

At the height of the "harder must be better" golf course design craze, Pete Dye was hired to build a punishing layout that would show the golfer, and the golf world, who was boss. Dye was the man for the job, and he succeeded, if you can call it that.

Pete Dye has designed some of the most memorable golf courses in this country, and usually that is a good thing. Play Dye's Straits course in Wisconsin and you'll replay the holes over and over in your head for the rest of your golfing life. Dye's hand-built holes etched into the cliffs of the Dominican Republic at Casa de Campo create an equally indelible image. But memorable is not always a good thing in golf, and most visitors who play the Stadium course at PGA West remember it as a round they wish they could forget.

What makes the course so difficult is nor its length, nor lightning-fast greens, nor wind. It is the fact that nearly every single shot risks a penalty stroke. It is a not a course, like many of the greats, that tests every shot in the bag with different types of holes. Rather it is repetitive, requiring a perfect shot every time without the possibility for recovery; few golfers who visit, including pros, can maintain either the attention or performance required. Fairways are extremely difficult to hold, and less-than-perfect (and sometimes even perfect) shots go astray. From the tee it's often difficult to discern where the hole goes and where the shot should be aimed. All the par-3s are penal with ample use of water, including an island hole more daunting than its predecessor at Sawgrass. In general, the penalty for mistakes, even minor ones, is loss of ball. The course is as close to unplayable as we've seen in the world. If this were the first Dye-designed course we'd ever played, we would never have played another. In addition, the stadium aspects of the TPC course were wasted, since the pros, by popular consensus, will no longer return here to play. The upside is that the average player may well hit a career shot here: Any shot with a good outcome during a round here is an accomplishment.

The complex includes the La Quinta Resort & Club, which has two golf courses of its own, both Dye designs. Guests have access to the public courses at the nearby PGA West community. These include the nefarious Stadium course, the Nicklaus Tournament course, and the **_Greg Norman Course._** The Nicklaus course, while very difficult as well, allows recovery, is a lot of fun to play, and provides a stark contrast showcasing the differences between requiring good shots to score and requiring good shots to survive. The Norman course is the most user friendly of the three, as well as the sole resort course in the entire Palm Springs region to allow walking and offer caddies.

The Dye courses at La Quinta both have a loyal following, but neither is his best work. The Dunes is a straightforward resort layout, very playable and forgiving for Dye but with no special charms or features. The Mountain course, on the other hand, has some of the most memorable Dye holes in the nation, forming a short section of the course that winds into the steep-walled canyons behind the resort. It is rare in golf that you have to worry about hitting walls with your shots, and when it happens it is usually the clubhouse or golf course homes, not sheer stone cliffs. The sixteenth is one of the most photographed and photogenic in golf, a landlocked version of Dye's island hole, with the green set among a lunar landscape of huge boulders and no recovery possible from a setting even more dramatic and intimidating than water. The tee shot also drops substantially in elevation, something his wet island holes do not do. It is a great hole in a great stretch of holes that unfortunately is much too short; the holes outside the mountainous canyons are not even close in quality.

LA QUINTA/PGA WEST AT A GLANCE

(800) 598-3828, www.laquintaresort.com

Golf Course Info: Practice area, no walking (except Norman course).

Stadium: $$$$, 5,092–7,266 yards, five tees.

Jack Nicklaus Tournament Course: $$$$, 5,023–7,204 yards, five tees.

Greg Norman Course: $$$$, 4,997–7,156 yards, five tees.

Mountain: $$$$, 5,005–6,758 yards, five tees.

Dunes: $$$–$$$$, 4,997–6,747 yards, five tees.

Lodging Info: $$$$. La Quinta features guest rooms in individual casitas, arranged in clusters around numerous swimming pools set throughout the sprawling resort. Accommodations are spacious and comfortable; the facility also has a world-renowned spa and tennis center, plus a very good children's program.

Getting There: La Quinta is about forty-five minutes from the Palm Springs airport and less than two hours from Los Angeles.

When to Go: It gets quite hot in the summer but is delightful the rest of the year.

Golf Travel by Design Courses Nearby: Desert Springs Marriott (twenty-five minutes).

Other Notable Pete Dye Courses You Can Play

- **River course at Kingsmill,** Williamsburg, Virginia
- **Lost Canyons**, Simi, California (thirty-six holes)
- **Harbour Town,** Hilton Head, South Carolina
- **Westin Mission Hills,** Palm Springs, California
- **Mystic Rock,** Nemacolin Woodlands, Pennsylvania
- **Brickyard Crossing,** Indianapolis, Indiana

Jack Nicklaus (1940–   )
Golf's Greatest Champion Turns Designer

Even if Jack Nicklaus, also known as the Golden Bear, had never designed a golf course, his place as one of the sport's legends would be totally secure. Tiger Woods's recent record-setting successes notwithstanding, most who follow the game still regard Nicklaus as its greatest champion. He was certainly the most prolific, winning one hundred professional events, including an unprecedented eighteen majors: six Masters, four U.S. Opens, five PGA Championships, and three British Opens. The only player ever to win every major more than once, he also picked up six Australian Open crowns along the way. The fact that he won so much is impressive, but the astounding part is that he won in every type of golf setting imaginable, from the narrow fairways and high rough of the U.S. Open venues to the ultraslick greens of Augusta to the windswept links of the British Isles. He had the shots for every occasion, and his innate abilities would greatly influence his designs.

Portrait of the Designer as a Young Man

Every designer's style evolves over time and with additional experience, but few have switched gears as radically as Nicklaus. His early success stories were primarily private layouts such as Muirfield Village, Shoal Creek, Desert Highlands, and Desert Mountain. Private clubs typically look for more challenging layouts than public courses, but Nicklaus took this to the extreme, building layouts that were suited to his own game: That is, they required every shot to be hit high, long, and with a slight fade.

The entire design industry went through a phase where harder was better and bragging rights went to the most difficult courses. This led Nicklaus to punish players at both his private courses, such as the extremely tough Pinehurst National and his early resort courses like the Bear at Michigan's Grand Traverse resort—an excruciating test from the tips.

The Mellowing of a Designer

But Nicklaus underwent a sea change along the way. Known first for building scary private tournament venues, his current status is as the man behind some of the most beautiful and enjoyable resort layouts being built. He seems to have suddenly discovered the fun in golf, and it is evident in his playful routings, now featuring multiple tees for all abilities. Nowhere is this more evident than in Mexico, where Nicklaus single-handedly pioneered high-end public golf and until recently enjoyed a near monopoly on it. It is true that he had some incredible land to work with, but he has subsequently brought what he learned back home, crafting what may be his best public course of all outside Las Vegas. Along the way he has built courses in the Colorado Rockies, along the Atlantic coastline, in England and Scotland, and throughout the rest of the world. Few designers' names add so much value to projects, and Nicklaus spends more time than ever on

E SEEMS TO HAVE SUDDENLY DISCOVER

THE FUN IN GOLF, AND IT IS EVIDENT

N HIS PLAYFUL ROUTINGS, NOW FEATURI

his private jet laying out courses around the globe. He will soon surpass the 200-course mark. Each design varies greatly based on location and the era in which he built it, but common traits include:

- **Stiff challenge from the tips.** Even as Nicklaus has softened, he's remembered that there are high-caliber players looking for a daunting challenge, and he gives it, again and again. Many of his recent courses top 7,100 and even 7,200 yards.

- **Holes that dogleg right or tricky par-3s that set up left to right.** Nicklaus was famous for his prodigious length and consistent, repeatable swing, which produced a high fade. He is equally famous in design circles for building courses that ask for, and accommodate, such a shot shape.

- **Reachable par-5s.** A long hitter, Nicklaus picked up many strokes on his opponents by reaching long holes in a stroke less than his competitors. The lesson was not lost, and he tends to pass the privilege on to the public by designing one or two reachable par-5s on nearly every course he creates.

- **Dramatic finishes.** A veteran of heated tournament finishes, Nicklaus builds courses perfect for wagering, where a lot can happen on the final three holes. Unlike many designers, however, he does not save the best for last. His Mexican coastal courses are good examples, reaching the sea early on the front nine.

- **Innovation.** Just as Nicklaus never shied away from challenge while playing, he isn't afraid to break new ground on the course. At Desert Mountain he put two flags and holes on each green, an easy one and a hard one, to cater to players of different abilities. On Daufuskie Island, he uses an oasis of trees and rough in the middle of the fairway to force a risk-reward choice of paths off the tee. At Punta Mita, Mexico, an offshore island grabbed his attention and became the first natural island hole in the world.

- **Dramatic landscapes.** Despite the vast number of courses Nicklaus has designed, few are in "normal" golf course settings. Yes, he has done Carolina and Michigan parklands, but the bulk of his work is in exotic locales, from the Sonoran Desert to coastal Mexico, from Hawaiian lava fields to the highest peaks of the Rockies.

- **Immaculate conditioning.** An interesting by-product of Nicklaus's popularity is that he is the highest-paid designer out there, and also has a reputation for creating the most expensive designs to build. As a result, nearly every course he does is high profile, and the owners go into it with maintenance budgets to match.

Nicklaus's career shift from mostly private clubs to numerous resort courses has made his work much more accessible to the traveling golfer. Still, his affiliation with very high-end resorts and regions make him one of the most expensive architects to sample. In addition, he has begun to differentiate between courses designed by his firm and the more marketable

Jack Nicklaus Signature Designs, which add a hefty amount to the price and indicate that Nicklaus was more personally involved in the design. The Signature courses are the ones many golfers aspire to play, but they tend to be the most expensive. His recent Bear Trace Trail in Tennessee, that state's version of the **Robert Trent Jones Golf Trail,** has changed things, making Nicklaus, even Signature Nicklaus, much more affordable.

KAUAI LAGOONS, *Kauai, Hawaii*

These two Nicklaus beauties receive little press but are arguably the best in this golf-rich state.

Land in Hawaii is so expensive that every golf course built in the state is a big deal, so it amazes us that these two courses remain hidden gems. What Nicklaus did here is unique for a thirty-six-hole facility. There are two schools of thought at such places: first, to build courses as different from one another as possible—something easier said than done, and only rarely pulled off—and second, to build two courses indistinguishable from one another, something that is unfortunately all too easy. Nicklaus took a third approach at Kauai Lagoons. He built a "championship"-style course, the Kiele, that is both stunning and quite resistant to low scores, alongside its alter ego, the Mokihana, which offers the same views, scenery, and feeling but with greatly toned-down challenge. The result is a complex that truly offers something for everyone, and golfers in the middle of the skill spectrum will love both.

How Nicklaus accomplished this is a clinic in golf course architecture. On the tougher Kiele course, nearly every green complex is offset, tucked

It's All in the Angles

One design element is handled differently at the two courses at Kauai Lagoons, and it greatly changes the level of scoring difficulty. By tucking the greens to one side or the other rather than straight ahead at the end of the fairway, Nicklaus makes golfers on the Kiele course plan better from tee to green, favor one side of the fairway, and hit more accurate lofted approaches. At the same time, by using sand traps rather than water or woods as the hazard of choice, he ensures that even those who post high scores won't lose or spend time looking for balls.

right or left of the fairway with the elbow guarded by bunkers. This requires that the tee shot be placed in the correct part of the fairway to open up the approach angle, and requires the shot into the green to fly the hazard, precluding bump-and-run shots. The abundance of fairway and greenside bunkers and offset greens make approach angles and pin positions much more important considerations than on most courses. He also adds a few forced carries, such as the island green on the dramatic 403-yard par-4 eighteenth, which requires a lot of nerve to go for in regulation.

The Mokihana is a very similar layout, except that nearly every hole plays straight ahead and there are far fewer greenside bunkers. This small change makes all the difference: Placement off the tee is no longer important, and shots can be rolled to the green, making the course play much easier. There are also few forced carries or water hazards.

Kiele, with four stunning par-3s that would be the signature holes at many courses, the memorable eighteenth, and beautiful scenery, is a serious contender for the title of best course in Hawaii. It also has the prerequisite ultradramatic Hawaiian oceanfront hole, the sixteenth, a short downhill par-4 on a peninsula jutting into the sea, with black rocky cliffs on either side. The Mokihana offers the same surreal settings in a user-friendly version even the highest-handicappers will enjoy. The balance offered by the two layouts, and the subtle but all-important architectural differences between them, make Kauai Lagoons a world-class facility.

KAUAI LAGOONS GOLF CLUB AT A GLANCE

(800) 634-6400, www.kauailagoonsgolf.com

Golf Course Info: Practice area, carts only.

Kiele: $$$-$$$$, 5,417–7,070 yards, four tees.

Mokihana: $$-$$$, 5,607–6,960 yards, four tees.

Lodging Info: The golf club has no lodging of its own, but is adjacent to the Kauai Marriott (808–245–5050, www.marriott.com), which boasts the largest pool in the state and has special reduced rates for guests on both courses. Other quality resorts in the area include the stunning Hyatt Poipu Bay, which has its own scenic Robert Trent Jones Jr. course. Guests of the Hyatt and other select hotels receive a discount on golf, but not as much as the Marriott.

Getting There: Most flights to Kauai connect through Honolulu, but there is some direct service from Los Angeles.

When to Go: There is simply no bad time to golf on Hawaii, which has just two seasons: summer, from May through October with temperatures in the high eighties, and winter, with temperatures in the seventies and low eighties.

Travel Deals: Like many Hawaiian courses, Kauai Lagoons offers discounts to guests of its associated hotel, the Marriott, and even steeper discounts for those who possess a Hawaiian driver's license.

GRAND CYPRESS, *Orlando, Florida*

Nicklaus's well-known love for the world's first golf course, the Old course at St. Andrews, where he won the British Open, led to this unique tribute to the Scottish links—just outside the gates of Disney World!

Walt Disney World has some fine golf, and Orlando has become a hotbed for the sport, home to the likes of Tiger Woods and Mark O'Meara. There are many excellent courses in the region, including new works by Greg Norman and old ones by Dick Wilson. But the forty-five Nicklaus-designed holes at Grand Cypress remain the city's best.

Ironically, the three nines at Grand Cypress came first, and although they host an LPGA event and are held in high esteem, they have been overshadowed by Nicklaus's subsequent New course, his homage to Scotland. Both are quite different, and both well worth playing.

The New course remains somewhat controversial, as it attempts to re-create the aura of St. Andrews far from the British Isles. Many lesser American courses are erroneously passed off as "Scottish-style" or "links-style" in an attempt to build credibility and ensnare players, and this accusation has been leveled at the New course. Nicklaus, we are happy to report, does in fact know what links courses are all about, having hoisted the Claret Jug three times and having played most of the great links. He has a deep appreciation for the oldest form of the game, deeper than most players and many designers. His intent was not to swindle the public but to offer them a taste of the course he loves so much—and he succeeds admirably.

The Old course is also one of the easiest courses to reproduce, since it is largely flat, with no major natural features such as mountains or lakes, and has little in the way of coastline or ocean views. Many of its holes, including the first and last, lend themselves to Florida, and it is re-creations of these that Nicklaus opens and closes his course with. In between he designs mostly original holes with a Scottish flair, using double greens, pot bunkers, wee burns, and high rough. He also uses cart paths and GPS systems, two decidedly un-Scottish elements, but nonetheless he rewards the golfer with a taste, and a sweet taste at that, of St. Andrews. The best reproductions are of the Swilcan burn and bridge, the Road hole, and the infamous Hell bunker.

Most resort guests clamor for a tee time at the more expensive New course, and you should, too, if you've never been to St. Andrews. But if you have been or are going, the twenty-seven-hole "regular" course offers the better golf. The mounding that some critics abhor as contrived earth-moving helps clearly define corridors of play, and give the course a sense of

At Kauai Lagoons' Kiele course, Jack Nicklaus gives golfers a chance to drive the green on the stunning sixteenth, but makes them pay a hefty price if they miss.

KAUAI LAGOONS GOLF CLUB

wild isolation. Several holes features Nicklaus's unique elevated fairways, dropping off on both sides like his course at PGA West, a rarity in design that is both interesting and attractive. The well-maintained course makes excellent use of water hazards to create both one-of-a-kind holes and several risk-reward opportunities. In fact, the entire Grand Cypress golf club is a first-rate operation, with a gracious clubhouse and helpful, professional staff.

GRAND CYPRESS GOLF CLUB AT A GLANCE

(800) 835-7377, www.grandcypress.com

Golf Course Info: Practice area.

New: $$$–$$$$, 5,339–6,833 yards, three tees.

Nicklaus Nines: $$$–$$$$, 5,056–6,983 yards, three tees.

Lodging Info: $$$–$$$$. The Grand Cypress Resort includes two distinct lodging options. The Hyatt Grand Cypress is a full-blown resort in and of itself with a pitch-and-putt course, vast pool complex with waterfall and slides, and many restaurants. The Villas at Grand Cypress offer much more space. Both provide shuttle service to the golf clubhouse (800–835–7377, www.grand cypress.com).

Getting There: Grand Cypress is in Orlando, with one of the nation's largest airports.

When to Go: Golf is played year-round, but summers are hot and humid. Also, because it sits next to Disney World, summer and school holidays are very busy as well.

Golf Travel by Design Courses Nearby: None.

BEAR TRACE TRAIL, *Tennessee*

Normally high-priced Nicklaus golf designs can be played for a song throughout Tennessee.

After the success of Alabama's *Robert Trent Jones Trail,* nearby Tennessee decided to get in the act of offering affordable, high-quality daily fee golf. They chose the Golden Bear, and the trail's courses, all located in state parks, are a boon for the nation's value-oriented golf travelers. Combining a few rounds of Nicklaus golf with Elvis Presley's Graceland, the Grand Ol' Opry, or barbecued ribs in Memphis makes a perfect road trip.

Nicklaus just opened his fifth course on the trail, Ross Creek Landing, midway between Memphis and Nashville. A Signature course, like the others in the trail, it offers a taste of his best work for a pittance of the cost of his resort golf elsewhere. Play a top Nicklaus resort course in Hawaii or Mexico, and you can expect to lay out $200 or more for the privilege. Depending on season, the Bear Trace courses run just $35–60 a round.

While the Bear Trace Trail is clearly patterned after Alabama's, there are some discernible differences. First, each location has just one eighteen-hole course, while Alabama's feature multiple regulation courses plus a short course. The layouts were designed and built one at a time, rather than all at once, and as a result, the courses on Nicklaus's trail vary markedly and have much more individual character. While the Robert Trent Jones Trail has numerous tees and ample yardage separation, the predominantly uphill approaches and forced carries make them difficult for players of all abilities, while Nicklaus's layouts, with four tees each, are more playable for less skilled players. But as always, Nicklaus provides challenge from the tips for those who want it, with the back tees stretching more than 7,100 yards at several locations. All feature superior bent grass greens, which are sloped but not overly undulating.

Since the five locations (with more to come) are spread over a smaller geographical area and are far fewer in number than Alabama's trail, it is quite possible to play them all in a single trip—and you should. Four of the five were selected as Top Ten new courses of the year when they opened.

While they are carved from dense Tennessee forests, with abundant oak, hickory, cypress, and cedar trees, water is common in the designs. Chickasaw incorporates many natural wetlands, Tims Ford plays around a large lake, Harrison Bay has twelve holes along the water, and the newest, Ross Creek Landing, overlooks the Tennessee River.

BEAR TRACE TRAIL AT A GLANCE

(866) 770–BEAR, www.beartrace.com

Golf Course Info: Practice areas, walking allowed.

Ross Creek Landing (866–214–2327): $–$$V, 5,504–7,131 yards, four tees.

Chickasaw (888–944–BEAR): $–$$V, 5,375–7,118 yards, four tees.

Tims Ford (888–558–BEAR): $–$$V, 4,848–6,764 yards, four tees.

Cumberland Mountain (888–800–BEAR): $–$$V, 5,066–6,900 yards, four tees.

Harrison Bay (877–611–BEAR): $–$$V, 5,290–7,140 yards, four tees.

Lodging Info: $–$$. There are numerous hotels and motels along the trail, and several locations are within driving distance of Memphis, Chattanooga, and other major cities. For lodging and golf package info, call (800) 369–0922.

Getting There: Memphis and Nashville both have large airports.

When to Go: The courses on the trail are either closed or have limited play in January and February. The full season runs from March through December, but April through November offer the best weather—though summers can be hot and humid.

Travel Deals: As a municipal-style network operated by the state parks and recreation department, the Trail is moderately priced to begin with. Additional savings are available for multi-day play and lodging packages at nearby hotels and motels.

Golf Travel by Design Courses Nearby: None.

REFLECTION BAY, *Las Vegas, Nevada*

It is rare to find a hidden gem in an area with a shortage of golf courses. What makes it more rare is the fact that this layout goes toe-to-toe with 800-pound gorilla Shadow Creek and equally deserves the title of best course in Las Vegas.

t's not lack of media attention that keeps Nicklaus's Reflection Bay off the radar screen—the course hosted the Wendy's Three Tour challenge several times and jumped onto *Golf Magazine's* Top One Hundred Courses You Can Play list at number sixty-five. It seems to be an issue of location that keeps it out of the public eye. The vast bulk of the Las Vegas area courses radiate northwest from the city, especially around Summerlin, home to more than half the region's name layouts. In comparison, the Reflection Bay course, part of a resort complex called Lake Las Vegas, is situated all by itself to the southeast. Believe us, it's worth the trip.

Nicklaus's work in Cabo San Lucas was so successful because it is located where the Sonoran Desert meets the sea. Here the Sonoran desert meets the largest private human-made lake in Nevada. Like the Mexican courses, it combines the desert setting with mountainous foothills and a lot of waterfront exposure—but here the desert is even more dramatic, with deep ravines to which Nicklaus added flowing creeks and tumbling waterfalls. Since it is not on the ocean, the holes reach right to the water's edge, and there are several peninsula greens jutting out into the lake. Water effects are used beautifully: On one hole you walk across stepping-stones in a creek to putt out beneath a waterfall, a touch of Hawaii transported to the mainland. But Reflection Bay is more than beautiful; it also makes great use of multiple tee boxes, angled forced carries, and elevation changes to ensure fun and challenge for all abilities, with many strategic decisions along the way. As a result, it vies with Nicklaus's stunning Punta Mita course and Kauai's Kiele as his very best resort work to date.

REFLECTION BAY AT A GLANCE

(800) 564–1603, www.lakelasvegas.com

Golf Course Info: Practice area, no walking.

$$$$, 5,166–7,261 yards, five tees.

Lodging Info: Outside play is welcome, but guests of the Hyatt Regency Lake Las Vegas on site get preferred rates and tee times. The Hyatt is a first-rate hotel with luxurious rooms, a large spa, excellent dining, and a small casino (800–55–HYATT, www.hyatt.com).

Getting There: The Lake Las Vegas resort is thirty minutes from the Las Vegas airport.

When to Go: Golf is played year-round, but temperatures climb above one hundred degrees in summer, and can be uncomfortably cold in winter. In fall overseeding takes place and the course may close for maintenance. Early spring is ideal.

Golf Travel by Design Courses Nearby: Rio Secco (twenty minutes); Cascata (thirty minutes); Las Vegas Paiute Resort (twenty minutes); Primm Valley (sixty minutes); Shadow Creek (thirty minutes); Bear's Best (twenty minutes).

BEAR'S BEST, *Las Vegas, Nevada*

Jumping on the tribute-and-replica-course bandwagon, Nicklaus brings his "can't-play" and "must-play" holes to the public—again and again.

Tribute and replica courses—those re-creating famous holes from all over the world or those done in the style and spirit of a region or designer—have become all the rage. Such "designs" are popping up all over the country, from Myrtle Beach and Atlanta to Texas, Michigan, and New Jersey. Las Vegas has been a hotbed of replica and tribute activity with Royal Links, a collection of copies of British Open holes; Cloud Nine, replicas of famous par-3s; even the Links of Las Vegas, a putting course that replicates greens from Augusta, Shinnecock Hills, and elsewhere. The newest convert is Jack Nicklaus, who bravely goes where no designer has gone before, building a tribute course to himself.

It may appear to be vanity, but there is logic to the concept. Many of Nicklaus's top-ranked layouts are private, such as Muirfield Village, PGA West, and Desert Highlands. Even his public ones are in far-flung locales, from Montana to the tip of Mexico's Baja Peninsula. Known for his passionate love of the game and its courses, Nicklaus has rounded up all his favorite holes from the roughly 200 courses he has designed and re-created them in the Nevada desert.

Other Bear's Best courses are planned, with an Atlanta site under construction and possible venues coming to Orlando, Washington, D.C., and Dallas. For the most part Nicklaus plans to match the selection of holes to the terrain, so the Vegas site is heavy on his desert holes, mainly from Arizona's Desert Mountain and Desert Highlands and Mexico's Cabo del Sol, Palmilla, and *Eldorado.* Nonetheless, he couldn't help but include some of his very favorite designs even from radically different locales such as Montana's Anaconda Iron Works and Colorado's Castle Pines. The Las Vegas course opened in early 2002 and makes a perfect companion to the stellar Reflection Bay course nearby.

BEAR'S BEST AT A GLANCE

(866) 385–8500, www.bearsbest.com

Golf Course Info: Practice area, no walking.

$$$$+, 5,043–7,194 yards, four tees.

Lodging Info: $$–$$$$. There is a wide range of lodging at every level of style and price in the Las Vegas area. The course is located in Summerlin, about twenty minutes north of the city; the major resort in Summerlin is the J. W. Marriott Las Vegas, one of the city's most opulent. The Marriott also has special tee time, discount, and golf shuttle arrangements with many top area courses, and is located next to the TPC Canyons. If you want to stay in Summerlin, this is the best choice; otherwise there are ample options in the city.

Getting There: Bear's Best is in Summerlin, twenty minutes from the Las Vegas Strip or airport.

When to Go: Golf is played year-round, but temperatures climb above one hundred degrees in summer and can be uncomfortably cold in winter. In fall overseeding takes place, and the course may close for maintenance. Early spring is ideal.

Golf Travel by Design Courses Nearby: Rio Secco (twenty minutes); Cascata (twenty minutes); Las Vegas Paiute Resort (twenty minutes); Primm Valley (sixty minutes); Reflection Bay (forty minutes); Shadow Creek (twenty minutes).

NICKLAUS SOUTH OF THE BORDER

In the past decade Jack Nicklaus almost single-handedly turned Mexico from a golfer's no-man's-land into one of the hottest golf destinations.

Jack Nicklaus's metamorphous from designer of ultradifficult private layouts to revered crafter of public access resort courses is linked with his work in Mexico. Before he journeyed south to build the now legendary Cabo del Sol, golf in Mexico was a nonissue.

That has changed, and Nicklaus is the one responsible. Today such hot designers as Tom Weiskopf and Tom Doak are following in his footsteps, but they have a lot of ground to make up before they dethrone Nicklaus as the king of Mexican golf.

He first visited the Baja Peninsula's Los Cabos region, home to the vibrant town of Cabo San Lucas, in the early 1990s. Cabo has been called Mexico's Hawaii because of its wonderful year-round weather, upscale lodging and dining, remoteness from the mainland, and high cost of living. Before golf arrived it was best known for some of the world's finest big-game fishing, especially for marlin, and as a tropical party spot. Today it is a world-class golf destination.

Cabo's geography is unique. The Sonoran Desert travels south from Arizona all the way down the Baja Peninsula. There are many types of desert in the world, but it is the Sonoran, with its towering saguaro cacti, that makes the best setting for golf, as is seen in Scottsdale. But only in Baja does the Sonoran Desert meet the sea, and in Los Cabos the peninsula is so thin that the mountain ridge running down its spine also comes to the water. Here, unlike any place on earth, desert and mountain meet the ocean, bringing together golf's three most dramatic settings.

It was here that Nicklaus built Cabo del Sol and turned toward a design philosophy that embraced beauty and fun over difficulty. He also refined his penchant for dramatic finishes, and has said that the final three holes at Cabo del Sol are his best closers of all. The course sits on rocky coastline along the Sea of Cortez; it plays down to the sea on the fifth hole, alleviating suspense, then follows with an unusual but effective pair of back-to-back par-3s along the coast. While the front nine has unfortunately become overdeveloped with large hotels and construction, the better back nine remains unspoiled, culminating with a par-4 down to the sea, a par-3 over a rocky inlet, and a par-4 along the curving coast like the par-5 finisher at Pebble Beach, a Nicklaus favorite.

The success of Cabo del Sol made golf, and Nicklaus, very popular in the region. He quickly built the wonderful Palmilla course, a twenty-seven-hole layout using more of the mountain and arroyo setting and a little less of the sea. More recently, he opened Eldorado nearby, which plays in a more traditional links routing along the coast and, like the stellar new Kingsbarns in Scotland, elevates the inland holes to provide stunning views throughout. It is Nicklaus's most visual effort in Mexico.

Nicklaus also turned his attention to the west coast of mainland Mexico, where he built a stunning course at the Four Seasons Punta Mita resort outside Puerto Vallarta. The course is open only to resort guests, receives just a handful of rounds each day, and is maintained at an incredibly high level. Here Nicklaus outdid even Cabo del Sol, with eight holes playing along the ocean and an even better final three, including a similar Pebble Beach–style closer. But the real attraction is the world's only natural island green. An offshore rocky atoll was too tempting to pass up, so Nicklaus built a green on it, 190 yards offshore. Depending on the tide, guests can walk along a sandbar or take an amphibious golf cart. Realizing that with the high ocean winds, the hole might be too tough, Nicklaus built a shorter inland par-3 alternative, so when guests complete the second hole

Finishing in Style

Having played in so many tournaments that come down to the wire, Nicklaus knows the value of a good finish, so he wraps up his courses with a dramatic flair. Nowhere is this more evident than at his two top Mexican layouts, Cabo del Sol and Punta Mita. Both end in par-4, par-3, par-4 fashion along the ocean. Both play down to the sea on sixteen, across the ocean in heroic fashion on seventeen, and conclude with a long par-4 along curving coastline. Why fix what's not broken?

they have the option of playing 3A or the more memorable 3B, truly one of the game's greatest holes.

In nearby Puerto Vallarta, Nicklaus recently completed a course at the thirty-six-hole Vista Vallarta facility, where the second course was done by Tom Weiskopf, who also built the second course at Cabo del Sol. This layout features wide fairways and a desert feel, a very solid effort but without the oceanfront drama of his other Mexican wonders. Nicklaus is not done: He is completing his first work on the country's east coast, on Cozumel.

MEXICAN COURSES AT A GLANCE

Los Cabos Golf Courses

Cabo del Sol Ocean (800–386–2465, www.cabodelsol.com): $$$$+, 4,695–7,103 yards, four tees.

Palmilla (800–367–2226, www.palmillaresort.com; twenty-seven holes): $$$$, 4,858–7,150 yards, four tees.

Eldorado (800–393–0400): $$$$, 6,228–6,899, three tees.

Golf Course Info: Practice areas, no walking.

Lodging Info: $$–$$$$. The Los Cabos region has a wide range of lodging, from inexpensive to totally swank. There are several hotels located at the Cabo del Sol course. Palmilla is the only true golf resort, a fine hotel with its own course. Las Ventanas al Paraiso is simply one of the world's finest resorts, and the only choice in the region if you are splurging (800–VISIT–CABO, www.visitcabo.com).

Getting There: Los Cabos International Airport is served by many American and Mexican airlines. All the resorts and courses are a short cab ride from the airport.

When to Go: Golf season is year-round, but summer is very hot with a few days of intense rain, which close the courses. November through May are ideal months.

Golf Travel by Design Courses Nearby: Desert course at Cabo del Sol.

Puerto Vallarta Golf Courses

Punta Mita (800–819–5053, www.fourseasons.com): $$$–$$$$, 4,994–7,014 yards, four tees.

Vista Vallarta Nicklaus Course (52–3221–0546, www.foremexico.com): $$–$$$, 5,254–7,057 yards, four tees.

Golf Course Info: Practice areas, walking allowed.

Lodging Info: $$$$. The Four Seasons Punta Mita course is the main reason to visit, and it is only open to guests of the very luxurious resort (800–819–5053, www.fourseasons.com). There are several resort hotels of various prices in Puerto Vallarta itself for those visiting the Vista Vallarta facility (888–384–6822, www.puertovallarta.net).

Getting There: Puerto Vallarta has a new airport that is served by many carriers. The resorts and Vista Vallarta courses are just ten minutes away. Punta Mita is thirty to forty minutes north.

When to Go: November through May are near perfect; the rainy season begins in June, with occasional rain. In July and August it rains all the time. Do not go during this period.

Travel Deals: While Puerto Vallarta enjoys the same weather, fine dining and quality of accommodations as Mexico's Cabo del Sol, its golf is significantly less expensive. Further savings are offered with a three-course package that combines rounds at both the Nicklaus and Weiskopf courses at Vista Vallarta and the Marina course at nearby Marina Vallarta.

Golf Travel by Design Courses Nearby: Weiskopf course at Vista Vallarta.

Other Notable Jack Nicklaus Courses You Can Play

- **Four Seasons Hualalai,** Ka`upulehu-Kona, Hawaii
- **Manele Bay,** Lanai, Hawaii
- **Great Waters,** Reynolds Plantation, Greensboro, Georgia
- **Summit course,** Cordillera, Edwards, Colorado
- **Melrose,** Daufuskie Island, South Carolina
- **Old Works,** Anaconda, Montana
- **Nicklaus Tournament course,** PGA West, Palm Springs, California
- **Castle Pines,** Castle Rock, Colorado
- **Mount. Juliet,** Thomastown, Ireland

Ted Robinson Sr. (1923–)
and Ted Robinson Jr. (1951–)
Beautifying Golf and the Environment

The father-and-son team behind Robinson Golf have not strayed too far from their California home, designing dozens of top courses on the West Coast and throughout the Southwest. If you have been to Palm Springs, you have probably already played a Robinson course, since no other designer has been as prolific in this golf boomtown. Ted Robinson Sr. has built approximately 170 resort courses, including some ranked among the nation's best. He's known for his extensive use of water hazards, as well as often elaborate aquatic features such as waterfalls and artificial creeks. But since his son joined the family firm, they have stepped into the limelight at the forefront of the new trend toward environmentally friendly golf. This is the biggest fundamental change to the golf course design industry since the advent of earthmoving equipment. It's causing architects to rethink every aspect of the business, from irrigation to the number of fairway acres planted. As Tom Fazio has demonstrated, the major limitation facing designers is not the land or natural features, but the permits and zoning required. As legal constraints tighten, more and more designers are starting, by choice or by need, to follow the Robinsons' innovations.

Earth-Friendly Earthmoving

Ted Sr. is a past president of the American Society of Golf Course Architects and a modern designer in every sense, embracing earthmoving equipment to create topography, installing abundant human-made water features, and using nongolf elements such as flowers and fountains to make his courses more scenic. Ted Jr., a longtime member of environmental advocacy organizations including the Sierra Club and The Nature Conservancy, has steered their business toward cutting-edge earth-friendly technologies. They make an unlikely pair, but are demonstrating that even moving vast amounts of earth can be done in a beneficial way.

When golf course design entered the modern era, enhanced subsurface irrigation changed the appearance of the game from British Islands brown to constant lush green, and golfers came to expect this condition, albeit unnatural, on their courses. In their latest effort the Robinsons are trying to turn back the clock. They are increasingly blending fairway grasses into the native vegetation of the natural setting; in their most extreme recent work, they're allowing the Bermuda grass to go dormant and stay brown throughout the winter playing season, a shock to many first-time visitors.

Their theories culminated with the thirty-six-hole Robinson Ranch public facility outside Los Angeles, developed by the family themselves. "Usually we have to address the client's wishes, but Robinson Ranch was our project, we owned it, and we approached it differently," said Ted Jr. The

ROBINSON GOLF

THEY HAVE STEPPED INTO THE LIMELIGHT AT THE

FOREFRONT OF THE NEW TREND TOWARD

ENVIRONMENTALLY FRIENDLY GOLF. THIS IS

THE BIGGEST FUNDAMENTAL CHANGE TO THE

GOLF COURSE DESIGN INDUSTRY SINCE

THE ADVENT OF EARTHMOVING EQUIPMENT

courses are the most advanced example of eco-friendly design ever undertaken in this country.

The eco-friendly philosophy is a relatively new phenomenon. When you visit a Robinson course, it is more likely to have been designed by Ted Sr. and feature:

- **Wide fairways and large landing areas.** This throwback to classical design is needed to counter a love of water hazards. It works well since the Robinsons design so many resort courses, which have to be more user friendly than private clubs.

- **Water hazards.** From creeks to lakes to waterfalls, water hazards, both natural and human-made, turn up in abundance on Robinson courses, especially at the end of the round.

- **Demanding and dramatic par-3s.** These are often the most memorable holes on Robinson courses, usually incorporating water, including island greens or long carries from the tips.

- **Strong risk-reward finishing holes.** Nearly every designer strives for a memorable closer, but the Robinsons succeed again and again, often requiring a water hazard to be carried on the approach, ensuring that matches can change right up to the very end.

- **Elaborate landscaping and beautification.** The Robinsons tend to beautify their courses, and like Nicklaus and Fazio, they're prone to elaborate water features—including cascades—for purely scenic purposes.

- **Elevation changes.** The famous downhill hole at the Experience at Koele, a 444-yard hole that Greg Norman drove the green on (due in part to a 250-foot vertical drop) is the most glaring example, but ups and downs are part of Robinson golf. They're not afraid to move earth either, such as the 1.2 million cubic yards used to create mounds and elevation changes at the thirty-six-hole Desert Springs Marriott resort.

Currently the Robinsons are focusing more and more on the environmental side of the design process, but the following courses span the breadth of their career.

THE EXPERIENCE AT KOELE, *Lanai, Hawaii*

This one-of-a-kind Hawaiian layout is the only course in the state with bent grass greens. It sits high in the mountains and far from the sea.

Hawaii is famous for its breathtaking oceanfront golf courses, but the Experience is not one of them. Sitting at an elevation of more than 2,000 feet, in mountainous terrain that is often cloudy and misty, it is not the popular image of a Hawaiian paradise. With its dense woods and glaring lack of real estate development, it would seem more at home in northern Michigan. But the course is so good it warrants a diversion from the state's sunny shores. It features severe and dramatic elevation changes, unique hole designs, and the state's best greens, the only bent grass putting surfaces in Hawaii.

The Experience straddles the fine line between fun and challenge as it rises and falls through the mountainous setting. It's so enjoyable to play, golfers may be surprised at its high slope and course ratings. Water is frequently in play, often arrayed at distances that tempt you to carry just a bit more than is feasible. The famous tee shot from a 250-foot elevation to a fairway in the valley below is made more menacing by the lake down the right-hand side. Although the fairway is very wide, many golfers overcompensate and place their shot in the rough and bushes to the left, negating the added distance from the severe drop. Other features include split and tiered fairways, seven lakes, and enough waterfalls for several golf courses.

The island of Lanai is unique in Hawaii. It is almost entirely owned by one company, which developed the two resort hotels and golf courses, but since guests share them all, it is really one big resort. The second layout is as different from the Experience as night and day. The Jack Nicklaus–designed Challenge at Manele runs along towering rocky cliffs over the Pacific and is the most visual example of the stereotypical Hawaiian oceanfront golf course. Coastal real estate is so expensive here that even the most famous courses usually offer but one or two ocean holes before turning back inland to cheaper terrain, but the Challenge has five. It also lives up to its name as vintage Nicklaus, requiring long carries into the wind. While it's very difficult from the blue tees, it's also a stiff challenge from any set. There may be no course in the state as beautiful—but when the wind blows, which is often, few are more difficult.

Not a Greg Norman Design

Greg Norman, one of the most popular and likable stars of the PGA Tour, has emerged in recent years as an equally popular golf course designer, clothing producer, and even winemaker. His name is quite marketable, so it is no surprise that it is frequently attached to the Experience at Koele, even by the resort itself. But while he is often listed as the Robinsons' codesigner, and sometimes as the course's sole designer, Norman himself is adamant in explaining that he was merely a consultant on the project and used the opportunity to learn the trade for himself. Fortunately, Norman's many recent solo successes have focused the spotlight on his own designs.

(800) 321-4666, www.lanai-resorts.com

Golf Course Info: Practice area, walking allowed.

Experience at Koele: $$$$, 6,217–7,014 yards, four tees. *Slope rating* 130–141. *Course rating 69.7–73.3.*

Challenge at Manele: $$$$, 5,024–7,039 yards, five tees. *Slope rating* 114–132. *Course rating 64.0–73.3.*

Lodging Info: $$$$+. There are two sister resorts on the island, 12 miles apart and a world away in terms of setting. The oceanfront Manele Bay is a beach resort; the Lodge at Koele sits in the forested mountains and is the state's largest wood-framed building, offering much more of a New England than a Hawaiian ambience. Both are true luxury hotels, with fine dining and first-rate amenities. Each has one golf course located on site, with free shuttle transportation between them; guests can use all the facilities of both interchangeably. It is possible to come over on the ferry from Maui's Lahaina and play the courses as an outside guest, but this is a full-day proposition for one round.

Getting There: Aloha and Hawaiian Airlines fly to Lanai from the other islands, and there is regular ferry service from Maui's Lahaina.

When to Go: Weather is moderate, sunny, and perfect for golf all year long.

Travel Deals: Since almost everyone who plays the course is a guest at one of the two resorts on the island, discounts are hard to come by here. However, there is a unique fringe benefit. Next to the course's hotel, the Lodge at Koele, is the only completely free course we have ever seen. The Cavendish Golf Club is a nine-hole course left over from the banana plantation days. It has no clubhouse or carts, but it is maintained by the same staff that keeps up the exquisite Experience course—and the price is right for a warm-up round or half day of golf.

Golf Travel by Design Courses Nearby: None.

DESERT SPRINGS MARRIOTT,
Palm Springs, California

Palm Springs boasts numerous upscale resorts with multiple courses, but the Desert Springs Marriott and its thirty-six Robinson-designed holes is simply the best.

Ted Robinson Sr. has built many golf courses, public and private, in the greater Palm Springs region, but Desert Springs is the highlight of his portfolio. The 400-acre resort site includes 23 acres of private lakes, which are used to great effect on and off the courses. This is the rare instance in which both courses are well above average, and either would justify a trip to Palm Springs to play. Still, there is no discernible quality difference between the two; if you go, plan on playing both.

Both typify the Robinson experience, with numerous water features, flower beds, and tons of scenery. The par-3s are memorable, each with an island version as well as another that requires a carry over water from tee to green. Water is the predominant theme here; the Palms layout uses waterfalls, pools, and lakes to create an oasis atmosphere, with constant views of the surrounding mountains offering perspective. All in all there is water on nine holes—and it is used beautifully, especially on the final four in a trademark strong Robinson finish. Fifteen is a short par-4 doglegging to a peninsula green, sixteen a midlength par-4 over water to an island fairway and over water again to the green. Seventeen is the best human-made island green we've seen. Architectural purists shake their heads at such holes, but if you are going to build an island, it might as well be dramatic. In this one the back of the green is flanked with a semicircle of palm trees—an unusual feature on island holes, which usually have a flat, raftlike green. In between tee and green are rocky outcrops in the water planted with desert flowers. It sets golfers up for the memorable finish, a par-4 that doglegs left around a lake running from tee to green.

The Valley course has slightly less water, but it is used in equally dramatic fashion. Numerous forced carries aren't long, but they can be daunting. It too features a memorable par-3 over water from tee to green, plus several longer holes over water on the approach shot; there's also an island-green par-3 on sixteen. Eighteen finishes with a second shot to an islandlike green over several waterfalls. This is fun, beautiful, and entirely artificial resort golf at its best.

The Marriott is also one of the region's top hotels. It continues the watery theme of the resort with a lake that enters the hotel lobby and boats to shuttle guests to island restaurants.

DESERT SPRINGS MARRIOTT AT A GLANCE

(800) 228-9290, www.desertspringsresort.com

Golf Course Info: Practice areas.

Palm: $$$–$$$$, 5,492–6,761 yards, four tees. *Slope rating* 116–130. *Course rating* 69.2–72.1.

Valley: $$$–$$$$, 5,262–6,627 yards, four tees. *Slope rating* 118-127. *Course rating* 69.6–71.5.

Lodging Info: The Marriott is a very large full-service resort hotel with a wide assortment of restaurants and amenities, including tennis and a spa. Guests of the nearby Marriott Rancho Las Palmas, a smaller, more subdued resort with a first-rate spa, also have golf privileges. The public is welcome, but hotel guests receive preferential tee times and discounts.

Getting There: The hotel is 15 miles from the Palm Springs airport and two hours from Los Angeles.

When to Go: Golf is played year-round with delightful weather, but summer months can be quite hot.

Golf Travel by Design Courses Nearby: La Quinta/PGA West (twenty-five minutes).

KO OLINA, *Oahu, Hawaii*

The least well known of Hawaii's golfing islands has some hidden gems, including Ted Robinson Sr.'s Ko Olina course outside of Honolulu.

With the famed beaches of Waimea Bay, Pipeline, and Sunset, Oahu is better known for surfing than golf. After all, the island sport was invented here, and the island still hosts some of its biggest championships. But if you are a golfer visiting Honolulu, the state's largest city, you are just a short drive from the Robinsons' lush Ko Olina layout.

The course features a vast quantity of gorgeous, but penal, water hazards. In true Robinson fashion it finishes dramatically, with a final hole featuring seven pools that tumble across the fairway into a lake and a waterfall that guard the left side of the green. On the memorable twelfth hole, golfers drive their carts underneath another tumbling waterfall. Besides water presented in myriad ways, the layout features generous landing areas that give you the chance to keep your ball dry; well-spaced tees offer everything from a resort round to a tournament challenge. Greens that are not protected by water are well bunkered. As on many Hawaiian layouts, tradewinds are a major factor.

The course is part of the J. W. Marriott Ihilani resort, and golfers stressed out by the prospect of hitting over all that water and skirting all the sand will be happy to know that the property has one of Hawaii's top spas. The resort is located just outside Honolulu, on the tip of the next major peninsula to the west; its waterfront location features gorgeous lagoons and vast expanses of beach.

J. W. MARRIOTT IHILANI RESORT & SPA AT A GLANCE

(808) 679-0079, www.ihilani.com

Golf Course Info: Practice areas, no walking.

$$$, 5,392–6,867 yards, four tees. *Slope rating* 125–137. *Course rating* 69.2–70.8.

Lodging Info: The Marriott is a full-service resort hotel with a very good spa and nice beaches. Guests receive substantial golf discounts, but the course is public and available to those staying at one of the many hotels of Honolulu.

Getting There: Ihilani is thirty minutes from Honolulu, Hawaii's biggest city.

When to Go: Weather is excellent year-round.

Golf Travel by Design Courses Nearby: None.

THE PHOENICIAN, *Scottsdale, Arizona*

The Robinsons bring their groomed resort golf to one of the nation's most luxurious hotels in the Sonoran Desert.

There is no shortage of first-rate public golf in the "Valley of the Sun," as the Phoenix/Scottsdale region is known. The first, and very best, examples of pure desert golf—including *Troon North,* the Boulders, and Grayhawk—can be found here. Rather than compete with these rugged limited-turf designs, the Robinsons did what they do best, crafting twenty-seven scenic, player-friendly holes at the Phoenician.

At this resort golf takes a sideline to the main event, the hotel itself. Built with borrowed money at the height of the S&L crisis, the resort embodies pure decadence. No expense was spared in its construction. The vast stretches of marble are often gilded with gold; the hotel houses an $8 million art collection and no less than eleven Steinway grand pianos. There are eleven restaurants and nine swimming pools, luxurious poolside cabanas, one of the nation's top spas, a championship croquet court, and a two-acre cactus garden with more than 350 varieties. The Phoenician also offers a world-class tennis facility with four different surfaces: grass, red clay, Har-Tru, and hard courts identical to those used for the Australian Open.

With all these first-rate facilities, the resort needed high-quality golf, and the Robinsons delivered. The three nines epitomize resort golf and are fun, beautiful, and very well maintained. While there is far less water than on most of their courses, the nines are challenging enough to be interesting

A Star in the Arizona Desert

The nation's most prominent hotel rating publication, the *Mobil Guide*, loves the Phoenician. The only resort in Arizona to capture five Mobil stars for lodging, it also has the state's only five-star restaurant, Mary Elaine's. Less than ten hotels have equaled this double-five-star feat. But add the four stars awarded to the resort's Terrace restaurant, for a total of fourteen, and the Phoenician receives more Mobil stars than any other property. It also captures five diamonds from the AAA.

to the serious golfer, but playable and scenic enough to please anyone. To create the desired parklike setting, the layout uses lush fairways, fountains, lakes, and the desert itself, featuring frequent elevation changes as it rolls through the desert foothills. Excellent bent grass greens are an unusual luxury in the desert climate. The nines are all equal in quality but different in character: The Oasis has the most water hazards, the Desert is a target-style nine with more exposed waste areas, and the Canyons features the most elevation change, climbing over rugged terrain. If there is one weakness, it is that the courses are unusually short. We suggest playing them all for a twenty-seven-hole day.

THE PHOENICIAN AT A GLANCE

(800) 880-8234, www.thephoenician.com

Golf Course Info: Practice area.

$$$$, 5,024–6,310 yards, three tees. *Slope rating* 107-131. *Course rating* 63.5–70.3.

Lodging Info: $$$$+. One of the nation's most luxurious hotels, the Phoenician spares no expense offering guests the best in lodging, dining, and accommodations. Guests spare no expense receiving these.

Getting There: The Phoenician is the closest major resort to the Phoenix Sky Harbor Airport, twenty minutes away.

When to Go: Golf is played year-round, but summer gets extremely hot.

Travel Deals: The Phoenician is one of the most luxurious and expensive hotels in the nation, but prices drop in summer when temperatures soar well over 100 degrees. Packages with unlimited golf are discounted by as much as two-thirds during the off-season.

Golf Travel by Design Courses Nearby: Troon North (thirty minutes); TPC Scottsdale (thirty minutes).

ROBINSON RANCH, *Santa Clarita, California*

Golf's most ecologically advanced course is a lesson for the future of the game.

Ted Robinson Sr. has worked on more than 170 golf courses, including many in recent years with his son, but this is the highlight of their family efforts. Opened in 2000, it merges a father's design experience with a son's enthusiasm and respect for the environment, and the result is a showcase of responsible development for the future of golf.

The industry has turned increasingly to positive environmental practices, often as a result of having no other choice. The most prominent example is the Audubon Cooperative Sanctuary Program, administered by Audubon International (different from the National Audubon Society). Meeting these standards allows a course to be recognized as achieving various tiers of responsibility. Robinson Ranch is the first course in the nation to receive the higher Audubon Silver Sanctuary certification. Yet while he is proud of this accomplishment, it wasn't enough for Ted Robinson Jr., who took it into his own hands to craft more demanding criteria. "We laid out the course to preserve as much of what we classified as A habitat as possible, utilizing as much as we could of the C habitat. We had a biologist identify animal corridors for the migrations of everything from snakes to bobcats. In terms of design and some other features, we really have the state of the art."

They used less than 80 acres of turf per course, while typical layouts might use 150. This cuts down on irrigation needs, and to further reduce water usage, Robinson Ranch uses a recirculating capture irrigation system. The limited amount of turf also means less fertilizer, pesticides, and herbicides. Rather than overseeding and watering the fairways in winter, as is typical with Bermuda grass, they are left to go dormant and stay brown. Even the garbage cans and driving range mats are made from biodegradable materials.

But environmental concerns aside, these are still golf courses, and the Robinsons wanted to offer the public a first-rate, private club experience. For this reason, they installed high-quality bent grass greens, built a top-notch clubhouse, and offer GPS systems to navigate the course. The Mountain course has more elevation change and, of course, plenty of water hazards. It reaches its high point on the eleventh tee, from which you can see more than half the holes on the course, as well as many on the adjacent layout. While the Mountain course is fairly forgiving and offers a relaxed golf experience, the Valley course is a different story. Intended to offer skilled golfers all the challenge they could want, it closes with six tough holes, one after another, so daunting that this stretch is nicknamed Death Row. The course, although only 6,903 yards—moderate by today's standards—comes in with a scary slope of 140 and rating of 74.5. It is longer and much tougher than its sibling, and ample stands of native trees, mainly sycamores and oaks, are in play; in typical Robinson style, so are many native wetlands.

ROBINSON RANCH AT A GLANCE

(661) 252-8484, www.robinsonranchgolf.com

Golf Course Info: Practice area, walking allowed.

Mountain: $$–$$$, 5,076–6,508 yards, four tees. *Slope rating* 121–133. *Course rating* 68.4–72.1.

Valley: $$–$$$, 5,408–6,903 yards, four tees. *Slope rating* 126–140. *Course rating* 70.0–74.5.

Ted Robinson's trademark use of water hazards beautifies the desert course at the Phoenician. THE PHOENICIAN

Lodging Info: There is no lodging at Robinson Ranch, but the facility is just 25 miles north of downtown Los Angeles.

Getting There: The course is 25 miles north of Los Angeles.

When to Go: Golf is played year-round, but summer brings high temperatures.

Golf Travel by Design Courses Nearby: None.

Other Notable Ted Robinson Courses You Can Play

- **Inn of the Mountain Gods,** Mescalero, New Mexico
- **Hyatt DFW Bear Creek,** Dallas, Texas
- **Indian Wells Resort,** Palms Springs, California (thirty-six holes)
- **Pelican Lakes,** Windsor, Colorado
- **Black Lake Golf Resort,** Nipomo, California (twenty-seven holes)
- **Fountain Grove Resort,** Santa Rosa, California

Arthur Hills (1930–)
Quietly Building Classic Courses for the Modern Era

Hardly a household name among the golfing public, Arthur Hills has never enjoyed the popular recognition of his contemporaries such as Pete Dye and Tom Fazio. Yet he has designed more than 120 golf courses, including award-winning designs at marquee resorts in golf travel's most popular destinations. Even as he enters his mid-seventies, Hills is at the height of his game, and in 2000 debuted two new public designs on *Golf Magazine's* Top Ten New Courses You Can Play list. A famously laid-back and soft-spoken man, Hills has not sought the limelight. With his work in demand more than ever, he is content to let his designs speak for themselves.

Composing a Golf Course

Hills has a background in landscape design, and studied horticulture at Michigan State. It comes as no surprise, then, that his courses emphasize the natural setting. Without much fanfare he has placed himself on the cutting edge of the environmentally friendly golf movement, preserving the highlights of the sites he finds and reclaiming those already damaged. His best courses are also among the nation's most visual, from the epic Links at Lighthouse Sound to the stunning Bay Harbor and Half Moon Bay courses.

Part of the reason Hills has stayed out of the limelight is that many of his early successes were at private clubs. He is responsible for so many country club layouts in golf-crazed Naples, Florida, that Pete Dye is reputed to have called him "the mayor of Naples." His highest profile private work was the Mountain course at Bighorn, which hosted the Skins Game several times. But in recent years his work has expanded to include many public and resort courses, and you can now play Hills designs from coast to coast.

The one thing you will be hard-pressed to find is a Hills course that can be labeled "radical." He is a traditionalist, and while he has publicly proclaimed his admiration for Pete Dye, his design philosophy is much more along the lines of Alister MacKenzie or Stanley Thompson. His first priority is the routing itself, making the best use of the land in the layout of the holes. The order of the holes and the mood it creates for the golfer is equally important, and Hills sees the course as a complete work—a symphony, so to speak—where each hole plays a part in the rhythm. He is less concerned with green complexes than many modern designers, at least to the extent that he does not feel that even the best greens can make up for a less-than-stellar routing.

Perhaps his greatest contribution to the game has been his ability to impose his classical beliefs on difficult sites, be they abandoned cement plants or oilfields. While other architects faced with such challenges have

HILLS SEES THE COURSE AS A COMPLETE

WORK—A SYMPHONY, SO TO SPEAK—

WHERE EACH HOLE PLAYS A PART IN THE RHYTHM

often provided fun and interesting courses by incorporating these challenged landscapes, Hills walks the finer line of building a traditional course as he might have done on ideal land, but in an environmentally sensitive manner. Whether he has a perfect site or not, you can expect to see the following on his layouts:

- **A player-friendly opening hole.** Like Ross before him, Hills designs for all abilities of players and likes to start the round with an enjoyable rhythm.

- **Wide fairways.** Like many old links courses, or the early parkland and heathland designs of Australia and England, Hills gives golfers room to play.

- **Irregular and menacing bunkers.** While flat-bottomed bunkers have come into vogue, being easier to build and maintain, Hills likes the older, more natural kind that have both irregular lips and interior contours.

- **Wooded tees and, when possible, courses.** Given his horticultural training, Hills is loathe to remove trees, and tries to create the feeling that a player is enjoying golf in the great outdoors by locating the teeing ground in a natural, wooded setting.

Golf's Higher Purpose

In recent years environmentalists, once fierce opponents of golf course development, have looked at the game as a savior. Golf courses can be used to keep undeveloped land open, but they have also proven a valuable way to convert polluted sites back to a natural setting. In Montana Jack Nicklaus converted a Superfund site at the Anaconda Iron Works into a top public course. Widow's Walk in Massachusetts was an illegal waste dump before golf. And Arthur Hills's stunningly beautiful Bay Harbor is built on a former cement factory site that once saw sixty acres of land contaminated by kiln dust, plus another fifty that were a defunct quarry. With the help of the Army Corp of Engineers, Hills encapsulated the dust under rubble and topsoil, grading the entire site

- **Strategic holes.** Hills would rather reward good shots than penalize bad ones, so he creates holes that offer rewards for executing better shots and multiple options off the tee.

Arthur Hills does not have as many famous courses as other top modern designers, but many of the following are recognizable. Even those that aren't are well worth a round.

BAY HARBOR, *Bay Harbor, Michigan*

In 1998 Arthur Hills turned a polluted industrial site into the best twenty-seven-hole course in the country.

Michigan is fanatical about its golf, consistently ranking near the very top in the number of new courses, per-capita courses, and golf participation by residents. It also has a disproportionate number of public access courses and large destination golf resorts. With hundreds of miles of lake shoreline and rolling, sandy, forested terrain, it is a near-perfect location for building golf courses, and there are many good ones. But Arthur Hills's Bay Harbor stands out as the state's best public course.

It was not always so beautiful—Bay Harbor was once a polluted cement plant and quarry. Today it boasts not only one of the nation's most beautiful golf courses but also Michigan's toniest golf resort and a very exclusive private community.

There are three nines at Bay Harbor, unusual among top courses, and it is the only twenty-seven-hole routing on *Golf Magazine*'s Top Ten list. Each has a unique feel, and while the Links and Quarry nines are the two best, we suggest playing all three, especially in northern Michigan where summer sunlight allows golf until ten at night. The Quarry routing, as you would expect, is built through the old quarry, incorporating 40-foot-high cliffs and exposed shale in its canyonlike design. The Preserve nine is a wooded parkland effort, a very traditional layout with an emphasis on strategic shotmaking. But the one you always see in pictures is the Links nine, built along 150-foot-high cliffs above Lake Michigan and the state's answer to the **Straits course** at Wisconsin's American Club. Besides the omnipresent water, it includes expanses of gorse and heather, rolling fairway mounds, and windswept sand dunes, completing the links experience. The only things missing at the Links are pot bunkers, but Hills protects the greens with his more typical deep, irregular bunkers, which are even harder to extricate shots from. Hills has always designed courses to be playable by golfers of all abilities; the tee separations are so severe at Bay Harbor that the nines play nearly double the length from the back tees as from the front.

Bay Harbor is a large planned community comprised of both luxury homes and condos and upscale lodging. It has a fully-featured deep-water marina, a retail complex, restaurants, and other sporting facilities.

(888) BAY-HARBOR, www.bayharbor.com, or www.bayharborgolf.com

Golf Course Info: Practice area, walking allowed.

$$$$, 3,881–6,810 yards, five tees.

Lodging Info: $$$$. The Inn at Bay Harbor is a luxury condominium hotel; rooms are rented out when not in use by owners. Another alternative is the Marina District, one of the residential developments within the complex, which has rental condominiums. The golf club is operated by Boyne USA resorts, which has several other golf resorts in the region, including Boyne Highlands and Boyne Mountain. Guests of these properties enjoy the same access and discounts on golf as Bay Harbor guests (www.boyneusa.com). There is also limited availability for nonguest public play.

Getting There: Bay Harbor is 63 miles from the Traverse City, Michigan, airport, which offers numerous commuter flights on several major carriers in spring through fall.

When to Go: The season is April through October, but May through September are the most reliable months. Some early- and late-season discounts are available.

Golf Travel by Design Courses Nearby: None.

SHEPHERD'S HOLLOW, *Clarkston, Michigan*

To find one of the nation's best remaining traditional golf course sites, Hills relied on divine intervention. God provided, and now there is a low-cost, high-quality twenty-seven-hole complex that carries golfers back to the game's Golden Age.

Historically, anyone from the Detroit area looking to play golf headed far north, to the public golf mecca of northern Michigan. But two years ago Arthur Hills gave Motor City residents—and visitors—a very good reason to stay home.

The site for the new Shepherd's Hollow is everything that Hills, a classically inspired designer, could want. It features 350 acres of undisturbed mature hardwoods mixed with pines on rolling, heavily wooded terrain, an absolutely perfect parkland setting. That such a piece of land went undeveloped in Detroit's wealthy northern suburbs for so long is surprising, but it is owned by a Jesuit order that used it as a spiritual retreat. Seeking to improve the land in a way beneficial to the community,

Arthur Hills's Ocean course at Half Moon Bay enjoys both a stunning cliff-top location and a new Ritz-Carlton hotel. © JOANN DOST

they chose public recreation, and leased it at a rate and under terms that ensured the golf would be affordable. The result is one of the great values in the high-end daily fee realm.

Hills laid out a very traditional routing that would make MacKenzie proud, following the natural contours of the land, making no two holes the same, and featuring wide fairways and clearly defined playing corridors through the trees. It offers visitors a chance to experience pure golf in the classic American style, and as a result, Shepherd's Hollow has quickly won praise and awards in the industry. The third nine, completed in 2001, equals the first two in quality and style.

SHEPHERD'S HOLLOW AT A GLANCE

(248) 922–0300, www.shepherdshollow.com

Golf Course Info: Practice areas, walking allowed.

$–$$V, 4,906–7,236 yards, five tees.

Lodging Info: Shepherd's Hollow is a daily fee course with no lodging attached, but it is in the suburbs of a major city, with ample lodging choices in all price ranges nearby.

Getting There: Shepherd's Hollow is thirty minutes from central Detroit and the airport.

When to Go: The spring through fall months are golf season in the region.

Travel Deals: This course is always a bargain, but on weekday early morning (7:00–10:00 A.M.) tee times are discounted, the opposite of what most courses do. Lower-priced replay rounds are always available as well.

Golf Travel by Design Courses Nearby: None.

THE LINKS AT LIGHTHOUSE SOUND,
Ocean City, Maryland

Ocean City is poised to join Myrtle Beach and Hilton Head as a major eastern golf destination, led by this Hills design described by one major golf magazine as "the Pebble Beach of the East."

One of the most acclaimed courses to open in 2000, this layout threatens to surpass Bay Harbor as Hills's crowning achievement. The 1,000-acre waterfront site was on the development drawing board for quite some time before an environmentally friendly low-density plan with less than a hundred homesites was approved. In an unusual twist for such communities, the very best land was left for the golf course.

Lighthouse Sound is change-of-pace layout for Hills, mixing holes from several design schools, including classical, modern, and links. The reason for this diversity is the land itself. Varied terrain is frequently cited as a positive factor on golf courses, but the Links at Lighthouse Sound takes this to the extreme. Holes are cut through tidal marsh, laid out on the waterfront along the bay, and set in heavily wooded inland sites, some of which play along a river. Half the holes sit on an archipelago of marsh and coastline linked to the mainland by the world's longest cart bridge; two holes jut out into the bay itself. From the first tee to the eighteenth green, it is a golf experience that elevates that stature of fast-growing Ocean City.

The routing is unusual in that the holes are built in separate clusters with quite a bit of space between them. This makes carts mandatory, but also allows Hills to visit and revisit the bay and marshes, whereas many waterfront courses have just a single stretch of dramatic holes. After his customary gentle opening hole, he jumps right into the meat of the course: Holes two through seven play around a bayfront peninsula and through tidal marshes. Eleven and twelve return to the bay, reaching the most extreme promontory on the layout. Although eleven plays to the bay, with water behind the green, it is a very traditional redan hole, even named such by Hills, his homage to tradition in a modern setting. This is just one of the many design highlights awaiting players at the Links at Lighthouse Sound.

LINKS AT LIGHTHOUSE SOUND AT A GLANCE

(888) 55–HILLS, www.lighthousesound.com

Golf Course Info: Practice areas, no walking.

$$–$$$, 5,548–7,031 yards, three tees. *Slope rating* 133–144. *Course rating* 71.1–73.7.

Lodging Info: There is no lodging affiliated with the course, but Ocean City is a major beach vacation destination with a wide variety of lodging in all price ranges, including many waterfront resorts and motels. For more information visit www.ocvisitor.com.

Getting There: Ocean City is on the east side of Maryland's Atlantic peninsula, 145 miles east of Washington, D.C., and 140 miles southeast of Baltimore.

When to Go: Golf is played year-round, but spring and fall are best. Winters can get chilly, and summers quite hot and humid.

Golf Travel by Design Courses Nearby: None.

OCEAN COURSE AT HALF MOON BAY,
Half Moon Bay, California

With a new high-end resort hotel and two courses, Half Moon Bay provides Bay Area golfers with a much closer coastal alternative to the famed layouts of Carmel and the Monterey Peninsula.

I n a very unusual move, the first layout at this thirty-six-hole facility along the Pacific coast was built on the inland site, the reverse of the usual development scheme seen at such revered resorts as ***Cabo del Sol*** and ***Whistling Straits.*** The nondescript Arnold Palmer and Ed Seay parkland routing wanders through a housing development, and as a result, Half Moon Bay at first stayed off the radar screen of most traveling golfers.

Not anymore. In 1997 Hills arrived and built a seaside layout with a stunning finish that put Half Moon Bay on the map. Two years later he did his best to refurbish Palmer's Old course into a suitable companion. Then in 2001 Ritz-Carlton arrived, elevating Half Moon Bay from a daily fee golf facility to a full-blown resort.

Frankly, Half Moon Bay has struggled to emerge from the pack in a region with many great courses, public and private, and no one has mistaken it for Pebble Beach. The lodging is extremely expensive, as is the golf, and there are no practice facilities, a surprising oversight. The weather in the region is as fickle as could be—fog can easily stop play here. The Old course, despite a dramatic finishing hole along the coast, is simply not worth the green fees it commands. But the Ocean course remains the highlight of Half Moon Bay, and is worth a visit.

It is a wide-open links layout combining Hill's tendency toward playability with traditional Scottish elements. It has ample elevation changes throughout; as a result, nearly all the holes, including the inland ones, have expansive ocean views. Like his layout at Lighthouse Sound, the course heads to the water right away, rather than keeping the golfer in suspense, and the opening and closing holes are stunning. The course concludes with a classic par-4, par-3, par-5 finish along the cliffs overlooking the Pacific, a finish that will wipe the resort's shortcomings from a your memory. Seventeen is the quintessential coastal par-3; like its famous neighbor at nearby Cypress Point, it's all carry, with no fairway between tee and green.

One word of caution. Despite its very strong start and finish, the middle of the Ocean course is somewhat dull—but worse, it can be dangerous. Six holes play side by side, and on the open links design, with no trees screening them, slices and hooks inevitably find their way into the wrong fairways. While this same problem is commonplace in the British Isles, here it is made even worse by the frequent fog, which hinders visibility and puts golfers on the defensive.

HALF MOON BAY AT A GLANCE

(800) 241–3333, www.halfmoonbaygolf.com

Golf Course Info: No practice area.

Ocean: $$$, 5,109–6,732 yards, three tees.

Old: $$$, 5,305–7,090 yards, three tees.

Lodging Info: $$$$+. Both courses are public and get quite crowded, but guests of the on-site Ritz-Carlton get preferential tee times and discounts. The hotel has an excellent spa, quality dining, and a very pleasant atmosphere (www.ritzcarlton.com).

Getting There: Half Moon Bay is forty-five minutes south of San Francisco and thirty minutes from the airport.

When to Go: Golf is played year-round, but the rainy season is from December through March, and temperatures drop anytime the fog rolls in.

Golf Travel by Design Courses Nearby: Pasatiempo (one hour).

PALMETTO HALL AND PALMETTO DUNES,
Hilton Head Island, South Carolina

**Hilton Head's largest golf resort has one
course each from several renowned architects,
but two classic Arthur Hills designs.**

These twin resort and residential communities have five courses
between them, including works by Robert Trent Jones Sr. and Bob
Cupp, but almost all the locals acknowledge that the highlights of the
complexes are its two Arthur Hills tracts, which are different enough
to cover the bases for all types of golfers.

The Arthur Hills course at Palmetto Dunes is relatively short, just
6,651 yards from the tips, but fully displays Hills's penchant for classical
design. With an emphasis on strategy, Hills's routing is contoured to the
land's natural features, weaving through an impressive mix of pine, oak,
and palmetto trees interspersed with lagoons and rolling sand dunes. It is
built on the sandy terrain perfect for golf courses, and as a result is usually
in very good shape. Palmetto Dunes features wide fairways among the
visually impressive dunes and marshes. While the course does not require
great length off the tee to navigate, it mandates course management
decisions such as forgoing the driver on many tees. Water is in play on ten
holes, and there are a few forced carries, both off the tee and on
approaches.

The Palmetto Hall course is quite a different story. For better players
it's usually the island's second choice after the renowned Harbour Town. It
is an unusual design for Hills, difficult and fraught with danger. Forced
carries abound, fairways are narrower, and there is an abundance of water
in play. Greens are often elevated and tiered, requiring high lofted shots to

Golf's Most Shapely Course?

In a bizarre experiment that has yet to be repeated, developers at
Palmetto Hall enlisted Bob Cupp, known as the preeminent user of
computer-assisted design in laying out golf courses, to build a
geometric course. The result is a truly one-of-a-kind layout that has
square and rectangular greens and tees, trapezoidal bunkers, and
grass-covered pyramids instead of mounds. For better or worse,
playing here will let you put another notch in your putter.

reach. Far more difficult than the typical Hills design, it draws players looking for a challenge. Whether or not you choose to play this layout is entirely a matter of talent. Good players will love it, while high-handicappers would be better served on the Palmetto Dunes layout.

The other three courses here offer up a wealth of variety. The George Fazio layout at Palmetto Dunes is the most difficult and should be attempted only by skilled players, while the resort's Robert Trent Jones Sr. design is the least intimidating, surprising given his flair for penal hazards and shots requiring both power and accuracy.

But the Bob Cupp "geometric" course at Palmetto Hall is the most unique layout of all, not just in Hilton Head but perhaps in all of golf. Unique is not always a positive trait, of course: Cupp's course has been denounced by many critics, and the only lists it shows up on are those of the worst courses. In any case, it will give you ammunition for endless nineteenth-hole discussions.

Palmetto Dunes is a mixed resort-and-residential community that includes both resort hotels and rental condos. Guests have access to the courses at sister development Palmetto Hall, a community without a lodging component. It is one of the only facilities in the Southeast that allows walking—on all of the courses except the Hills's layout at Palmetto Hall.

PALMETTO HALL AND PALMETTO DUNES AT A GLANCE

(800) 827-3006, www.palmettodunesresort.com

Golf Course Info: Practice area, walking allowed (except Hills at Palmetto Hall).

Palmetto Dunes Courses

Arthur Hills Course: $$-$$$, 4,999–6,651 yards, three tees. *Slope rating* 113–127. *Course rating 68.5–71.4.*

George Fazio Course: $$, 5,273–6,873 yards, four tees. *Slope rating* 123–132. *Course rating 70.8–74.2.*

Robert Trent Jones Course: $$, 5,425–6,710 yards, three tees. *Slope rating 117–123. Course rating 69.3–72.2.*

Palmetto Hall Courses

Arthur Hills Course: $$V, 4,956–6,918 yards, four tees. *Slope rating* 117–132. *Course rating 68.6–72.2.*

Bob Cupp Course: $$, 5,220–7,079 yards, four tees. *Slope rating* 126–141. *Course rating 71.1–74.8.*

Lodging Info: $$-$$$$. There are two resort hotels within Palmetto Dunes. The Hyatt Regency, which while touted as among the island's best, is tired and blasé compared to the many fine Hyatt golf resorts in the country (800–554–9288, www.hyatthiltonhead.com). A more luxurious choice is the Hilton, which sits in a gated community within the greater community

(800–845–8001, www.hiltonheadhilton.com). There are also a wide selection of rental condos, homes, and villas in the resort (800–845–6130, www.palmettodunesresort.com). Guests receive preferential tee times at both Palmetto Hall and Palmetto Dunes.

Getting There: Hilton Head has a small airport served by US Airways, and shuttle service is available from the nearby airport in Savannah, Georgia.

When to Go: Golf is played year-round, but summer brings high temperatures and humidity. June through November is hurricane season, and while the island is rarely hit, high winds and rain are not uncommon.

Travel Deals: Both courses, as well their affiliated resorts, lower prices in the hot, humid summer and the fall hurricane season.

Golf Travel by Design Courses Nearby: Ocean course at Kiawah Island (two hours); Wild Dunes (two hours).

Other Notable Arthur Hill Courses You Can Play

- **Marriott Camelback,** Scottsdale, Arizona
- **Walking Stick,** Pueblo, Colorado
- **Legends course,** LPGA International Resort, Daytona Beach, Florida
- **Hyatt Regency Hill Country,** San Antonio, Texas
- **Black Gold,** Yorba Linda, California
- **Sheraton Tamarron,** Durango, Colorado
- **El Conquistador,** Fajardo, Puerto Rico

Robert Trent Jones Jr.

(1939–   )

The Legend Continues

f Robert Trent Jones Sr. ushered in the modern era of golf course architecture, then his son has done as much as anyone to keep the age alive. Jones Jr. is by all accounts a workaholic, a tireless designer, industry spokesperson, author, and promoter. He has been especially effective at the latter, and no golf course designer is more famous for being a designer than Jones, whose name both draws daily fee golfers and sells real estate at private clubs. Working with his father, he developed the Asian market for golf courses; he has continued to expand the game's horizons, opening the first full-sized courses in Russia and mainland China. With more than 200 designs under his belt since he stepped out on his own, it is easier to list countries and states where he has *not* worked than vice versa.

A Seven-Day-a-Week Job

Like Jones Sr., he has occasionally been criticized for spreading himself too thin and rolling out the occasional bland, cookie-cutter design. But he has also laid out many critical successes. Other architects have done as well or better in terms of putting courses on the various magazine ranking lists, but where Jones Jr. has excelled is at creating one-of-a-kind layouts that stand out not just for their routing but also for the overall setting and experience. From the unique Prince course in Kauai to the peak of Maine's Sugarloaf Mountain, Jones has always embraced a sense of place in his courses, not just using the natural setting but glorifying it.

For Jones, golf is a seven-day-a-week job, and his penchant for working in the Pacific Rim and Hawaii, where he has ten layouts, keeps him on the road. He also designs courses throughout the United States, Caribbean, and Europe, and has even had the "audacity" to lay out courses in Ireland and Wales. When he is not designing courses or attending the increasingly frequent grand openings of his layouts, he is busy serving the game and community in other ways. He has been president of the American Society of Golf Course Architects and chairman of the California Parks and Recreation Department, has served on various land planning committees, and is a frequent participant in various conferences on the environment, land use, and golf course design. His book, *Golf Course Design*, is intended for average golfers to gain a better understanding of the principles of the design science in a way that will help them score better. He has also devoted considerable energy to developing affordable public golf, from his design of Poppy Ridge, home course of the Northern California Golf Association, to Eagle Point, a daily fee course he built and owns in southern Oregon. As a name-brand designer Jones is too flashy for some in the industry, but there is little doubt that his impact on the game has been vast, and for the better.

ROBERT TRENT JONES II, LLC

WHILE MANY ARCHITECTS START THE EXPERIENCE

WITH A GENTLE HOLE, JONES IS WILLING

TO SET THE TONE WITH A BOGEY, OR WORSE,

For someone with such a lengthy track record, Jones has never developed a trademark style that is easy to pin down. Because he has truly worked in every environment, his courses run the gamut from barely touching the setting to massive earthmoving, from links to parkland to tropical designs. But what you will most often notice about Jones's work is:

- **Bunkers in play.** Aiming bunkers are for MacKenzie. Jones puts his in play off the tee, and has continued to refine the art of bunkering. Well schooled in the economics of golf course development, he has put an emphasis on cost-effective maintainability while producing ever-more-elaborate bunker designs, blending every element from classical contours to very modern hazards. Some of his fairways are studded with bunkers from tee to green.

- **Sense of place.** Besides fitting his courses to the environment, Jones celebrates their surroundings and prominent features. From incorporating ancient lava rock walls and sacred ground at Poipu Bay to taking the third dimension of height to new limits at Sugarloaf, from the sprawling jungle course of Princeville to the widespread use of native flora at Spanish Bay, Jones seeks to make a statement with each course about its place in the region. By incorporating the ruins of Roman aqueducts in his Penha Longa course in Portugal, for instance, he puts the player in Continental Europe in spirit as well as body.

- **Difficulty.** While Jones does create a large number of public and resort courses, he does not hesitate to challenge the golfer, and often ignores the prevailing theory that resort courses, especially from the middle tees, should be less penal than private clubs. A visit to his Prince course, the very public Poppy Hills, or Spanish Bay will be memorable, but it is unlikely to produce a personal-best score.

- **Tough openers.** While many architects start the experience with a gentle hole, Jones is willing to set the tone with a bogey, or worse, right out of the gate. This is not a rule of his, and he certainly has courses with friendly starts, but he has shown repeatedly that if the routing dictates it, he will ask golfers for their A game on the first shot.

Jones's work spans a broader geographical spectrum than any other designer's, and you can enjoy his work in all the corners of the globe. Here are some of his best.

With no constraints on space and no housing development, Jones has built one of the world's biggest, most beautiful, and most difficult courses in a fantasy setting on Hawaii's Garden Isle.

N o matter how many more courses Robert Trent Jones Jr. builds, he will forever be remembered for his two masterpieces, Spanish Bay and the Prince course. The latter is almost without fail the highest-ranked layout in the state of Hawaii and holds a special spot in Jones's heart, since he has a home nearby and believes it contains some of his finest holes.

What makes the Prince course so special is its site, which is not just beautiful but also huge. Few architects will ever have the opportunity to build on the scale that Jones did here. While full-sized eighteen-hole courses have been built on lots as small as 100 acres, and entire thirty-six-hole resorts, including hotels, have been put on 400 acres, Jones used this vast amount for just the eighteen-hole Prince, which wanders through a huge coastal stretch of rain forest and jungle. Like Pine Valley, no hole is

A Personal Best

Robert Trent Jones Jr. told The Golf Insider that he considers the par-5 fifteenth at the Prince course the best 3-shot hole he has ever designed—and he has done a lot of them.

Like a desert course, the hole is broken into three distinct islands by the junglelike foliage. From the tee area players must carry the ball between 100 and 195 yards to reach the fairway. Big hitters, however, also risk clearing the first landing area and reaching a stream at the end of it, just 240 yards from the white middle tees. The second shot must clear the stream and a ravine of thick underbrush about 40 yards wide, then carry far enough and stay left enough to open an approach angle to the green, which is offset to the right side. Only a lone bunker guards the front of the green, but this effectively takes the ground game away, forcing players to loft a shot to a green that has a cliff drop-off behind it.

visible from another; so dense is the surrounding vegetation that each appears as almost its own course. As the course sprawls through the site, golfers are rewarded with waterfalls—naturally occurring, for a change— rock-filled ravines, vistas of the remote Na Pali coastline, beaches, and the ocean. It is a one-of-a-kind site, unspoiled and beautiful.

It is also one of the most difficult courses you can play, and the first two holes are the toughest start we've seen on a public course. The opener is 408 yards from the easier white tees to a narrow fairway with out-of-bounds on both sides. The second shot is more difficult, a long iron or fairway wood to a small offset green behind a penal ravine hazard more than 50 yards deep, with out-of-bounds behind and to the sides. The second hole is a similar challenge: It's not difficult for an average player with an 18 handicap to lose four balls and rack up 16 or more strokes before the third tee. This can set the tone for a long round of golf.

The Prince's critical acclaim comes from its unusual setting, which allowed Jones to utilize his sense of place, and it boldly says *Hawaii* from the first tee to the last green. But while single-digit players will love it, high-handicap resort golfers will not be cheated by skipping it, as they might be at other famous "must-plays." Fortunately, the Princeville resort has another surprise up its sleeve, the less well-publicized Makai course, a very solid twenty-seven-hole routing by Jones that emphasizes playability and will be enjoyed by all golfers. The three nines can be played in enough eighteen-hole combinations to fill several days at this beautiful resort. Even those up for the challenge of the Prince should try this underrated routing at least once.

PRINCEVILLE AT A GLANCE

(800) 325-3589, www.princeville.com

Golf Course Info: Practice area, walking allowed.

Prince: $$$–$$$$, 5,338–7,309 yards, five tees. *Slope rating* 127–144. *Course rating* 72.0–75.6.

Makai (twenty-seven holes): $$–$$$, 5,516–6,901 yards, three tees. *Slope rating* 115–132. *Course rating* 69.6–73.2.

Lodging Info: $$$$+. The Princeville Resort has a very contemporary Marriott hotel, but it's fairly remote by Hawaiian standards—on the northern coast of Kauai, far from the island's other resort areas. While outside play is allowed, it is most convenient to stay here, and hotel guests receive a discount.

Getting There: Aloha and Hawaiian Airlines fly to Kauai from the other islands, and there are direct flights from Los Angeles. Princeville is about forty-five minutes from the airport.

When to Go: There is simply no bad time to golf on Hawaii, which has just two seasons: summer, from May through October with temperatures in the high eighties, and winter, with temperatures in the seventies and low eighties.

Golf Travel by Design

Travel Deals: Like many Hawaiian courses, Princeville offers discounts to guests of its hotel, and even steeper discounts for those who possess a Hawaiian driver's license.

Golf Travel by Design Courses Nearby: Kiele Lagoons (forty-five minutes).

THE LINKS AT SPANISH BAY,
Pebble Beach, California

Simply one of the nation's greatest courses, Spanish Bay is considered by its fans superior to famous neighbor Pebble Beach.

Robert Trent Jones Sr. faced one of the biggest challenges in golf when he was asked to design the follow-up to the internationally acclaimed Pebble Beach Golf Links, and he rose to the occasion with his best design, Spyglass Hill. It was only fitting that Robert Trent Jones Jr. was given the opportunity to design the resort's third course, and he too delivered with his best work, the Links at Spanish Bay. Which of these renowned three is the best is an argument that will never be resolved—each has equally adamant fans—but there is no doubt that these are the best three courses at any single resort. Spanish Bay is among the world's top golfing experiences, public or private.

Jones tried to live up to the *Links* name in his course, something that despite its beloved reputation, Pebble Beach does not do except on a few

Don't Fence Me In

After the construction of the course, new plantings of native vegetation did not take hold as well as the designers had planned; several parts of the course have thus been fenced off as environmentally sensitive areas. While the fences are obviously not an attractive part of the landscaping, they play a role in protecting the sensitive environment at Spanish Bay. Critics have called them a major weakness of the course, yet many newer layouts incorporate similar environmental areas into which golfers cannot tread, even to retrieve visible balls.

holes. To achieve this, he installed sandy dunes—but in such a manner as to make them appear naturally occurring. Many courses have built dunes in this country in an attempt to re-create the Scottish experience, but Jones, along with codesigner Sandy Tatum, succeeded by blending dunes, sandy waste area, apparently windswept contours, and native vegetation growing throughout the sand. In addition, the course was planted from tee to green with fescue grasses, the same strain that the great links courses use, and fairways and greens are meant to be dry and firm. Greens are left open to encourage the bump and run; winds sweep across the course; and in almost every respect, Jones achieved his goal of re-creating the Scottish experience on the Monterey Peninsula. Yet in keeping with his sense of place, Jones makes the course fit the region by incorporating native Monterey pines, many more than 100 feet tall. The only drawback is exposure to the road and some golf course homes, but these are quickly forgotten amid the beauty of the course. Several holes hug the Pacific coast; when the weather is good, views are stunning.

Like its neighbors, the course encourages walking. Caddies are available as well to complete one of golf's great experiences, a pilgrimage to the Pebble Beach resort.

THE LINKS AT SPANISH BAY AT A GLANCE

(800) 654-3900, www.pebblebeach.com

Golf Course Info: See Spyglass Hill.

Links at Spanish Bay: $$$$, 5,309–6,820 yards, three tees. Slope rating 129–146. Course rating 70.6–74.8.

FOUR SEASONS NEVIS, *Nevis, West Indies*

Robert Trent Jones Jr. ventured to the Caribbean to build one of the region's best courses at one of the world's best resorts.

Golf travel can be an expensive proposition, and while there are plenty of bargains available, certain courses simply cannot be played on a low budget. Some resorts justify the $400-a-night tariffs, and others are best skipped over. If you can afford it, the Four Seasons Nevis and its beautiful Robert Trent Jones Jr. course are not to be missed.

Nevis is a tiny island that forms half of the independent confederation of Nevis and St. Kitts, a former English colonial holding. While St. Kitts is considerably more developed, with several large resort hotels, a casino, and new golf courses, Nevis, just a ferry ride away, remains one of the

Dramatic elevation changes help make the Chateau Whistler course one of the world's best mountain designs. FAIRMONT HOTELS & RESORTS

Caribbean's last unspoiled gems. Lodging on Nevis consists of just a handful of wonderful manor houses, small inns that are left over from the island's cotton plantation days, and one modern resort, the Four Seasons.

The hotel sits on Pinney's Beach, a 7-mile-long stretch of sand that is one of the world's finest, yet the hotel is the only one on it. The resort is so luxurious, secluded, and relaxing, it can be difficult for guests to roust themselves for a round of golf. Fortunately, when they do, tee times are largely unnecessary, because the course is open only to hotel guests and a handful of homeowners at the resort. The result is a leisurely, uncrowded experience on a very good golf course.

The course is set in the heavily wooded, junglelike foothills above the resort and has no coastal exposure, but does offer sweeping views of the ocean and across the straits to the island of St. Kitts. The layout is a mix of isolated junglelike holes, such as those found at Jones's **Prince** course, and open elevated holes with views, more like his **Makena** design. Flora-filled ravines slice through the course, and Jones builds several carries over them. Throughout the layout he uses his favorite hazard, bunkers made from

The Modern Masters

gleaming white sand, in play off the tee and surrounding many greens. Swaying palms grace the course, which also incorporates the stone ruins of an old sugar mill, tying it to the fabric of the island. In an unusual twist, an extra tee box is added to the fifteenth hole to allow long hitters the opportunity to carry a huge ravine en route to the fairway. Many resort players tee one up here, knock it into the hazard, and quickly "forget" their shot, proceeding to the tee they were playing.

Two years ago a hurricane ravaged the resort and golf course, which have since been rebuilt and reopened, better than ever. From fine dining to one of the world's best beaches, the Four Seasons Nevis offers a superlative, and expensive, golf escape.

FOUR SEASONS NEVIS AT A GLANCE

(800) 819-5053, www.fourseasons.com

Golf Course Info: Practice areas, walking allowed.

$$$, 5,153–6,766 yards, four tees. *Slope rating* 128–132. *Course rating* 68.3–73.6.

Lodging Info: Only guests of the Four Seasons have access to the course, and it is the only resort hotel on the island. Still, the hotel offers dine-around plans allowing guests to have dinner at and experience the charming manor home inns of Nevis.

Getting There: Commuter air service is available into Nevis. The better option, however, is to fly to the larger airport on St. Kitts, where Four Seasons guests are met and shuttled to the hotel by private motor launch, a faster, cheaper, and more memorable option.

When to Go: Golf is played year-round, but summer though late fall are hurricane season. Winter is ideal.

Golf Travel by Design Courses Nearby: Royal St. Kitts (one hour).

MAKENA, *Maui, Hawaii*

In the shadow of more famous Kapalua and Wailea sits Makena, Maui's best thirty-six-hole resort.

The term *resort* takes on a whole new meaning in Hawaii, where many of the top golf complexes are in enormous communities combining hotels, retail spaces, and residential components. On Maui this is taken to extremes: Kaanapali has a Sheraton, Westin, Hyatt, and several other hotels, while Wailea has a Four Seasons, the Grand Wailea, and a few more. Maybe this explains why visitors to Maui often overlook quiet

Makena, with just its one hotel. This is a shame, because it has two of the state's top layouts, among Robert Trent Jones Jr.'s best.

Makena began with just one Jones layout, which was later split and expanded into two, both incorporating holes from the original. They are equally good and include all the things we expect of Jones, including numerous and strategically placed bunkers, views of the major Maui features—including Holeakala's volcanic crater and the ocean—integration of existing ancient stone walls, and a routing that incorporates ravines, streams, and native vegetation.

The North course is farther inland; as a result, it's hillier with more dramatic elevation changes and covers more rugged ground, including a deep rock-strewn ravine on the wonderful sixth hole. Jones uses this diagonal hazard to split the hole into two fairways, a classic risk-reward scenario. Hit to the larger, safer right-side landing area and you are faced with a tricky pitch across the heart of the gully to the thin side of a green protected by a deep front bunker. Play the more dangerous left side off the tee and the ravine is fully in play, especially for slicers, but if you pull it off you land just short of the unprotected green and have the fat part left to work with. Long hitters can even reach the front.

The South has more ocean views and two holes, fifteen and sixteen, that play along the coast. The toss-up is between a more dramatic inland routing and a more scenic coastal layout, both well worth your attention. They are also much less subject to the strong Hawaiian tradewinds than Maui's other top courses at Wailea and Kapalua.

The Maui Prince Makena is small by Maui standards, with less than 400 rooms, giving guests relatively easy access to the courses even in peak season. It is operated by Japanese hotel chain Prince Hotels and attracts a strong Japanese clientele. As a result, the five-diamond hotel is home to the island's best sushi and Japanese cuisine. Prince also owns the Mauna Kea and Hapuna golf resorts.

MAKENA AT A GLANCE

(800) 321–6248, www.princeresortshawaii.com

Golf Course Info: Practice area, walking allowed.

North: $$–$$$V, 5,303–6,914 yards, four tees. *Slope rating* 128–139. *Course rating* 70.9–72.1.

South: $$–$$$V, 5,529–7,017 yards, four tees. *Slope rating* 130–138. *Course rating* 71.1–72.6.

Lodging Info: $$$. One of Hawaii's hidden gems, the Makena Prince is a quiet and secluded choice for those put off by the hustle and bustle of larger resorts like nearby Wailea. It is a good value, and offers substantial discounts on golf to hotel guests.

Getting There: Makena is less than half an hour from Maui's large airport, which has flights from both Honolulu and the mainland.

When to Go: Weather in Hawaii is excellent year-round.

Travel Deals: Like many Hawaiian courses, Makena offers discounts to guests of its hotel, and even steeper discounts for those who possess a Hawaiian driver's license. Prince Hotels also offers golf packages that combine play and lodging at Makena with its other resorts on Oahu and the Big Island.

Golf Travel by Design Courses Nearby: None.

CHATEAU WHISTLER, *Whistler, British Columbia*

Canada's top ski resort comes alive in summer as the country's top golf destination.

With a dollar that is worth just more than half of its U.S. counterpart in recent years, Canada represents one of the great opportunities for bargain golf travel, and few Canadian resorts can hold a candle to Whistler, with four top courses to choose from. Whistler is a completely human-made village—an enclave of resort hotels, shops, and restaurants designed to be entirely accessible by and mostly limited to pedestrians. Stay anywhere in the village and you have easy access to a wide variety of shopping, dining, and golf. All the courses allow public access, but only one hotel in Whistler has its own golf course, and that is the Chateau Whistler, part of the Canadian Pacific chain (now merged with Fairmont hotels), which also operates such esteemed resorts as *Banff Springs* and the *Jasper Park Lodge*.

At Whistler Robert Trent Jones Jr. had the chance to go toe-to-toe with other name-brand designers such as Jack Nicklaus and Arnold Palmer, and he came out on top. This is, after all, the mountains, and his Chateau Whistler course has the most mountainous setting—and he never lets golfers forget it. The severe elevation changes are used to provide stunning panoramic views of the surrounding peaks, snow covered even in summer. Exposed rock ledges are used throughout the course to connect it with its surroundings, mountain lakes create strategically placed hazards, and fields of summer wildflowers rival the landscaping of Augusta National. It is a beautiful and well-groomed course that is also a lot of fun to play, typified by the eighth hole, a long par-3 that plays downhill to a small green flanked by a pond on one side and a granite cliff on the other. From the back tees it is also a very difficult test of golf and should be reserved for single-digit players.

Whistler's other golf offerings include Nicklaus North, the resort area's newest, which is a spacious layout sprawling through wooded areas and taking advantage of natural water features. It has extensive and attractive bunkering, but the many homes intrude on the golf experience, especially in such a rugged and rustic setting. The Arnold Palmer–designed Whistler Golf Club is a municipal course owned by the village; it just underwent a major face lift to celebrate its twentieth birthday. It sits on a flat piece of land at the base of the valley but is filled with lakes, ponds, and other water hazards. These three courses are within minutes of each other. The fourth, Big Sky, is located twenty-five minutes away and rivals the Chateau Whistler course in quality. A Bob Cupp layout, it sits at the base of an 8,000-foot stone peak, offers 360-degree views, and is incredibly scenic.

WHISTLER AT A GLANCE

(800) 441–1414, www.chateauwhistlerresort.com

Golf Course Info: Practice area, walking allowed.

Chateau Whistler: $$–$$$, 5,157–6,635 yards, four tees. *Slope rating* 124–142. *Course rating* 70–73.

Big Sky (www.bigskygolf.com): $$V, 5,208–7,001 yards, four tees. *Slope rating* 114–133. *Course rating* 70–73.

Nicklaus North (www.nicklausnorth.com): $$–$$$, 4,732–6,908 yards, five tees. *Slope rating* 113–138. *Course rating* 66.3–73.8.

Whistler Golf Club (www.whistlergolf.com): $$, 5,348–6,597 yards, four tees. *Slope rating* 120–132. *Course rating* 70.5–71.3.

Lodging Info: The Chateau Whistler course is located at the hotel, and guests receive discounts and preferential tee times. The Chateau and Pan Pacific (800–533–6465, www.panpac.com) are Whistler's top two hotels. There are many other choices, including a Westin, several smaller hotels, and rental condos. A new Four Seasons luxury hotel is under construction. For more lodging information: see 800–WHISTLER, www.tourismwhistler.com.

Getting There: Whistler is two hours north of the Vancouver airport, and shuttle service is available.

When to Go: Because of all the snow at the ski resort, the golf season is short—May through October—but June, July, and August are best.

Travel Deals: The Chateau Whistler resort offers numerous golf packages, some that combine play on its course with the other two layouts in the village, Nicklaus North and the Whistler Golf Club. Because Whistler is primarily a ski town, lodging rates are lower in the summer.

Golf Travel by Design Courses Nearby: None.

PEHNA LONGA, *Sintra, Portugal*

Visitors to Portugal can play one of the nation's top courses just outside Lisbon without traveling to the golf-rich Algarve.

When it comes to golf travel, Portugal is best known for its Algarve resort region, where beautiful cork trees and public courses abound. But we have never been too impressed with the quality of golf in the Algarve; it's also overrun with tourists and lacks a distinct Portuguese flavor. A better choice is to visit the wonderful coastal city of Lisbon, rich in charm, history, and cuisine, and play golf at nearby Pehna Longa, one of the nation's best layouts.

His father traveled to Spain to build such courses as Sotogrande and Valderrama before other golf designers had become as global, and Robert Trent Jones Jr. followed in his path with many top courses throughout the Continent. The Atlantic course at Pehna Longa is unique in its incorporation of ancient ruins into the site, including stone walls from a Roman aqueduct. These arched walls run down one side of the fairways on six, the signature hole, while the other side is flanked by water. Golfers who hit the green tucked behind the lake and guarded by a nest of bunkers will have conquered a hole rated among the top 500 on earth.

But there is more here than old stone. The layout is aimed at better players and requires both distance and accuracy to navigate the water hazards, sharp elevation changes, and extensive bunkering. The first three and the last three holes are located in a wooded valley studded with granite outcroppings, while the twelve holes in between rise above the woods on a series of hillsides with sweeping views to the Atlantic and Lisbon. The greens are large, undulating, and tricky to putt. While the course is located several miles inland from the coast, it sits on an elevated piece of ground; wind is frequently a factor.

This was Jones's first course in Portugal, and he returned in 1995 to lay out another routing, the nine-hole Monastery course named for the historic building ruins it passes. This is a much gentler resort layout for less skilled players. The resort sits within a national park and includes the Caesar Park hotel, one of Portugal's best. It is located in Sintra, a wealthy suburb of Lisbon, near the Estoril Casino, the grandest in the nation.

CAESAR PARK AT A GLANCE

+351 21-924-9011 or through Leading Hotels of the World (www.lhw.com)

Golf Course Info: Practice area, walking only.

Atlantic: $$V, 5,600–6,910 yards, three tees.

Monastery (nine holes): $.

Lodging Info: $$–$$$. One of Portugal's top resorts, the Caesar Park is a full-service hotel. The course is also open to the public.

Getting There: Pehna Longa is twenty minutes from Lisbon and less than half an hour from the airport.

When to Go: Weather is good year-round.

Golf Travel by Design Courses Nearby: None.

Other Notable Robert Trent Jones Jr. Courses You Can Play

- **Raven at Sabino Springs,** Scottsdale, Arizona
- **Raven at South Mountain,** Scottsdale, Arizona
- **Sugarloaf,** Carrabassett, Maine
- **Beach course,** Waikoloa, Hawaii
- **Poipu Bay,** Kauai, Hawaii
- **Gold course,** Wailea, Hawaii
- **Emerald course,** Wailea, Hawaii
- **Squaw Creek,** Lake Tahoe, Nevada
- **Celtic Manor,** Newport, Wales

The Next Generation

In recent years golf course construction in the United States and abroad has been growing at a record pace. National Golf Foundation statistics showed that as we entered the new millennium, more than one new course a day was being opened in this country, and 90 percent of these new layouts were public. That's a lot of golf courses for the traveling golfer to play.

Technology has also continued to advance to the point at which golf courses can be built—and in many cases opened for play—faster. Once upon a time it was common for courses to be left idle for a year after completion to grow in. The economics of the golf industry make such an admirable course of action impractical for almost every developer, but nonetheless new courses are being opened in a much more polished state than was the case just a few years ago. As a result, new layouts are jumping right onto the various "best" lists, a phenomenon that was rare in the past. This has upped the ante among both designers and developers, a trend that continues to feed on itself, with the traveling golfer reaping the benefit of all these new gems. At the same time, the golf industry has observed that if people are willing to journey to remote places like Royal Dornoch, Melbourne, or Northern Ireland to play the great classic courses, they will go to rural Mexico, the Oregon coast, or Prince Edward Island to play the new classics. More and more, sites are being chosen for their natural features, with location and ease of access secondary considerations. This liberated thinking has done no less than produce what some critics called the world's best golf course less than a year after it opened.

There is no coherent theme to the future of golf course design as there was with the modern era. Up-and-coming architects continue to take golf in new directions, while many of the modern masters are still plugging away with great success. If there are some major underlying trends we can look forward to, they include a return to classic style—but often with a very modern spin. Today more formally trained architects are entering the field, and many have done historical research into MacKenzie's bunkering and other classic elements. In an effort to capture the magic of the earliest British Isles courses, new artists are building higher and higher dunes, seeking out prime coastal land, and returning to unconventional routings dictated by the flow of the terrain, resulting in courses with a wider range of pars and less balanced configurations of par-3s, -4s, and -5s.

Modern innovations also continue to appear. While multiple tee boxes have become the rule rather than the exception, we are seeing more courses with holes featuring either two completely different sets of teeing areas that alternate by days, or two different greens—an increasingly common way for architects to keep the golfing experience fresh for repeat visitors. Optional nineteenth holes, like Nicklaus's work at **Punta Mita,** are starting to crop up as well. One other notable trend is that the new architects are shying away from Ted Robinson–style beautification, with fewer fountains, artificial waterfalls, and flower beds, and using more of the raw site in waste areas, lava fields, deserts, or even vineyards.

As the race to build more and more acclaimed courses heats up, developers are turning to some unfamiliar faces and, in some cases, gambling on fresh talent. But the next generation of great designers are not the young guns you might expect. In many cases they have worked for other big-name architects, or even themselves, for years, but are only now stepping into the limelight. Rees Jones, for instance, might be surprised to find himself grouped with this cast of lesser-known designers, but despite his formidable experience remodeling U.S. Open venues, the vast majority of his best public courses have been turned out in the past decade, and he continues to accelerate his pace. Tom Weiskopf is no stranger to competitive golf or golf course design, but since breaking off his partnership with the more established Jay Morrish he has begun to roll out prized public gems of his own.

Following are the names you can expect to hear more great things from, and those behind some of the best new courses that have opened in recent years. In truth, they are some of the best courses, period.

Honorable Mention

Some other designers who are knocking on fame's door and have made a big splash with their first attempts include:

Kyle Phillips. This American had the nerve to go to Scotland—St. Andrews, no less—and build what many visitors are finding to be the most enjoyable course they play across the pond. Kingsbarns immediately jumped onto the "best courses" lists, onto the covers of golf magazines, and into the international spotlight as the first course in all of Scotland with ocean views from every hole. A human-made product built on flat potato fields, it is a perfect example of the return to classic style being made possible with modern technology. Phillips is currently working on the new layout at the red-hot Bandon Dunes resort in Oregon.

David McLay Kidd. In almost the reverse scenario, this aspiring Scottish designer with exactly one course to his credit came to our shores and built Bandon Dunes, a course so lauded it debuted on *Golf Magazine*'s Top One Hundred list at number three, behind only Pinehurst Number Two and Pebble Beach. It has been heralded as nothing less than the second coming of links golf.

Sam Torrance. Given the almost impossible task of building a new links course in St. Andrews, Torrance was faced with not just historical competition but also the widely acclaimed new Kingsbarns course next door. A former European Tour player and current Ryder Cup captain, Torrance's first design effort resulted in an understated, subtle links along the lines of the Old course itself, a layout that opened looking like it had been there forever. As hard as it is to believe, the Torrance course holds its own with the flashier Kingsbarns.

Jim Engh. Quietly carving a reputation as an unapologetic modernist who has created several high-end private layouts, Engh jumped into the public eye with Redlands Mesa, an ultradramatic course in rugged western Colorado. The layout is so good, so beautiful, and such a good value that it stole the thunder from what was supposed to be the state's biggest golf event, the opening of Jack Nicklaus's Summit course at ***Cordillera***. Not only has Redlands Mesa emerged as the consensus pick for the state's course of the year, many who have played it think it is the state's finest, period.

Greg Norman (1955–   )
Improving on Tradition

G reg Norman doesn't need to design golf courses. The first player ever to surpass $10 million in career winnings, Norman is one of the game's all-time greatest players. He has won eighty-seven golf tournaments worldwide, including the 1986 and 1993 British Open Championships, in addition to eighteen titles on the PGA Tour. Despite his success on the course, he may end up making more of a splash on Wall Street: Norman is currently enjoying the greatest business success of any professional golfer, with lucrative ventures in real estate development, equipment, clothing, and even wine. Compared to his growing sales of luxury homes and homesites both here and in Australia, the golf course design business is small potatoes. So why has he spent so much time designing golf courses around the world? Because Norman loves the game.

A Student of the Game

As a student of golf history and tradition, it comes as no surprise that Norman is most influenced by Alister MacKenzie and A. W. Tillinghast. Norman grew up as Australia's most successful player competing on classic courses like MacKenzie's *Royal Melbourne, Kingston Heath,* and *Royal Adelaide.* Traditional elements permeate his work, but he has also developed a style of his own. Norman has enjoyed as much success building courses as he did playing them, stepping onto the scene in consultation with Ted Robinson on the gorgeous *Experience at Koele.*

Considering how few courses Norman has created, he has built them in a lot of different places, including the United States, Ireland, the Bahamas, Australia, and the Far East. As a result, he has a wide variety of settings under his belt. Still, as you travel and visit Norman's courses—which all look much different on the surface—there are some underlying things you will recognize, including:

- **Limited turf designs.** Taking the desert golf trend—which reduced the amount of grass planted due to irrigation concerns—a step farther, Norman has carved out a niche as a specialist in "limited-turf" designs, even where he could plant grass. Rather than raw desert, he tends to fill in the gaps with waste areas made of sand, decomposed granite, or other substances. The effect is to create attractive visual relief while reducing the amount of maintenance, irrigation, and chemicals needed on the course. These waste areas also serve another purpose—keeping balls that leave the fairway in play—which is important since he:

- **Uses little rough.** Despite his success with the thick rough at the British Open, his courses tend to feature little or no high grass. This is also true around the greens, where he uses:

KEEPING THE FRONTS OF THE GREEN

OPEN IS A PRIORITY FOR NORMAN, WHO

ENCOURAGES BUMP AND RUN PLAY.

- **Shaved collars.** The height of the grass around the green is indistinguishable from the green itself, so when you miss the target on a Norman course, you usually have the option of putting, chipping, or pitching your ball onto the green. This actively encourages the ground game; balls can be putt on some Norman courses from 50 yards off the green.

- **Wide fairways and aiming bunkers.** In a nod to the beloved tradition of MacKenzie and Tillinghast, Norman embraces the classic look, but his lack of rough means that although he presents you with a wide target, there is nothing to hold balls that leave the fairway; you still need to try to hit the middle.

- **Sneaky long.** Norman mixes short and long holes to make courses play longer than the yardage indicates. By using short par-3s that put a high premium on accuracy, some of which require shaped shots to get near the pins, he gains extra length to use elsewhere without sacrificing any challenge to par. A drivable par-4 is often a part of his design—which also frees up yardage, but requires near-perfect execution. He adds the extra yards to par-5s and some par-4s that play like –5s, such as 460-yard uphill par-4 (from the middle tees) at his Moonah course.

- **Ample greenside bunkers.** Keeping the fronts of the green open is a priority for Norman, who encourages bump-and-run play. But if you get out of position off the tee, he usually leaves you the choice of approaching the green from the side, through the air. Deep bunkers beside the green keep players honest, ensuring that if you choose this route, you'd better reach the putting surface.

When playing Norman's courses, aim for the far-off fairway bunkers, keep the ball between you and the hole, and work on your short game. Here are some places you can try this strategy out.

WENTE VINEYARDS, *Livermore, California*

Norman, a wine lover and vintner himself, has built the best wine-country course in the world.

One good thing about grapes is that they tend to grow in beautiful settings, which is why visiting wine country anywhere in the world is usually a good idea. Vines grow best on hillsides—and terraced vineyards make a beautiful backdrop to golf; wine grapes do best in mild climates, too, just as golfers do. So it always struck us as odd that there are so few good wine-country golf courses. Perhaps prime grape soil, such as that in California's Napa and Sonoma Valleys, is too expensive, and golf courses there, like Silverado, are given the worst land.

But happily, there is one exception, although it has remained a surprising secret. Considering that there is a dearth of high-quality public golf in the San Francisco suburbs, and Livermore is one of the closer golf destinations, Wente Vineyards has not gotten a lot of press. It is not on any of the Top One Hundred lists, but it deserves to be. Cut right through the heart of the vineyards, with rows of vines forming one of the game's more unusual hazards, it is simply the world's finest public wine-country course.

The course has three distinct sections, including an impressive stretch of holes on a mountain ridge. The very first tee sets the tone, dropping to a fairway that looks wider than it is, more than 100 feet below. As with many holes on the course, the length and elevation change allow for numerous attack strategies; and players can make par or birdie here with everything from a 5-iron to a driver off the tee.

On longer holes Norman honors MacKenzie with aiming bunkers; on shorter holes, like the par-three second, he takes a cue from Donald Ross with greens that are easy to hit but hard to hold, and harder still to get near the pin. As a result, the course is very fair, allowing average players to have fun but making low scores difficult. The tenth through twelfth holes play on top of a high mountain ridge before plunging back down for the finish. The unique risk-reward tenth is a dogleg par-4 of just 284 yards that requires a perfect tee shot over a penal abyss to reach. Most players, even good ones, settle for a low iron to set up a short approach.

Livermore Valley is an up-and-coming region for both wine and golf, and is home to Rees Jones's public Poppy Ridge course. More than a dozen wineries are located here, of which Wente is the largest. The vineyard complex includes the course, an open-air concert venue, a tasting room, and a fine-dining restaurant. After a strong finishing hole, players can enjoy one of Wente's many wines on a veranda abutting the eighteenth green—or head into the clubhouse, built for Norman's course and designed to resemble an Australian cattle station.

THE COURSE AT WENTE VINEYARDS AT A GLANCE

(925) 456-2476, www.wentegolf.com

Golf Course Info: Practice area, no walking.

$$$, 4,975–6,945 yards, four tees. *Slope rating* 122–142. *Course rating* 69.4–74.5.

Lodging Info: There is no lodging at the course, but Wente Vineyards is located forty minutes from San Francisco.

Getting There: Wente Vineyards is located forty minutes from San Francisco.

When to Go: Golf is played year-round, but winters bring more rain.

Golf Travel by Design Courses Nearby: Links at Spanish Bay (two hours); Spyglass Hill (two hours); Half Moon Bay (two hours); Pasatiempo (two hours).

GREG NORMAN COURSE AT PGA WEST,
Palm Springs, California

With public play limited to the daunting Nicklaus Tournament course and the impossible Stadium course, PGA West brought in Norman to design a course resort guests could easily enjoy.

For a desert region, Palm Springs is surprisingly lush, and while there are a few recent desert-style efforts, most courses use wall-to-wall grass. Norman chose a different route, following his limited-turf philosophy but taking it to an extreme: There are only sixty-five acres of turf on the course, twenty-five of which consist of tees and greens. The rest of the layout is covered with less welcoming surfaces, such as water, bunkers, and sandlike decomposed granite.

Despite the lack of grass, landing areas are generous where Norman wants you to play. This is the secret to good target design. Nearly every green is surrounded by waste area, but the surface is not penal, and you can still get up and down from it. The waste areas also provide a buffer between fairways and desert foliage, keeping errant shots in play. Norman

Norman by the Numbers

Limited-turf designs are often used because they can save money, both in initial construction and down the road: They require less irrigation, fertilizer, and mowing labor. But at PGA West the design was chosen more for its beauty and playability, and a premium on aesthetics drove the price of the course to more than $20 million, a staggering figure. To achieve the pleasing design, which is among the most visually memorable in Palm Springs, Norman used 56,000 tons of decomposed granite for his waste areas. Due to its high cost, this is often called DG or "desert gold." During site inspections, Norman toyed with the design, increasing the number of bunkers from the original 32 to 120. Rather than leave the waste areas barren, he planted them with desert flora, including 65,000 individually drip-irrigated plants. These are big numbers—but par is still just 72 strokes.

The Score's Not the Thing

Americans grow up on stroke play in golf, which simply means keeping score by counting strokes. It's the way almost every tournament on the PGA Tour is conducted, how course records are set, how handicaps are maintained. Some are surprised to find the game played any other way. But in the British Isles, where virtually everyone who plays belongs to a club, match play is most common. This is where the object is not to post the best score, but to beat your opponent on each hole. If you hit the green on a par-3 and your opponent dumps his shot in the pond, he or she will usually concede the hole, presuming you will win, and you move on. If you get to the seventeenth tee with a three-hole lead, the match is over. It is a difficult concept for those used to stroke play to grasp, but it allows you to recover from bad holes, and no one errant shot "ruins" your round as when you are keeping score. Stableford is an alternative scoring system that awards points for bogeys, pars, birdies, and eagles, and dismisses all other holes, highlighting only good play.

uses shaved collars, so you can putt even if you miss the green. The result is a course that is hard to score well on but plays just fine. The experience is heightened by the fact that this is the only resort course in Palm Springs with caddies.

Norman also tinkers with the relative length of the holes to make the course play longer than the scorecard indicates. Short par-3s put a high premium on accuracy, and he adds the yardage he saves to par-5s such as the eighth, which plays 599 yards from the blues (not the tips). He also saves yardage with the tenth, a short par-4 (308 yards) that taunts long hitters to go for it over a minefield of bunkers. This clever mix of short and long holes is a Norman trait. In both cases golfers must repeatedly decide whether or not to go for it—adding to the fun.

(800) 598-3828, www.laquintaresort.com

Golf Course Info: Practice area, no walking (except Norman course).

Stadium: $$$$, 5,092–7,266 yards, five tees.

Jack Nicklaus Tournament Course: $$$$, 5,023–7,204 yards, five tees.

Greg Norman Course: $$$$, 4,997–7,156 yards, five tees.

Mountain: $$$$, 5,005–6,758 yards, five tees.

Dunes: $$$–$$$$, 4,997–6,747 yards, five tees.

Lodging Info: $$$$. Accommodations at La Quinta are spacious and comfortable.

Getting There: La Quinta is about forty-five minutes from the Palm Springs airport and less than two hours from Los Angeles.

When to Go: It gets hot in the summer but is delightful the rest of the year.

Golf Travel by Design Courses Nearby: Desert Springs Marriott (twenty-five minutes).

DOONBEG, *County Clare, Ireland*

More than a century ago this coastal linksland in southwestern Ireland was considered one of the world's great golf sites—yet it was never developed. Now Greg Norman has chosen it for his masterpiece.

t was bound to happen. Sooner or later, the two-time British Open Champion would take a stab at designing a real links course—and in every sense of the word, Doonbeg is a real links course. This choice piece of land was originally selected by the Black Watch Regiment in the 1850s for its golf course, but it was too far from the railroad, so as a second choice the group built nearby built **Lahinch,** considered one of the world's greats. The special feature that drew the Black Watch was a mile and a half of uninterrupted crescent-shaped coastline lined with gigantic, sandy dunes. When Norman first laid eyes on this linksland, he was stunned. "If I spend the rest of my life building courses, I don't think I'd find a comparable site anywhere."

Doonbeg is more than a classical course; it was built in the classical style. Norman approached the task in the most traditional manner possible, letting nature do most of the work. He placed greens and tees where sites were naturally available, moving very little earth. Most of the fairways were simply mown down from native grasses, with no seeding—almost unheard of today. Norman used a very traditional out-and-back routing, and the course is never more than two holes wide. It's what the Irish might have done centuries ago. But there are some surprises. Unlike many links, the water is clearly visible, and can be seen from all but two holes. The layout follows the coast; from the first tee you can see straight across the horseshoe-shaped bay to the ninth green. Ancient sand dunes tower more than 100 feet high, with greens set beneath, between, and occasionally atop them. It is a spectacular, one-of-a-kind site, and if measured on looks and feel alone would certainly be in the world's handful of top tracts.

The caveat is that Doonbeg is an extremely difficult course—one on which the average golfer will struggle, at best, and the low-handicapper will become frustrated. In local tradition, the staff is encouraging Americans to try their hand at match play or Stableford scoring rather than counting strokes, because they simply amass too many. Doonbeg is more challenging than *Royal County Down,* which many consider the most difficult in the British Isles. Because of the natural style of the course, it has the highest and thickest rough we have ever seen. This makes the task of extricating your ball impossible—not because you can't swing the club, but because you can never find the ball once it leaves the fairway. In Norman's style, there is no first cut of rough to slow the ball down, and rock-hard links fairways encourage balls to roll out of sight. Only the straightest, most consistent of hitters will be able to tackle the course.

Nonetheless, Doonbeg is links golf on an epic scale, and since it is located in prime Irish golfing country, between Lahinch and Ballybunion, and the closest major course to the Shannon airport, it would be hard to skip. Take a caddie, take the local advice, try match play, and enjoy the ride!

DOONBEG AT A GLANCE

+353 65-9055247, doonbeggolfclub.com

Golf Course Info: Practice area, caddies available, walking only.

$$$, 4,860–6,818 yards, four tees.

Lodging Info: $–$$. A hotel is under construction at the course, which should open in 2003–2005. There are a few bed-and-breakfasts in the small town of Doonbeg, near the course, but the closest small city is Ennis, about 20 miles away.

Getting There: Doonbeg is 40 miles from Shannon International Airport.

When to Go: Golf season is year-round, but the best weather is from April through November.

European Travel Tips: See Prestwick.

Golf Travel by Design Courses Nearby: Ballybunion New course (sixty minutes); Lahinch (thirty minutes).

Greg Norman likes to use short par-3s that require a very precise shot to get close to the hole, as on the thirteenth at his namesake layout at PGA West.

MOONAH COURSE AT THE NATIONAL,
Mornington Peninsula, Australia

Melbourne has the richest collection of parkland courses of any city on earth, so when the Shark returned home he added a much-needed links outside the city.

As Alister MacKenzie discovered, Melbourne has the perfect sandy terrain for building heathland or parkland courses. But today's designers are realizing that the Mornington Peninsula, a popular beach getaway destination for city residents, has near-perfect linksland. This combination is too good for traveling golfers to pass up. The peninsula starts just south of the city, with its heart just over an hour from downtown.

There are several notable courses, mostly new, on the peninsula, but the highlight is the National, a private club that—like many outside the United States—welcomes foreign visitors. The National has three courses, and on any given day two are open to outside play. The best of the three is the Moonah course, designed by Greg Norman and named for the moonah tree, a beautiful and revered native species resembling the cork trees of Spain and Portugal.

Like most Scottish links, the Moonah sits on coastal terrain but is separated by a beach and strip of thick bushes from the sea. The course itself is open and relatively flat—more like the Old course at St. Andrews than the massive dunescape of Norman's *Doonbeg.* As a result, the wind rolls in off the sea and regularly affects play. The fairways are narrow by Norman's standards, but the sparse rough allows recovery from errant shots. There is extensive bunkering, both in the fairways and around the greens. Still, as is his style, Norman has created approaches that are almost all open, encouraging bump-and-run play. He uses the native moonah trees (which cannot legally be removed) to great visual and strategic effect, building some holes around them, using them to frame tee boxes, and creating angled corridors of play.

While there are no towering dunes, the site's rolling undulation and ridges are evocative of some of the most revered Scottish links layouts. It is a dramatic course that is also a lot of fun to play, offering suitable challenge for all abilities. Norman mixes his long and short holes to offer everything from drivable par-4s to true 2-shot tests, such as a 460-yard uphill par-4—from the white tees. On the highest piece of ground on the course, he locates the tee for the par-3 sixteenth with its views to the sea and over the rest of the layout—just as the par-3 at Turnberry, where Norman won one of his British Opens, overlooks the course. A round at the Moonah is one the traveling golfer will not soon forget.

Adjacent to the Moonah is the Ocean course, on the same piece of land but closer to the sea. Opened along with the Moonah (2000), it was designed by five-time British Open Champion Peter Thompson, Australia's most prolific golf architect. Another true links layout, the Ocean course has similar topography—although a bit flatter—but features a much different design. Thompson uses wider fairways, because his course is windier. Nearly every green is protected in front by bunkers, requiring shots to be flown to the green. And while Norman's course is long with flat landing areas, Thompson fills his shorter fairways with dips, mounds, and undulations in the irregular style of the earliest links, forcing players to hit off a variety of lies. The third and oldest course at the National is an inland Robert Trent Jones Sr. design that is nearby, but on radically different land. A wooded mountain course, it is more reminiscent of the courses of Alabama's *Robert Trent Jones Trail* than seaside links. It features uphill approaches to nearly every green and, of course, water hazards throughout. Since it was the first layout here, it is now called the Old course. All three are first-rate. The National should be an addition to every Melbourne golfing trip.

THE NATIONAL GOLF CLUB AT A GLANCE

+61 3-5988-6666, www.nationalgolf.com.au

Golf Course Info: Practice area, walking only (except Old course).

Moonah: $$V, 5,803–7,334 yards, four tees.

Ocean: $$V, 5,509–6,669 yards, three tees.

Old: $$V, 5,873–6,313 yards, three tees.

Lodging Info: $$–$$$. There is one inn on site at the National, within walking distance of the clubhouse; guests get discounted green fees (The Grange at Cape Shank, +61 3–5988–2333, www.grangecc.com.au). Two excellent luxury hotels on the Mornington Peninsula are Lindenderry at Red Hill (+61 3–5989–2933, www.lindenderry.com.au) and Pepper's Delgany (+61 3–5984–4000, www.peppers.com.au).

Getting There: The heart of the Mornington Peninsula is seventy minutes from the Melbourne airport.

When to Go: It doesn't get very cold in Melbourne—rarely dropping below fifty—and golf is played year-round. Still, it does get quite hot in their summer (December–February). Spring (November) and fall (March) are the best times.

Australian Travel Tips: Australia seems like it is very far away, but from the West Coast, especially Los Angeles, it is closer than Europe, certainly Scotland. It also offers world-class lodging and dining far superior to any you will find in the British Isles. Because of the weak Australian dollar, it is even less expensive for U.S. golfers than Canada, and the best golf courses are bargains. Couple this with good weather, friendly and sophisticated residents, and a welcoming attitude toward North Americans, and you can understand why we think it is a great golf destination. Like many top courses abroad, the National has limited tee times for visitors. They are less formal than their sandbelt counterparts in Melbourne, but you may still find it easier to arrange a trip through a golf tour operator specializing in the region. Such an operator can make tee times and arrange transportation and, if you need it, lodging as well. The best choices are Koala Golfday (+61 3–92–598–2574) and Wide World of Golf (800–214–GOLF, www.wideworldofgolf.com).

Travel Deals: Golfers staying at the Grange at Cape Schank, located at the National Golf Club, can play the courses at a reduced price as guests of the owner, who is a member.

Golf Travel by Design Courses Nearby: Kingston Heath (seventy minutes); Royal Melbourne (seventy minutes).

GREAT WHITE COURSE AT DORAL, *Miami, Florida*

Now living in south Florida, Greg Norman gave his new neighbors something to be thankful for at the region's most famous golf resort.

Norman built two of his trademark limited-turf designs simultaneously, his namesake *Greg Norman Course at PGA West* and his nick-namesake Great White course at Doral. The two layouts show how the same concept can be executed well without repetition, because these resort tracts have little in common other than minimal turf.

Fittingly, the course was built on the site of the existing White course at Doral. It's not a renovation, however; the old layout was razed and rebuilt from scratch. A target-style desert course is a novel concept in south Florida, but it succeeds brilliantly and—if anything—is even better than its western counterpart in the actual desert. The gleaming white waste areas flanking the fairways are filled with palm trees. In addition to the usual purposes of containing shots, reducing the need for grass and maintenance, and adding visual relief, they function as natural cart paths, alleviating the need for unsightly blacktop. Where carts have to cross the fairway, Norman went so far as to blend strips of artificial grass in with the real thing to provide a wear-free surface for driving—and no asphalt.

Small touches can make a huge difference when it comes to golf course design, and here Norman's attention to detail really comes through. At PGA West in the desert, he used decomposed granite for his waste areas, a desert ingredient whose color and texture reflect the surroundings. Here he used crushed seashells, presenting the bright white tropical look of south Florida. While courses throughout the flat state regularly install ponds, lakes, and fountains, for his water hazards Norman chose shallow, but penal, Everglades-like marshes. These are filled with sea grasses and constantly come into play, a reminder of what the region is built on. They also make the course very tough from the tips—the resort's most difficult. Some highly unusual touches here are slightly incongruous but make the layout a memorable resort experience: a blind par-3 ringed with mounds like the one at Lahinch, a dramatic island par-3 that raises the bar for the genre, and a few double and even triple greens.

Doral is also home to the famous Blue Monster, which hosts a PGA Tour event Norman won three times, as well as three other layouts. The resort is the closest to Miami's airport. It offers a famous spa as well the headquarters of the renowned Jim McLean golf school, considered by many to be the nation's best.

DORAL AT A GLANCE

(800) 71–DORAL, www.doralgolf.com

Golf Course Info: Extensive practice area, no walking.

Great White: $$$$+, 5,026–7,171 yards, four tees. *Slope rating* 116–133. *Course rating* 69.4–75.1.

Blue Monster: $$$$+, 5,392–7,125 yards, four tees. *Slope rating* 124–130. *Course rating* 73.0–74.5.

Gold: $$$$, 5,179–6,602 yards, three tees. *Slope rating* 123–129. *Course rating* 71.4–73.3.

Red: $$$$, 5,216–6,614 yards, three tees. *Slope rating* 118–118. *Course rating* 67.1–72.5.

Ted Robinson's twenty-seven-hole layout at the Phoenician combines the stark beauty of desert golf with the fun and playability of a resort course.

ABOVE *The Chateau Whistler course showcases many of Jones's design traits, including penal hazards such as this creek in front of the green, forcing players to fly the ball to the target.*

OPPOSITE PAGE *One of the world's best mountain courses, Robert Trent Jones Jr's. Chateau Whistler layout has alpine lakes, exposed rock outcroppings, and endless wildflowers.*

RIGHT *Jones used boulders and views of surrounding peaks to accentuate the mountain feel of the Chateau Whistler course.*

This treeless coastal site on Australia's Mornington Peninsula mirrors the links land of the British Isles, and was the perfect spot for Greg Norman's Moonah Links.

Rather than the traditional railroad ties, Rees Jones used boulders to bulkhead his lakes at Naples Grande, greatly increasing the course's beauty.

ABOVE *Naples Grande is one of the few top Florida courses that are blissfully free from homes, accentuating the natural wild feel.*

BELOW *At Massachusetts's Pinehills, Rees Jones employs one of his favorite design tools, building a safe "ramp" between the severe greenside bunkers for those playing a bump-and-run shot from the fairway.*

RIGHT *This downhill par-3 to the edge of the sea is the signature hole at Thomas McBroom's Algonquin course in New Brunswick, but the other seventeen holes are excellent as well.*

PHOTO FAIRMONT HOTELS & RESORTS

BELOW *One of the first modern desert courses in the world, Troon North Monument is still the gold standard for the genre, where Tom Weiskopf and Jay Morrish created a work of art in a rugged, desolate setting.*

PHOTO ©MIKE KLEMME/ GOLFOTO

ABOVE *Thomas McBroom's best-known design trait is his frequent use of rock, from boulders to exposed ledge, as seen here at his Le Geant course at Mont Tremblant, Quebec.*

RIGHT *A trained artist, Mike Strantz designs his courses for maximum visual impact, as showcased at his stunning Tobacco Road layout near Pinehurst, North Carolina.*

Silver: $$$$, 4,661–6,614 yards, three tees. *Slope rating* 117–131. *Course rating* 67.1–72.5.

Lodging Info: $$$–$$$$. Doral is a full-service resort. The courses are open to outside play, but guests get discounts and preferential tee times.

Getting There: The resort is twenty minutes from the Miami airport.

When to Go: Golf season is year-round, but summer can be quite hot and humid, while summer through fall is hurricane season.

Golf Travel by Design Courses Nearby: None.

TIBURON, *Naples, Florida*

Norman brings much-needed public golf to the privateclub enclave of Naples, and his Franklin Templeton Shootout tournament along with it.

Naples, the ultrawealthy community on Florida's west coast, appears to the first-time visitor to be one giant strip of golf courses—which, in fact, it is. But the vast majority of these gates stay closed, because the bulk of Naples's golf resides in private clubs and communities. Fortunately, this has been changing with the recent addition of Rees Jones's wonderful *Naples Grande,* Ray Floyd's Raptor Bay, and the biggest recent development of them all, Norman's thirty-six-hole Tiburon.

Part of a residential community that also includes the brand-new Ritz-Carlton Naples Golf Resort, Norman's course is at press time a twenty-seven-hole layout with the fourth nine under construction. It is daunting enough from the tips that Norman moved his signature tournament, the Franklin Templeton Shootout, here to challenge the pros. While it is clearly a Florida course, Norman wanted to add some touches of British Isles play, so the layout is designed to be fast and firm and welcome the ground game as you approach the green. He filled the course with stacked sod-walled pot bunkers, rarely seen in Florida—or much of the United States, for that matter. But the bunkers are filled with orange-colored coquina sand and water runs rampant throughout the course, something not seen in the Old Country. Several greens jut into lakes; fairways are flanked by water.

In keeping with Norman's style, there is hardly a blade of rough to be found at Tiburon. Fairways are very wide—but with nothing to slow down rolling shots, you still need to keep the ball from the edges of the fairways, which inevitably lead to water. The current layout occupies a whopping 230 acres, but Norman did his best to leave as much of the native foliage and wetlands intact as possible. The playable area of the course is just ninety acres, earning him recognition from the Audubon Cooperative Sanctuary Program for his environmental efforts. Golf courses in Florida tend to lack character and be repetitive, but as he did at Doral, Norman integrates interesting features to keep the course fresh. Tiburon will reward visitors with both its beauty and stiff challenge.

RITZ-CARLTON GOLF RESORT AT A GLANCE

(800) 241-3333, www.ritzcarlton.com

Golf Course Info: Practice area, no walking

Tiburon (27 holes): $$$$, 4,988–7,193 yards, four tees. *Slope rating* 108–137. *Course rating* 66.9–74.5.

Lodging Info: The courses are associated with the new Ritz-Carlton Golf Resort (the second Ritz-Carlton in Naples), and guests receive discounts. Still, these layouts are also open to the public—and there are dozens of hotels throughout Naples.

Getting There: Naples is thirty minutes from the Fort Myers airport.

When to Go: Golf season is year-round, but summer can be hot and humid, while summer through fall is hurricane season.

Golf Travel by Design Courses Nearby: Naples Grande (ten minutes).

Other Notable Greg Norman Courses You Can Play

- **Champion's Gate,** Orlando, Florida (thirty-six holes)
- **Meadowbrook Farms,** Houston, Texas
- **Westin Rio Mar (River course),** Rio Grande, Puerto Rico
- **Elks Run** Batavia, Ohio
- **Four Seasons Emerald Bay,** Great Exuma Island, Bahamas (opening in 2003)

Rees Jones (1941–)
From Renovator to Innovator

Rees Jones joined his famous father, Robert Trent Jones Sr., in the design business more than thirty years ago and has remodeled or designed more than 125 courses. So how does he represent the next generation of architects? Jones's career has gone through two dramatically different stages. Jones Sr. got his big break in 1951 when he was asked to prepare Oakland Hills for the U.S. Open. For years he was known as an "Open doctor"; he became famous for these renovations before his original work surpassed it. In an eerily similar career trajectory, son Rees began the same way, but became even more famous for his "major preparations" than his father had been. Along the way Rees Jones updated Hazeltine, the Country Club, Baltusrol, Congressional, and even Pinehurst Number Two, all in advance of U.S. Opens. He continues to this day with the renovation of 2002 Open site Bethpage Black.

A Style of His Own

At the same time, Jones's original work began to prosper, but with the exception of Pinehurst Number Seven (1987)—his first publicized breakthrough—virtually all his notable work has been in the past decade, including his three very high-profile, very private oceanfront courses: Atlantic, Nantucket Golf Club, and Ocean Forest, all built since 1995 to great acclaim. His major resort designs are mostly brand new as well, including just opened layouts at Reynolds Plantation, Casacata, and the upcoming Pinehurst Number Nine. Despite Jones's long history in the business, most of his designs that will be played by traveling golfers are quite recent.

It is said that the apple does not fall far from the tree, but in Jones's case, his style is distinctly different from that of his father. While his brother, Robert Trent Jones Jr., has continued the modern era that Jones Sr. introduced, Rees Jones has championed a return to traditional design along with modern technology that has been called neoclassicism. Jones bears much responsibility for this trend, which is also reflected in the work of other hot architects such as Mike Strantz, Thomas McBroom, and Greg Norman.

Perhaps it was all the work he did on those U.S. Open venues—the Tillinghast, Ross, and Flynn classics—that influenced him. Whatever the reason, Rees Jones has emerged since the early 1990s as one of the game's best architects. When you visit his courses, you will find:

- **Visual definition.** Jones believes that seeing the entire target and the shot required helps the player visualize and achieve what is needed. "As he stands over the ball I want him to see the target and visualize his shot." Many of Jones's common design features are used to achieve this, including:

- **Elevated tees.** Whenever possible, his tees overlook the hole, helping

REES JONES HAS CHAMPIONED A RETURN

TO TRADITIONAL DESIGN ALONG WITH

MODERN TECHNOLOGY THAT HAS BEEN

the player to see it. This also has the side effect of increasing the natural beauty of his most stunning layouts, such as Rio Secco and Cascata.

- **Mounds and contour.** Mounds, berms, and grass bunkers provide three-dimensional relief that helps the player isolate target areas of the hole. On many earlier courses—including Pinehurst Number Seven, the Green course at Williamsburg, and Burnt Pines—he used extensive rows of mounding down either side of the fairway the way other designers use waste areas: to both frame the hole and contain errant shots. While he is using less of this mounding in more recent efforts, long parallel rows of mounds are a Jones signature touch.

- **Diagonal greens, ramped approaches, and an emphasis on the ground game.** In his nod to tradition, Jones is adamant about restoring the ground game to golf. "I've done so many coastal courses where you have to have shot options once the wind picks up. A lot of times I'll run greens on a diagonal, so that you can have an opening and not go at the flag [along the ground]. This gives you the option: Go for the flag and incur a penalty or take the easier route, 2-putt and get out of town." He also builds ramped approaches to greens between the greenside bunkers to encourage the ground approach.

- **Wide fairways with an advantageous side.** The broad target lets more players keep the ball in play—but by making one side of the fairway better for approaching the green, Jones is able to add hazards to this side to create a risk-reward scenario. One thing this leads to is:

- **Extensive bunkering.** One Jones trademark is a row of bunkers, ranging from many small pot bunkers to sculpted large shallow bunkers, running down the entire length of one side of the hole. If you flirt with hazards successfully, it rewards you with an easier approach. He also uses large, irregular and elaborately shaped bunkers reminiscent of MacKenzie's artistic style but with much more modern shapes, especially around greens.

- **Long layouts.** Jones usually provides a wide assortment of tees for all abilities, but you can count on his courses being unusually long, even by modern standards, from the tips. Only one of the following layouts clocks in at less than 7,100 yards.

Since making a splash with Pinehurst Number Seven, Rees Jones has not slowed. He has continued to unveil high-quality public courses, both at resorts and by themselves, throughout the United States. Here are some of his best.

PINEHURST NUMBER SEVEN,
Pinehurst, North Carolina

Rees Jones has developed a spiritual tie with Pinehurst, renovating the famed Number Two for the U.S. Open; designing Number Seven, the first great successor to the Ross gem; and now seeing his Number Nine under construction.

Pinehurst has a lot of good courses, but from 1903 when Donald Ross began on Number Two, it would be more than eighty years before another great one would be built. Rees Jones ended that drought—and made himself an instant star in the design world to boot—with Number Seven.

At Pinehurst Jones accomplished something rarely seen in the upper echelon of public courses: He designed a real-estate-driven, residential golf course where the homes are barely noticeable to the players. Many aspiring courses are ruined by the intrusion of homes, condos, fences, and swimming pools onto fairways, but not Number Seven. More important, it showcased the debut of his neoclassical style, a throwback that mixed small bunkers and hard-to-hold greens with a rugged site much different from the existing Pinehurst experience.

Five of the layouts at the resort, including Number Two, radiate from the main clubhouse with its Ryder Cup bar and historic aura. They share the mostly flat, sandy terrain with thinned-out pine forests, little water, and few penal features. Number Seven is several miles away, and a world apart topographically. It is hilly with severe elevation changes, thicker woods, huge sandy pits, and forced carries over water and ravines. You name it, and if it can swallow your ball, Number Seven has it. There is even an

His Airness

Michael Jordan is the greatest basketball player of all time, and he also happens to be a very good golfer. He picked up the game as a student at the University of North Carolina, so it is natural that Pinehurst became his early stomping grounds for golf. It is said that among its many charms, Pinehurst Number Seven is Jordan's favorite course, and the layout suits his personality: dramatic, bigger than life, and always capable of producing great shots.

abandoned tar pit in play. With enough 3-putts, you might get your score on Number Two as high as on Rees Jones's layout, but there is little doubt that Number Seven is the most difficult course at Pinehurst.

It is also beautiful, and far more dramatic than any of its predecessors. For example, the remarkable par-3 sixteenth features a tee to a green waste area down the right side with jagged fingers of fairways reaching into it—a wonderful effect. It was also built when Jones still loved his containment mounds, lines of which flank many fairways here and define the corridors of play. Most tees are elevated, as are most greens. Jones's designs have become more subtle since Pinehurst, but as long as you are up for a stiff challenge, this is a must-play layout that also makes many of Jones's design traits evident. The positive reception the course has received among the press, resort guests, and locals may explain why Jones was again chosen as a featured designer at Pinehurst: His new Number Nine should open in 2003.

PINEHURST RESORT & GOLF CLUB AT A GLANCE

Golf Course Info: See Pinehurst Number Two.

Travel Deals: Pinehurst offers a wide range of golf packages, most of which include a Modified American Plan. Less expensive packages include golf on courses One, Three, Five, and Six, with various additional surcharges for courses Two, Four, Seven, and Eight. If playing the four most desirable courses is your goal, more expensive packages that waive the surcharges are a better deal. Due to the popularity of Number Two, most packages limit guests to one round on this course per visit.

RIO SECCO, *Las Vegas, Nevada*

It was his great success at Rio Secco that led to Rees Jones's greatest achievement of all, the mythical Cascata.

Before *Shadow Creek* opened to the public, Rio Secco was "the" hotel course in Las Vegas, and it remains open only to guests of the Rio Hotel Casino, Harrah's Casino, and Las Vegas residents. It is also home to the golf school run by Butch Harmon, Tiger Woods's coach. Whether or not you need lessons, however, it's worth choosing to stay at the Rio to play this desert masterpiece.

Balance is important in golf, and balance is what Rio Secco offers, with six dramatic canyon holes, six plateau holes playing atop the desert, and six more winding through wide desert washes and ancient riverbeds. It is a rare site that can showcase such different aspects of the pure desert environment, and Jones used as many of the naturally occurring features as possible, devoting his improvements to adding slopes to connect the three differing elevations. He also demonstrated his emphasis on width amid the penal surroundings, creating very large landing areas.

The 240-acre site has 92 acres of grass, enough to fill in the generous fairways and undulating greens, along with 2 acres of water hazards and nearly 150 acres of scenic buttes, canyons, and starkly beautiful surroundings, all incorporated into the design. You'll also find eighty-eight of Jones's favorite hazards—sand traps—along the way. There are several forced carries, and the course is extremely long from the back tees (7,332 yards), but like his Pinehurst Number Seven it rewards those up for the challenge with an unforgettable setting and endless sequence of "signature" holes. Try your hand at seven, for instance: a long par-4 with the green cut into the face of a canyon wall.

RIO SECCO GOLF CLUB AT A GLANCE

(888) TO–SECCO, www.harrahs.com

Golf Course Info: Practice areas.

$$$$, 5,778–7,332 yards, five tees. *Slope rating* 127–142. *Course rating* 70.0–75.7.

Lodging Info: The Rio is an all-suite hotel casino. Guests of Harrah's, an older casino hotel that has the same owners, can also play the course.

Getting There: Las Vegas has one of the largest, most easily reached airports in the world, with direct flights from many cities. The hotels are all within a ten-minute cab ride of the airport; green fees include round-trip shuttle transfers from the hotel to and from the golf club.

When to Go: Golf is played year-round, but temperatures climb above one hundred degrees in summer and can be uncomfortably cold in winter. In fall overseeding takes place, and the course may close for maintenance. Early spring is ideal.

Travel Deals: Las Vegas room rates fluctuate wildly throughout the year based on what conventions and sporting events are going on, but rates are typically lower in the heat of summer. The Rio Hotel Casino regularly promotes lodging and golf packages on its Web site when occupancy is low. Those who are flexible with their travel dates can take advantage of these offers and realize significant savings.

Golf Travel by Design Courses Nearby: Shadow Creek (twenty minutes); Cascata (thirty minutes); Las Vegas Paiute Resort (twenty minutes); Primm Valley (sixty minutes); Reflection Bay (thirty minutes); Bear's Best (twenty minutes).

Waste areas increase the visual drama of Pinehurst Number Seven, but also help the player by containing shots, keeping balls in play and out of the woods. PINEHURST INC.

NAPLES GRANDE, *Naples, Florida*

Rees Jones introduced high-quality resort golf to a town known for its private clubs.

Wayne Huizenga is a billionaire famous for his high-profile ownership of professional sports teams, but he is also one of Florida's top hoteliers, with such standout properties as the Hyatt Pier 66, Boca Raton Resort & Club, Edgewater, and the Registry. The latter two sit side by side on one of the Gulf Coast's finest beaches, and they now have a golf course to match.

The relatively flat Florida setting works to Jones's advantage, and he is able to implement many of his favorite design features on the course. Almost all the tee boxes are elevated, giving players a very good look at the holes; the fairways are wide; and the bunkering is elaborate, including lipless shallow bunkers flashed right up to the fairway turf. He uses hazards to favor one side of the broad fairways, such as on the risk-reward par-5 ninth, which curves sharply around a lake. To get home in 2, players must drive as close to possible to the water's edge, while those looking for a drier route can simply follow the 3-shot path down the large fairway as it winds around the hazard.

Greens are elevated and guarded with bunkers on the side. In typical Jones fashion, several are set diagonally to the path of play, encouraging safer ground approaches or risky airborne attacks at the pin. Water is in play as well; several greens are beautifully bulkheaded with natural stone and raised well above the level of the lakes. The routing is also one of the more scenic in this heavily developed residential area, refreshingly free of homes, with many preserved older trees, including cypresses, pines, and oaks. Jones also did a good job of incorporating the water into the scenery, such as on the seventeenth hole, a unique par-3 with the tees on a peninsula jutting into the lake and the green on the mainland. Not only is this the reverse of the typical design, but it allows Jones to feature the water prominently without bringing it into play. He does, however, give the elevated green a huge and wildly shaped bunker protecting the front and left side.

NAPLES GRANDE GOLF CLUB AT A GLANCE

(888) 483-6800, (941) 659-3700, www.naplesgrande.com

Golf Course Info: Practice areas, walking allowed.

$$$-$$$$, 5,210-7,102 yards, four tees. *Course rating* 70-75.

Lodging Info: You must be a guest of one of the two associated hotels to play the course. Fortunately, they are the two finest properties in the area. The Registry (800-247-9810, www.registryhotel.com) is a large, grand, and fairly formal resort, while the neighboring Edgewater is smaller and more laid back (800-821-0196, www.edgewaternaples.com).

Getting There: Naples is thirty minutes from the Fort Myers airport.

When to Go: Golf season is year-round, but summer can be hot and humid, while summer through fall is hurricane season.

Golf Travel by Design Courses Nearby: Tiburon (ten minutes)

OCONEE COURSE AT REYNOLDS PLANTATION,
Greensboro, Georgia

Rees Jones joins Jack Nicklaus, Tom Fazio, and Bob Cupp with the newest layout at one of America's top golf resorts.

At Pinehurst, Rees Jones was asked to build the resort's seventh course, and he responded with its longest, most challenging layout on much different topography. At Reynolds Plantation, he was asked to build the fourth tract—and gave the resort its longest and most challenging, on much different topography. Sound familiar?

Reynolds Plantation is a vast residential and resort development encompassing more than 4,000 acres adjacent to huge Lake Oconee. While its four courses all have very different feels, they are linked by the first-class maintenance and landscaping that the resort is known for. The first course was the Plantation by Bob Cupp, a very attractive layout that is set mostly in the thicker woods inland from the lake. The shortest and easiest of the resort's courses, it has come to be somewhat overshadowed, but was highly acclaimed when it opened and is still well worth a round. With small greens and rolling fairways, it is a traditional parkland layout with little water in play.

It was Reynolds's second course, Great Waters, that really put it on the map as a golf resort. Designed by Jack Nicklaus, who likes the place so much he has a home here, the course's front nine begins in the thick woods and wanders down to the lake, emerging dramatically on nine and then playing the rest of its holes along the shoreline. The nines are very different looking but have the same penal character: Errant shots are lost on either side, in thick pine forests or in the lake. But the scenery is beautiful, with the back one of the most memorable inland nines in golf. With four distinct sets of tees, its playability reflects Nicklaus's kinder, gentler resort phase, even with the penal hazards. Despite the high ratings given to both the Cupp course and the Fazio work that followed Great Waters, the Nicklaus course has remained the must-play of the bunch—at least until Jones's design.

Fazio's National splits the difference between Reynolds' first two layouts, with a more wide-open layout that showcases the pines rather than carving its way through them. It is very much in keeping with Fazio's recent work. A large number of bunkers do not hesitate to leave the edges and come right across the landing areas. Tilted so they can be seen from the tees, these are visually intimidating, and the main defense of the course. They are also quite deep; at many other places they'd have steps built in. More than eighty of Fazio's elaborate traps guard both the landing areas and the greens, which are also quite undulating. There is more elevation change on this terrain, and although it is just off the lake, wind can still be a big factor. Fazio returned to Reynolds in 2000 and added a third nine, increasing the number of holes with lake views. The new nine is as strong as the other two; any combination of the National makes a fine round of golf. It is not the wonder that Great Waters is, but if you have the time, it is a fun and attractive course.

Jones's brand-new course is adjacent to the Ritz-Carlton resort that just opened at Reynolds Plantation. It's a bit removed from the other three, but with a prime spot on the banks of the lake. The complex also includes a campus of the respected Dave Pelz Scoring Game School, which emphasizes the short game. Like Great Waters, it mixes pine forest and lakeside holes— but with more dramatic elevation changes and more bushes, shrubs, and foliage. There is no prolonged stretch of waterfront holes like the nine at Great Waters, but it plays to and from the lake and finishes with two excellent lakeside closers. It remains to be seen whether Jones's offering will dethrone Great Waters as the best of the bunch, but it's clearly a must-play. Its stunning array of memorable holes includes the eighteenth: a long par-4 along the lake, 485 yards from the back tees. The drive plays over an inlet of the lake—a moderate but imposing forced carry—and must also clear a long bunker in the rough short of the fairway, which then turns and follows the coast to a deep green protected by bunkers in front and water behind, with a narrow entrance for Jones's favored ground assault. The greens complexes are exceptional, with subtle classic curves and some of the finest putting surfaces you will encounter in your travels. Other touches—ramped elevated greens, shapely bunkers, wide landing areas, and elevated tees—can be found throughout the stately layout, which stretches nearly 7,400 yards from the tips.

REYNOLDS PLANTATION AT A GLANCE

(800) 733-5257, www.reynoldsplantation.com

Golf Course Info: Practice area, walking.

Oconee: $$$–$$$$, 5,198–7,029 yards, five tees. *Slope rating 122–139. Course rating 67.7–73.8.*

Great Waters: $$$–$$$$, 5,057–7,048 yards, four tees. *Slope rating 114–135. Course rating 68.8–73.8.*

National (27 holes): $$$–$$$$, 5,292–7,015 yards, three tees. *Slope rating 116–127. Course rating 69.5–72.7.*

Plantation: $$$–$$$$, 5,162–6,656 yards, three tees. *Slope rating 115–127. Course rating 69.1–71.3.*

Lodging Info: Reynolds Plantation is a private community; the courses are open only to members and hotel and cottage guests. There are about 200 cottages, up to four bedrooms each, spread throughout three complexes on the vast property. You'll also find a wide range of facilities, including water sports, a marina, several restaurants, and other sporting diversions. The resort's sole hotel, the new Ritz-Carlton, opened in spring 2002 (800–241–3333, www.ritzcarlton.com).

Getting There: The resort is an hour west of Atlanta's Hartsfield Airport, the busiest in the United States and easy to get to from anywhere.

When to Go: Golf is played year-round, but prime season is March through November. Summer months are hot and humid.

Golf Travel by Design Courses Nearby: None.

BLACKSTONE NATIONAL AND PINEHILLS,
Massachusetts

**Jones returns to the site where he played
"U.S. Open doctor" on the Country Club to craft two
high-quality bargain layouts in Massachusetts.**

While almost every top golf course architect is based in Florida or California, Rees Jones continues to live and work in his hometown of Montclair, New Jersey. Perhaps this gave him an appreciation for the dearth of high-quality daily fee courses throughout the Northeast when compared to the nearby Middle Atlantic region or other parts of the country. Whatever the reason, it was a much-appreciated boon to golfers in Massachusetts and throughout southern New England when Jones opened two daily fee facilities in the Bay State in summer 2001.

The courses are quite different, but both are excellent—and good values as well. Blackstone National, in Sutton, is a very traditional New England course, a hilly parkland routing where even the clubhouse and maintenance buildings are designed to look like barns and farmhouses. It is a less intimidating routing than some of Jones's other courses, although it has a lot of elevation changes. The only water in play on the entire course is a pond on the par-3 eleventh. For the most part the routing is a quintessential classic eastern design, with two nine-hole loops of nongimmicky holes, wide fairways lined with stands of mature hardwoods, classical bunkering (mainly on one side of the fairway, as is Jones's habit), and numerous doglegs. Greens are large, often elevated, and only moderately undulating. He uses elevated tee boxes whenever possible, but because of the hills the views of each hole are not as comprehensive as in his typical designs. The course ends with a very unusual hole, especially for the lengthy Jones. Eighteen is a very reachable par-5, just 485 yards from the back tees. It requires a long drive to the right side of the landing area to open up the approach angle, with a second to a small green guarded by deep bunkers. With greens kept in excellent shape, GPS on the carts, and green fees often under $50, Blackstone is a champagne golf experience for the beer budget.

Pinehills, in Plymouth, is a little flashier and a little pricier—the first course at a larger complex that just opened a second layout, this one by Jack Nicklaus. It is also home to the largest practice facility in New England, with three complete golf academies, including a Dave Pelz Scoring Game School.

While Blackstone has fairways lined with sparser hardwoods, Pinehills is carved from thick pine forests in the Carolina style. Blackstone is quite hilly, but rolling, while Pinehills is more of a ridge-and-valley course with sharper natural features and contours. It is a slightly stiffer challenge, since balls disappear more readily in the dense underbrush; there is also more water in play, and more penal hazards. The rolling site has some severe glacial features, such as sharp ridges and ravines, all of which Jones incorporated. The fifteenth is a good example of his work: A drive from an elevated tee box must cross a tree-filled ravine immediately in front. The player can see the entire hole, yet the naturally occurring hazard is both beautiful and intimidating. Upon reaching the green complex, you will find Jones's slightly elevated green with ramped openings guarded on the sides by deep bunkers in the greenside slopes.

The Nicklaus course was slated to open in May 2002, and is intended to be a more modern contrast to Jones's neoclassical design. While Jones uses traditional square tee boxes, Nicklaus employs irregular free-flowing tees to set the mood immediately. The greens on the second layout are far more undulating, and the design includes hazards rarely seen in golf: cranberry bogs.

BLACKSTONE NATIONAL AT A GLANCE

(508) 865-2111, www.blackstonegolfclub.com

Golf Course Info: Practice area, walking allowed.

$–$$V, 5,203–6,909 yards, four tees. *Slope rating* 119–132. *Course rating* 69.5–73.5.

PINEHILLS GOLF CLUB AT A GLANCE

(866) 855-GOLF, www.pinehillsgolf.com

Golf Course Info: Extensive practice areas, walking allowed.

Jones Course: $$V, 5,380–7,175 yards. *Slope rating* 125–135. *Course rating* 69.6–73.8.

Nicklaus Course: $$V; other specifications to be announced.

Lodging Info: Neither facility has lodging on site, but both are in areas with abundant choices. Lodging info can be obtained through the clubs.

Getting There Blackstone National: The course is fifty minutes southwest of Boston, and also easily accessible from Hartford, Connecticut, and Providence, Rhode Island.

Getting There Pinehills: Plymouth is about an hour southeast of Boston.

When to Go: Golf season is from May through November.

Golf Travel by Design Courses Nearby: None.

A mystery in the golf world, Jones's Cascatamay become known as his greatest lifetime achievement—if anyone gets to play it.

When Steve Wynn and Tom Fazio built **Shadow Creek,** it gave Wynn's hotels an ace up their sleeve for attracting high-rolling gamblers—the promise of a coveted tee time. Wynn's biggest competitor, MGM Grand Resorts, decided it needed a comparable course and brought in Rees Jones to design the very exclusive, very expensive, and very secretive Cascata.

The first twist in the Cascata saga happened when the course, nearly finished, changed hands. MGM Grand bought Wynn's Mirage Resorts and merged the companies. Now MGM had the golf course it was trying to

What Are My Odds?

If Shadow Creek is as borderline "public" as you can get, with limited access and the nation's highest green fees, how should we describe Cascata? At press time the course was playable by invitation only, and the intended audience is very high rollers—gamblers who, according to one published report, are prepared to open credit lines in excess of $100,000 at the participating casinos. Theoretically, if you have enough money and are willing to risk losing it, you can play Cascata. Does this make it public? Not by our standards. But by the time you read this, things may well have changed. Faced with the very expensive proposition of maintaining what may be the world's costliest course for a dozen players each day, Park Place Entertainment was exploring options for following in the model of Shadow Creek and opening the course for "public" play. It has already taken the step of welcoming small corporate outings. In a city that thrives on more and more spectacular one-upmanship, we predict that nongamblers will be able to take on Cascata soon, probably for $1,000 a head.

outdo, and didn't need another layout, especially one rumored to have cost somewhere in the stratospheric ballpark of $60 million to build. They sold the nearly finished Cascata to rival Park Place Entertainment, which owns half a dozen casino hotels in Las Vegas. After some logistical glitches with the growing seasons and advance preparations, Cascata opened for play, very quietly, in 2001.

The level of maintenance, poshness, and beauty is clearly intended to rival Shadow Creek, but Cascata is very much a desert course, or, as Jones puts it, a "desert links." The MGM people behind the original design located a large desert site near Boulder City, 20 miles outside Las Vegas, that had both stunning topography and ample access to desert golf's most valuable asset, water, from nearby Lake Mead. The nearly 400-acre lot Jones had to work with is full of canyons. While much blasting was conducted, he found that—like the original links courses of Scotland—the landscape gave him natural tee, green, and fairway sites where the holes fit the land perfectly. "Choosing the best eighteen was the hard part," Jones joked about the job. "It looks like a desert links because the holes fit right through the valleys. It's a phenomenal piece of ground, the desert answer to Shadow Creek, the same type of spectacular setting, but a natural one." Like its competitor, virtually every hole is completely private in its canyon setting, and even fewer people, about a dozen a day, play it.

Cascata has landscape similar to Jones's beautiful **Rio Secco** course, only more of it is in the canyons and less on plateaus, immersing the player in the golf experience. Although radically different from any course he, or any other designer, has ever built, Jones's style is recognizable throughout. The course lends itself to the ground game, with no forced carries and open approaches to the greens. It's long. It has wide landing areas. It has elevated tees. It has classic routing elements in a very modern setting. It is very much a Rees Jones course.

The course is named for a 417-foot waterfall that flows through the center of the clubhouse. Water features are very much an integral part of the course, used on the first and last holes to set the atmosphere, and in many locations in between. An ancient riverbed conveniently ran throughout the property, which Jones proceeded to pump water into and restore to its former glory. The lush fairways are lined with thin stands of palm trees, which form a visual buffer between the verdant grass and the rugged desert; along with the flowing river, they create the illusion of an oasis, especially when viewed from Jones's trademark elevated tee boxes. It is simply one of the most visually spectacular courses ever built. As it becomes more accessible to play, it should cement Jones's reputation as one of the game's top designers.

Access through Park Place Entertainment Properties (www.parkplace. com): Bally's (800–634–3434, www.ballyslv.com); Caesar's Palace (800–634–6661, www.caesars.com); Flamingo (800–732–2111, www. flamingolasvegas.com); Paris (800–BONJOUR, www.parislasvegas.com)

Golf Course Info: Practice area, walking allowed.

$$$$+, 5,591–7,137 yards, four tees.

Lodging Info: Only guests of the Park Place properties above can be invited to play Cascata.

Getting There: Las Vegas has one of the largest, most easily reached airports in the world, with direct flights from many cities. The hotels are all within a ten-minute cab ride of the airport. The golf club provides round-trip transportation to and from the course for invited hotel guests.

When to Go: Golf is played year-round, but temperatures climb above one hundred degrees in summer and can be uncomfortably cold in winter. In fall overseeding takes place, and the course may close for maintenance. Early spring is ideal.

Golf Travel by Design Courses Nearby: Rio Secco (twenty minutes); Shadow Creek (thirty minutes); Las Vegas Paiute Resort (twenty minutes); Primm Valley (sixty minutes); Reflection Bay (thirty minutes); Bear's Best (twenty minutes).

Other Notable Rees Jones Courses You Can Play

- **Poppy Ridge,** Livermore, California (twenty-seven holes)
- **Burnt Pines,** Sandestin, Florida
- **Falcon's Fire,** Kissimmee, Florida
- **Palmas del Mar,** Humacao, Puerto Rico
- **Montauk Downs,** Montauk, New York
- **Sandpines,** Florence, Oregon
- **Legend Trail,** Scottsdale, Arizona

Tom Weiskopf (1942–   )
Player-Friendly Designs from a Great Player

Few designers and even fewer golf travelers will ever be able to hit the kind of shots that Tom Weiskopf's silky-smooth swing produced. His PGA Tour career yielded fifteen victories and five foreign titles, including the 1973 British Open. Before he retired to devote himself to golf course design, his short Senior Tour career was equally memorable, with five victories in as many years, including another major, the 1995 U.S. Senior Open. But despite his obvious talents, Weiskopf, perhaps more than any other designer, understands how the average person plays golf, and the dichotomy between his private courses and public designs is unrivaled by anyone except his former competitor Jack Nicklaus.

Each Hole Is Memorable

Weiskopf recognizes what few others do about the nature of resort-based golf: Not only is the talent level of players lower, but many will play the course just once. Toward that end, his public designs are intentionally less severe and feature fewer bunkers, fewer penal hazards, and nary a blind shot. At the same time, he knows that the traveling golfer collects memories along with scorecards, and strives to make each of his holes as memorable as possible.

When he first got into the design business, Weiskopf partnered with Jay Morrish. They enjoyed immediate success with a Scottsdale private club named Troon, rated best of the year. The duo followed this up with the acclaimed public Troon North course. Both, not coincidentally, bear the name of the site where he won the British Open. While Morrish had established a very good desert track record at the nearby Boulders, Troon North has become the industry benchmark for excellence in desert design, and quickly accelerated Weiskopf's career. He and Morrish laid out twenty-five courses before parting amicably. Since striking out on his own, Weiskopf has earned a place alongside the next generation of great golf architects.

While his hometown of Scottsdale has been the setting for many of his design triumphs, Weiskopf has not limited himself geographically, building courses from the Bahamas to Scotland where his private Loch Lomond stunned the locals and is already heralded as one of Britain's best. Considering that he won his major in Scotland, and is a big fan of traditional architecture and the likes of Donald Ross, Alister MacKenzie, and C. B. Macdonald, it is not so surprising that he easily adapted to the British Isles setting for this effort. But no matter where you play his public courses, you can expect to find:

HE KNOWS THAT THE TRAVELING GOLFER

COLLECTS MEMORIES ALONG WITH

SCORECARDS, AND STRIVES TO MAKE EACH

- **Few penal hazards.** Weiskopf likes to give the player room. Toward this end, he believes that bunkers should be shallow, and that there should be no more than six holes with water in play. He also adds:

- **Buffer zones, especially around the greens, for near misses.** He thinks that even on holes with penal hazards, slightly inaccurate shots should not have drastic results, so he adds bunkers or rough to keep balls in play. Around the greens, he often builds grass hollows.

- **No drastic climbs to the green.** Weiskopf strongly dislikes the kinds of elevation changes up to the green that Robert Trent Jones Sr. embraced, and limits the ascent to 30 feet. Beyond this, he feels that a climb adds too much length to the hole, and also reduces visibility—violating another of his design rules, that there be:

- **No blind shots.** Litigation is as much a reason for this as aesthetics, but the rule also fits with Weiskopf's understanding that public courses often receive one-time play.

- **Large, open greens, often with false fronts.** On public courses he builds larger putting surfaces to handle the increased amount of foot traffic, and leaves the fronts open to promote bump-and-run shots. At the same time, he likes false fronts, so if you approach the greens with a high lofted shot, you have to land the ball beyond the initial slope.

- **No penalty for straight shots.** It sounds simple, but many designers use either cross hazards, such as a body of water in the fairway, or a sharp dogleg to force the player to either lay up or carry the hazard. Weiskopf believes you should not be penalized for a straight shot being short or long. In the same vein he designs:

- **Holes playing into or with the wind.** Since he admires straight shots, he is not a fan of crosswinds, and tries to lay out his holes so they play either directly into or away from prevailing winds.

- **Reliance on natural features.** While many public golfers think of Weiskopf primarily as a desert designer, where almost everything in play is artificial, his many private courses and more recent public works have taken him into the mountains and to the islands, where he carefully identifies prominent natural features—mature trees, rock outcroppings, ravines, and streams—and builds his holes to incorporate them.

- **A variety of lengths,** including a reachable par-4, a par-5 reachable in 2, and a par-5 *not* reachable in 2. These are three hole types he considers vital.

While many of Weiskopf's early successes were private courses, he is working on more and more public layouts, including a second course to join Jack Nicklaus's **Reflection Bay.** Between his solo designs and his work with Jay Morrish, the traveling golfer will have no trouble finding worthwhile Weiskopf courses to play.

TROON NORTH, *Scottsdale, Arizona*

Despite a slew of imitators, immaculately maintained Troon North remains the gold standard by which desert golf courses worldwide are judged.

Troon North may have been Tom Weiskopf's first high-profile public course with partner Jay Morrish, but it already showed the design characteristics he favors. The original course is now called Troon North Monument; its newer sibling, an equally acclaimed solo effort by Weiskopf, is the Pinnacle.

While many earlier Scottsdale designs merely re-created parkland layouts in the desert through abundant grass seed and water, Troon North came about as water restrictions were forcing the advent of limited-turf designs. Monument is a pure desert golf course, with its fairways laid out in stark contrast to the rugged surroundings; it features the target aspect of forced carries over natural areas to reach the fairways. But while visually impressive, the carries are far less demanding than those over lakes on many more "traditional" courses. Reflecting Weiskopf's often stated ideals, one of the things that make the course great is that it is eminently fair. Collection areas and bunkers do their best to keep errant tee shots away from the rattlesnakes, and high-quality bent grass greens are receptive to both airborne and running shots. In fact, despite the unusual setting, the course is an homage to Scotland's Royal Troon, where Weiskopf hoisted the Claret Jug. We are reminded of this on the Postage Stamp hole, which, needless to say, is a short par-3 surrounded by deep bunkers.

Weiskopf also stresses memorability, and few holes in golf are as vivid as the third, the namesake Monument hole, which features a single boulder so big it could be described as a rock mountain in the fairway at the bend in the dogleg. This red desert edifice is sufficiently far along that it cannot be flown, yet close enough so that players have to choose a side to go around. In either case, the monolith is so unique as to create an everlasting impression. Another example is the par-5 eleventh, Saddle, which doglegs between two stunning granite formations. As a result of these fantastic holes and the constantly wonderful conditioning, the course has been ranked in the Top Twenty since it opened.

Weiskopf's newer Pinnacle has been cited as even better than the original by fans who favor shot value and shot execution. Some find it too hard, however—and it *is* the most testing of his public efforts. Named for Pinnacle Peak, which it approaches and winds around, the layout boasts far more elevation changes and grander sweeping views of its surroundings, though it's not as visually stunning as its sibling. It has narrower fairways, and nearly twice as many bunkers. All four par-3s are on the long side, making it a tough course for average players—and an excellent one for single-digit handicappers. If Monument is Royal Troon, with its broad flat fairways, than Pinnacle is **Royal County Down**, requiring well-struck shots on precise lines over ridges.

(480) 585-5300, www.troongolf.com

Golf Course Info: Practice area, no walking.

Monument: $$$$+, 5,050–7,028 yards, five tees. *Slope rating* 117–147. *Course rating* 68.5–73.3.

Pinnacle: $$$$+, 4,980–7,044 yards, five tees. *Slope rating* 116–147. *Course rating* 68.5–73.4.

Lodging Info: There is a relatively new Four Seasons resort located at the facility, with a block of tee times reserved for guests. We are big fans of this luxury chain, which operates some of the best golf resort hotels in the world, but this is not its best property (800–819–5053, www.fourseasons.com). The course is also open to the public, but tee times require advance reservations.

Getting There: Troon North is fifty minutes from the Phoenix Sky Harbor Airport.

When to Go: Golf is played year-round, but summer temperatures routinely climb above one hundred degrees. Still, prices drop by more than half, and courses are less crowded.

Golf Travel by Design Courses Nearby: Phoenician (thirty-five minutes); TPC Scottsdale (twenty minutes).

TPC SCOTTSDALE, *Scottsdale, Arizona*

In his hometown, Weiskopf and Jay Morrish designed the course that is home to the most popular event on the entire PGA Tour, the Phoenix Open.

Tom Weiskopf has repeatedly stressed his belief in playable courses when talking about design, and nowhere is this more evident than at the two courses he and Jay Morrish designed for the Tournament Players Club in Scottsdale. While PGA Tour pros sweat the brutal finish at the *TPC Sawgrass,* and the *TPC Stadium course at PGA West* has been deemed too difficult for a tournament, winners at Scottsdale routinely shoot in the low 60s. The course is so popular with pros that more than two dozen of them call the course home.

It is also popular with traveling golfers, one of the most navigable TPC courses in the United States. Unlike its neighbors and the famous pair of Weiskopf designs at Troon North, the Stadium course, where the tournament is played, is not a true desert course. There are some forced carries over natural areas from the tees, especially the pro tees, but desert does not line the fairways, which feature wall-to-wall grass, and there is no target element. Still, it's no cakewalk, thanks mainly to some of Weiskopf's design traits. He reaches his personal limit by including six holes with water in play, the most he will put on a course. While he includes his trademark reachable par-5, at just 468 yards from the blue tees, the second shot is to an island green, fitting his risk-reward style. There is also a drivable par-4, the seventeenth, which at 292 yards from the blues helps create an exciting finish with potential for eagle, birdie, or bogey, or worse. More than seventy bunkers guard the course, many "flashed" in the classic Tillinghast style Weiskopf admires, meaning the backs are higher than the fronts. While the course is of moderate length from all but the long back tees, Weiskopf follows another of his rules by building several holes—including the longest par-4 on the course (470 yards from the tips)—directly into the prevailing wind.

While very user friendly, the Stadium course's tough and watery finish can be a bit much for less skilled traveling golfers. The solution for them is found at the TPC Scottsdale's second eighteen, the Desert course, also designed by Weiskopf and Morrish. A completely different layout from the Stadium, it is a true desert course, with rugged natural areas framing most fairways and more of a target element. But it is quite short, with generous landing areas and no water, making it extremely forgiving. It is also an extremely reasonable value for a high-quality daily fee desert course in expensive Scottsdale, with green fees never rising above $53 in peak season. In a unique situation, the TPC Scottsdale is owned by the city,

A Place for Records

The TPC Scottsdale Stadium course is a place where records are set with amazing frequency. It perennially boasts the highest attendance of any PGA Tour event: Crowds often swell to better than 400,000, even though the tournament usually conflicts with the Superbowl. Low scores are de rigueur here. Mark Calcavecchia's 28-under winning performance in 2001 was a PGA Tour record, as were his thirty-two birdies. Tiger Woods wowed fans when he aced a par-3 here, but the real excitement in 2001 came from the longest hole-in-one ever recorded on the Tour. Andrew Magee hit his historic shot on the drivable par-4 seventeenth, which plays 332 yards from the pro tees, for a rare double eagle.

Troon North is not just one of the nation's best courses, it is consistently among the best maintained. © MIKE KLEMME/GOLFOTO

the only municipal Tournament Players Club in the nation. While the Stadium course demands green fees more in line with the prestigious Troon North, Grayhawk, and other nearby gems—more than $200 in peak season—when summer comes you can play thirty-six holes on both TPC courses here for about $120.

TPC SCOTTSDALE AT A GLANCE

(888) 400–4001, www.tpc.com

Golf Course Info: Practice areas, no walking.

Stadium: $$$$, 5,455–7,089 yards, four tees. *Slope rating* 120–135. *Course rating* 68.9–74.5.

Desert: $V, 4,715–6,552 yards, four tees. *Slope rating* 103–112. *Course rating* 64.8–71.4.

Lodging Info: There is no lodging at the course, but the elegant Fairmont Scottsdale Princess is just two minutes away and offers packages (800–223–1818, www.fairmont.com). There are dozens of other choices in nearby Scottsdale and Phoenix.

Getting There: The courses are thirty minutes from the Phoenix Sky Harbor Airport.

When to Go: Golf is played year-round, but summer temperatures routinely climb above one hundred degrees. Still, prices drop by more than half, and courses are less crowded.

Golf Travel by Design

Travel Deals: The TPC Scottsdale is owned by the city, the only municipal Tournament Players Club in the nation, and greens fees are priced accordingly. The less acclaimed Desert course is an excellent value for a high quality, daily fee course in traditionally pricey Scottsdale, with maximum greens fees of $53. In the summer off-season packages offer thirty-six-holes on both of the TPC courses for about $120.

Golf Travel by Design Courses Nearby: Phoenician (thirty-five minutes); Troon North (twenty minutes).

DESERT COURSE AT CABO DEL SOL,
Cabo San Lucas, Mexico

Soon to have three courses by three of our showcased designers, Cabo del Sol is without a doubt the premier golf facility in Mexico.

When Jack Nicklaus built the *Ocean course at Cabo del Sol,* it instantly put Mexico on the golf map. Weiskopf was chosen to create Cabo's second layout, his highest-profile public solo effort to date. Mexico, Nicklaus, and Weiskopf seem to go well together, since the latter followed this effort with another thirty-six-hole facility featuring a Nicklaus course, *Vista Vallarta.*

Nicklaus has often said that the coastal exposure he had at Cabo del Sol was the finest he's seen, and its developers did not try to top that experience with the second course. Instead, Cabo del Sol is creating unique and individual golf experiences, with Weiskopf's Desert course and Tom Doak's upcoming very hilly Vista course. When complete it will be not just Mexico's premier golf resort, but one of the best in the world.

Weiskopf's course, which opened in 2002, combines his desert experience with his love of the links. While any attempt to duplicate the pure links experience in a desert setting is bound to fail, Weiskopf has wisely chosen to include only those features that are replicable. This is his best opportunity to date, since the course, which sits just inland of the Ocean layout, is but a driver away from the sea and features both dramatic views and high winds. He created a traditional out-and-back links routing, with two sets of parallel holes, including a couple that are joined into double fairways. The prominent natural features are the desert arroyos: dry river washes that, along with two small lakes, are the sole penal hazards, in keeping with Weiskopf's reluctance to punish golfers. Greens are classically styled, slightly elevated with open fronts to receive bump-and-run shots and intricate bunkering alongside to capture errant shots. Like the Scottsdale designs he had so much success with, the course is carved from the Sonoran Desert, but Weiskopf adds plenty of his grassy "buffer zones" around the green complexes to keep missed approaches from finding the hostile desert.

The course is on slightly higher, more rolling ground than Nicklaus's and features subtle elevation changes throughout, but none of the severe climbs Weiskopf dislikes. As a result of its elevation, panoramic views of the sea can be found on nearly every hole, helping to achieve what Weiskopf strives for on every course he designs: a memorable experience.

CABO DEL SOL AT A GLANCE

800–386–2465, www.cabodelsol.com

Golf Course Info: Practice areas, no walking.

$$$$+, 4,695–7,103 yards, four tees.

Lodging Info: $$–$$$$. The Los Cabos region has a wide range of lodging, from inexpensive to totally swank. There are several hotels located at the Cabo del Sol course. Palmilla is the only true golf resort, a fine hotel with its own course. Las Ventanas al Paraiso is simply one of the world's finest resorts, and the only choice in the region if you are splurging (800–VISIT–CABO, www.visitcabo.com).

Getting There: Los Cabos International Airport is served by many American and Mexican airlines. All the resorts and courses are a short cab ride from the airport.

When to Go: Golf season is year-round, but summer is very hot with a few days of intense rain, which close the courses. November through May are ideal months.

Golf Travel by Design Courses Nearby: Desert course at Cabo del Sol.

VISTA VALLARTA, *Puerto Vallarta, Mexico*

Weiskopf's second resort effort south of the border makes him the runner-up to Jack Nicklaus as Mexico's top golf designer.

At Cabo del Sol, Weiskopf gets second billing to Jack Nicklaus, but at the new Vista Vallarta the tables are turned. The latest entry in the rapidly growing field of high-end Mexican golf venues, Vista Vallarta is a pure daily fee facility just outside Puerto Vallarta. Two courses opened at about the same time, in early 2002—one each by Nicklaus and Weiskopf.

Nicklaus got the hillier and more open lot, and has built a fun but not especially dramatic resort-style layout. Weiskopf worked in a more memorable junglelike setting reminiscent of *Kauai's Prince* course. The land is more epic, and as is his style, Weiskopf incorporated as much of the existing landscape and as many natural features as possible, with almost no earthmoving. He also did a fantastic job of using the existing palm trees to frame or backdrop several greens, resulting in some stunning approaches. The course crosses several ravines filled with thick native foliage and has more water than its neighbor, but not enough to surpass Weiskopf's self-imposed limits. The setting allowed him to design some of his cherished memorable holes, especially the par-3 thirteenth, with a green carved from the jungle and seemingly perched on the edge of a hillside precipice. Due to the junglelike vegetation, Weiskopf was able to create one of his more visually intimidating courses while still quietly building in buffer zones to give players more room than it appears from the tee.

In a bit of a twist, Weiskopf put his requisite drivable par-4 at the end of the course, creating a final-hole finish that will be hotly contested in match play—or allow folks having a good day to take their shot at a personal best.

VISTA VALLARTA AT A GLANCE

+52 3221–0546, www.foremexico.com

Golf Course Info: Practice area, walking.

$$$, 7,153 yards, four tees.

Lodging Info: There is not yet lodging associated with the course, but two hotels will eventually be built on site. A wide assortment of lodging is available in nearby Puerto Vallarta (888–384–6822, www.puertovallarta.net).

Getting There: Puerto Vallarta has a new airport that is served by many carriers. The resorts and Vista Vallarta courses are just ten minutes away.

When to Go: November through May are nearly perfect months here, but the rainy season begins in June with occasional rain. By July and August it rains all the time. Do not go during this period.

Travel Deals: While Puerto Vallarta enjoys the same weather, fine dining, and quality of accommodations as Mexico's Cabo del Sol, its golf is significantly less expensive. Further savings are offered with a three-course package that combines rounds at both the Nicklaus and Weiskopf courses at Vista Vallarta and the Marina course in nearby Marina Vallarta.

Golf Travel by Design Courses Nearby: Nicklaus course at Vista Vallarta.

OCEAN CLUB, *Paradise Island, Bahamas*

Resident pro and U.S. Open Champion Ernie Els will be getting company: Both Tiger Woods and Michael Jordan are said to be building golf course homes here.

Just a few years ago, Paradise Island's low-key residents included the sleepy Ocean Club boutique hotel, Merv Griffin's nondescript high-rise casino hotel, and the run-of-the-mill Paradise Island Golf Club. Things sure have changed.

Sun International, the casino and resort giant that originally developed the acclaimed South African casino and golf resort Sun City, took over Mr. Griffin's operation and acquired three-quarters of Paradise Island, a beach enclave just a short bridge away from Nassau and much larger New Providence Island. Three years ago Sun more than doubled the size of the casino hotel and relaunched it as Atlantis, a towering pink 2,000-room resort with an aquatic theme, including the most elaborate pool and lagoon complexes on earth. For fans of water slides, river pools, and sunbathing, there is simply nothing that can compare. In 2001 Sun doubled the size of the Ocean Club, its much more expensive and private boutique hotel next door, then brought in Tom Weiskopf to bulldoze the old Paradise Island Golf Club plus the small airport adjacent to it and lay out the new Ocean Club course.

The site is almost completely flat, and unfortunately lacks the drama of top island courses like Teeth of the Dog at *Casa de Campo* or the *Four Seasons Nevis.* Nonetheless, it benefits from the almost surreal turquoise water the Bahamas is famous for and showcases many of Weiskopf's design traits. Despite the oceanfront setting and a couple of human-made lakes, water is in play on only five holes, and there are no other penal hazards. Fifteen is the requisite drivable par-4 that many resort guests can safely go for, playing just 283 yards downhill. A second such hole is much more of a risk-reward proposition: The signature seventeenth plays directly along the ocean, which swallows missed drives. Likewise, there are both reachable and unreachable par-5s for variety, and the par-3s are widely differing lengths. Greens are open in front and welcome running shots; the numerous fairway bunkers are flashed and shallow, as his public course mentality dictates. Perhaps the most noticeable of the Weiskopf traits here is how almost every hole plays directly upwind or downwind, even when the prevailing winds change direction in this always windy setting.

Few holes are as memorable as the fourth here, a longish par-4 that plays downhill (but into the prevailing wind) along a peninsula that tapers until the green is left jutting into the sea. Views of the gorgeous turquoise water frame both sides of the hole; waves crash up against the right side of the green complex, challenging the approach.

*(800) 321–3000, www.oceanclub.com,
www.atlantisresort.com*

Golf Course Info: Practice area, no walking.

$$$$+, 4,995–7,159 yards, five tees.

Lodging Info: The Atlantis Casino Hotel has an enormous number of restaurants and attractions and is a large, flamboyant Las Vegas–style resort. The Ocean Club is a very expensive and private hundred-room boutique hotel next door. Both are a short shuttle ride from the course.

Getting There: The Ocean Club course is thirty minutes from the Nassau airport.

When to Go: Golf is played year-round, but summer through fall is hurricane season; rain is more likely.

Golf Travel by Design Courses Nearby: None.

Other Notable Tom Weiskopf Courses You Can Play

- **Waikoloa Kings course,** Waikoloa, Hawaii
- **La Cantera,** San Antonia, Texas
- **Cedar River course, Shanty Creek,** Bellaire, Michigan
- **Zimbali Resort,** Durban, South Africa

Thomas McBroom (1953–   )
The Future of Canadian Golf

L
ike his idol, Stanley Thompson, Thomas McBroom is not exactly a household name in the United States. The situation is much, much different north of the border, where, along with Thompson, McBroom has more top-ranked Canadian courses than anyone. At last count Canada's largest golf magazine, *Score,* had given him eight of the top forty spots, and he designed one of the nation's only two courses to receive five stars from *Golf Digest.* McBroom has quietly and steadily built a reputation as a top designer while laying out nearly five dozen courses. Many of McBroom's best layouts are for private clubs, but he has done more than enough public and resort courses to give the traveling golfer a taste of his work, and he is expanding geographically as well. While he has not designed any U.S. courses yet, he has some on the drawing board—and is currently building layouts in Europe and the Caribbean as well.

Using Technology to Accentuate Nature

His work follows in Thompson's footsteps, with classically styled strategic routings that not only reflect but also emphasize the natural beauty of the surroundings. Just as Thompson contoured his bunkers to mirror nearby mountain ranges, McBroom will unearth rock formations to accent the rugged nature of a Canadian site. He also uses classical elements such as aiming bunkers, but works with a thoroughly modern style, using technology to achieve his goals.

It is hard to fathom that such a young designer would already have been through various phases in his career, but when McBroom burst onto the scene he liked to build elaborate tiered and undulating green complexes. He still does, but after seeing the taste for such designs decline in the marketplace, he's gone more conventional and yielded to economic realities. McBroom formally studied landscape architecture before working for Bob Cupp, from whom he learned a great deal about golf course design. In the very short time since, he has built a surprisingly large number of courses throughout Canada, from the Rockies to one of the most remote spots in Nova Scotia. When you visit them, you will notice:

- **Rocks.** It may just be the coincidence of having built so many courses on the Canadian Shield—a giant rock formation that extends from Ontario through Quebec and into the Maritimes—but a substantial number of McBroom's designs use rock as the defining feature. One of his most acclaimed successes, Rocky Crest, was aptly named: It is built on 250 acres of mostly solid rock. "I've done a lot of interesting things with rocks, framing holes, requiring people to hit over it. We've unearthed rock and even washed it."

- **Diversity.** McBroom loathes repetition and tries to create eighteen different holes on each course. To avoid an unnatural flow or gimmicky

JUST AS THOMPSON CONTOURED HIS

BUNKERS TO MIRROR NEARBY MOUNTAIN

RANGES, McBROOM WILL UNEARTH ROCK

FORMATIONS TO ACCENT THE RUGGED

appearance, he tries to link the holes with a theme, such as the bunkering style. But expect a lot of different lengths, shapes, and features in a single McBroom course.

- **Framed targets.** Golfers visiting McBroom courses needn't worry about where to go. He believes that the fairway and the target need to be framed visually, whether by trees, bunkers, or rocks. Toward this end, he uses:

- **A lot of bunkering that does not come into play.** Aiming and target bunkers, or those put aside to frame the edges of a hole, are common on his layouts.

- **Classical elements.** Like many of the new-generation designers, McBroom is well schooled in golf history and admittedly "hugely influenced by Stanley Thompson." As a result, he frequently employs classic elements, from aiming bunkers to nonreturning nines and alternate approach routes to greens.

McBroom offers one special benefit to the traveling U.S. golfer: Because his fine layouts are in Canada, visiting and playing them can often be done at bargain rates. Here are some of the best.

THE LINKS AT CROWBUSH COVE,
Morell, Prince Edward Island

One of only two courses in all of Canada to win a five-star rating from *Golf Digest*, this modern dunes layout has put tiny Prince Edward Island on the map as a major golf destination.

The jewel in Thomas McBroom's crown, the Links at Crowbush Cove has won accolades throughout the golf world. The course has been praised so loudly that people are venturing to Prince Edward Island just to play it. When they get there, they are finding that the tiny island has a surprising amount of good golf and great food, all at bargain prices—but the Links remains its prize.

McBroom calls it "a modern dunes course," and it is by no means an attempt to re-create a British Isles links course, as are *Pacific Dunes* or *Whistling Straits.* While it is on the coast, the course has little waterfront exposure; it uses a winding parkland routing, with each hole isolated from the others and lined with trees. But inside the tree line, between the woods and the fairways, are naturally occurring dunes, which in McBroom's style frame the corridors of play on almost every hole. Rather than the epic towering dunes of a Ballybunion or Pacific Dunes, it is a subdued course, rolling, with a very private feel. Just as McBroom constantly strives for in his work, each hole is an individual adventure.

Risk-reward choices abound, and it is the little strategic elements that make this course a magnet for critical acclaim. The third hole is a very reachable par-5, only 500 yards from the tips, but it has extensive fairway bunkering around the first- and second-shot landing areas. Avoiding the former is a must to get home in 2. In the traditional style, the green on a short par-5 is small and drops off in all directions, requiring a very accurate approach to reap the reward. In contrast, eleven is a massive par-5 with a large marsh—70 yards long—two-thirds of the way down the hole. Players who do not hit a very good tee shot have to seriously consider laying up and playing for bogey. This hole illustrates how a golf course can demand players execute tough shots but also give them a chance to avoid risk by playing for bogey. It also exemplifies McBroom's penchant for crafting varied holes, in this case two par-5s that stress much different things.

The course has ocean views from several holes; a handful play along

Coming Soon, More McBroom by the Sea!

Thomas McBroom must be the hardest-working architect in Canada, having worked on nearly sixty courses. But he has never opened one outside his own country—until now. With several European and American projects under construction, McBroom's first foray onto foreign soil will be Royal St. Kitts, part of a new Marriott resort on the sister island to Nevis, home to the stunning Four Seasons Nevis. This will complete one of the Caribbean's most compelling duos when the course and new hotel open in early 2003. As often happens, McBroom got a unique site—this one on a sandy peninsula that lets him route holes along both the Caribbean Sea and the Atlantic Ocean, with five holes running along the coast for their full length. The links-style, nonreturning layout will feature wide fairways and large greens, in part because the course is subject to high winds, and the features, as McBroom puts it, are on "a big scale." Expect a lot of inland water hazards, palm trees, and big clusters of bunkers that will come into play on "more aggressive lines." The acreage McBroom has been given is substantial, and he is building a big-time course to suit it.

inlets from the sea. The most noteworthy is eight, an absolutely stunning par-3 that plays over a watery cove or adjacent marsh (depending on tee and pin position) to a green set beneath an elevated ridge with shapely and elaborate bunkers cut into its face.

Tees, greens, and fairways at Crowbush Cove are all excellent-quality bent grass. While many golfers will not notice it, among these dunes and classic touches lies a very modern drainage and irrigation system, which ensures that the course is kept in first-rate condition despite very heavy play.

THE LINKS AT CROWBUSH COVE AT A GLANCE

(800) 377-8337

Golf Course Info: Practice area, walking allowed.

$-$$V, 4,965–6,903 yards, four tees. *Slope rating* 108–148. *Course rating* 67.3–75.2.

Lodging Info: There is a resort hotel at the course, the Rodd Crowbush. Prince Edward Island is small enough that you can drive almost anywhere in the main tourism district in forty-five minutes or less. The Links is less than twenty minutes from Charlottetown, the island's main city, so you can easily stay downtown. The top hotels are the Delta (800–268–1133, www.deltahotels.com) and the Rodd (800–565–RODD, www.Rodd-hotels.ca), both full-service urban branches of Canadian chains. For more information on the island, try 888–PEI–PLAY or www.peiplay.com.

Getting There: Drivers can take the Confederation Bridge from New Brunswick, while those flying can come right into Charlottetown on Air Canada.

When to Go: The golf season runs from late May through early October, but June, July, and August are the best months.

Travel Deals: Golf in Canada is generally a bargain, but the Links is a standout, with high-season rates of less than $50 for a world-class course. The Links is operated by a group that owns several other high-end, daily fee courses on Prince Edward Island, and multi-round passes offer further discounts. Lodging packages are also available at the on-site Rodd resort.

Golf Travel by Design Courses Nearby: Green Gables (fifteen minutes); the Algonquin (three hours).

Three excellent golf courses, a charming pedestrian resort village, and thoroughly French flair make Mont Tremblant the top golf destination in eastern Canada.

Mont Tremblant is the sister property to British Columbia's *Whistler* resort, and like its sibling it features a walking-only village comprised of shops, hotels, and restaurants. The resort has four golf courses (three of which are excellent), is in the heart of French Canada, and is a first-class destination that offers third-class prices for visiting Americans.

Two of the courses are right at the Tremblant village, while the other two are at the neighboring Gray Rock resort, a few minutes away. McBroom's effort, which translates to the Giant, was the first of the Tremblant pair, and despite its fearsome name it isn't overly long. Cut through dense forest in a parkland style, it has few parallel fairways. The site is wooded but was once covered by glaciers; as a result, there are ravines, valleys, and upthrust plateaus, all of which McBroom incorporates.

In classic style, the fairways are quite wide. Greens are simple by McBroom standards, with little undulation. This accommodates the resort player, while skilled golfers will be challenged from the back tees by the strategically placed carries over lakes and ravines. For instance, seventeen is a par-5 measuring just 491 yards, but the green is fronted by a deep and penal ravine.

It Takes a Village

Intrawest is Canada's leading ski resort developer—and among the world's most successful. The company has a unique formula that involves the construction of a pedestrian facility where everything from skiing to dining, lodging to shopping is available on foot; guests never need to drive once they arrive. The flagship village is in Whistler, but this was so successful that the company built versions at Tremblant as well as its golf-only resort, Sandestin. Competitors have started imitating the concept, and resort villages are cropping up from coast to coast.

In New Brunswick, Thomas McBroom got choice oceanfront land for the back nine of his Algonquin course. FAIRMONT HOTELS & RESORTS

While the site isn't as rocky as many of his more recent efforts, the extensive formation known as the Canadian Shield does poke its head above ground at Le Geant, where McBroom has incorporated some granite ledges as his trademark framing device. Like its newer sibling, the course is maintained in excellent shape despite heavy play, and since Tremblant is primarily a ski resort, tee markers on the course cleverly reflect this, with green circles, blue squares, black diamonds, and double black diamonds indicating increasing levels of difficulty.

The second course at the village is Le Diable (the Devil), designed by Michael Hurdzan and Dana Fry. Its name is derived from the many red waste areas carved from the iron-rich sand along the fairways. It is longer but with less elevation change than Le Geant. Most golf packages at the resort also include the two courses at Gray Rocks—La Belle and La Bête, or Beauty and the Beast. They got the names wrong, as La Belle is a tired and bland layout, not worth playing, while La Bête is an exceptional and original design from Canada's second best-known architect, Graham Cook. The Beast is a must-play addition to Tremblant's two home courses.

MONT TREMBLANT RESORT AT A GLANCE

(877) TREMBLANT, www.tremblant.ca

Golf Course Info: Practice areas, walking allowed.

Le Geant: $–$$V, 5,115–6,826 yards, four tees. *Slope rating* 113–131. *Course rating* 68.2–73.0.

Le Diable: $–$$V, 4,651–7,056 yards, four tees. *Slope rating* 122–131. *Course rating* 69–73.

La Belle: $–$$, 5,623–6,330 yards, four tees. *Slope rating* 118–119. *Course rating* 70–72.

Le Bête: $–$$V, 5,150–6,825 yards, four tees. *Slope rating* 119–131. *Course rating* 69.8–73.0.

Lodging Info: Tremblant village has several condos and hotels, the most luxurious of which is the Chateau Tremblant (800–441–1414, www.fairmont. com). Gray Rocks is a more rustic and traditional family mountain resort nearby (800–567–6767, www.grayrocks.com). Both offer packages including golf on all four courses, which are excellent values.

Getting There: Tremblant is ninety minutes from Montreal.

When to Go: Midspring to midfall. September features foliage season and stunning vistas.

Travel Deals: The Mont Tremblant Resort teams up with the nearby Gray Rocks Resort to offer unbeatable packages with seventy-two holes of golf. The Big Fore package lets you choose accommodations at either resort and play the combined four courses—for bargain prices that would be notable before the strong exchange rate but are fantastic after applying it.

Golf Travel by Design Courses Nearby: Le Chateau Montebello (forty minutes).

THE ALGONQUIN,
St. Andrews-By-The-Sea, New Brunswick

Next-generation architect Thomas McBroom breathes new life into a tired mail-order design from the revered Donald Ross.

Donald Ross may be the most respected of all golf course architects, but he is responsible for more courses than he ever could have visited. One of these was the Algonquin hotel's seaside course in New Brunswick, which Ross is said to have laid out in his Pinehurst office after having been mailed a topographic map of the site, which he never visited.

Nearly a century later the hotel decided the coastal setting on the Bay of Fundy was worth something more suited to its unique character, so owner Fairmont hotels—which runs *Banff Springs,* the *Jasper Park Lodge,*

Canada's First Seaside Resort

St. Andrews-By-The-Sea was founded by British loyalists fleeing north during the American Revolution, and is the nation's first seaside resort village, retaining much of its English charm. The houses along its waterfront main street are remarkably well preserved. At the historic Algonquin hotel, staff members still wear kilts.

and many other top golf resorts—brought in McBroom. The result is more of a redesign than a renovation, with half of the holes entirely new.

The course starts off with a wooded parkland nine, on the original part of the course, which McBroom routed around a variety of hazards, including ponds and creeks, while taking advantage of the site's elevation changes. But it is the new back nine where he really wows the visiting golfer with a mix of sea-view and oceanfront holes, including the signature twelfth, a downhill par-3 to a well-bunkered green that appears to be dramatically suspended on the edge of the sea. After this short but stunning hole, McBroom, as he likes to do, mixes things up with the longest par-4 on the course—483 yards from the tips. Playing along the coast from tee to green, at least it's downhill.

ALGONQUIN RESORT AT A GLANCE

(888) 483-6800, www.fairmont.com

Golf Course Info: Practice area, walking allowed.

Algonquin: $$, 5,713–6,908 yards, four tees. *Slope rating* 120–134. *Course rating* 67.2–73.7.

Woodland: Nine-hole short course designed by Donald Ross.

Lodging Info: The Algonquin is New Brunswick's premier resort hotel and features a Scottish atmosphere.

Getting There: St. Andrews-By-The-Sea is in southern New Brunswick, just across the border from Calais, Maine.

When to Go: Midspring to midfall. In summer the region gets sixteen hours of daylight.

Golf Travel by Design Courses Nearby: The Links at Crowbush Cove (three hours); Green Gables (three hours).

BELL BAY, *Cape Breton Island, Nova Scotia*

In remote Nova Scotia, where Alexander Graham Bell invented the telephone, Thomas McBroom reinvents classic parkland golf.

Stanley Thompson's *Cape Breton Highlands* has long been regarded as Canada's premier public course, but it takes a serious effort to reach it. Now the trip is doubly worthwhile, because Cape Breton offers a new and distinctly different challenge at the inland Bell Bay.

On the wooded hillsides surrounding Nova Scotia's Bras d'Or Lake, McBroom has laid out a classic parkland routing that also provides stunning views from every single hole, a rare achievement. As with his other courses, he has designed a layout that is competition worthy from the tips but resort friendly from the lesser tees. Wide fairways and generous landing areas are protected by traditionally shaped fairway and greenside bunkers. McBroom's framing beliefs are showcased on seventeen, a par-3 that can play anywhere from 86 to 182 yards over a deep ravine through a clearly defined corridor of tall and impressive trees.

Golf in Canada is usually a bargain for the visiting U.S. golfer, and high-quality layouts do not come at much lower prices than this natural beauty. Although it is among McBroom's more recent masterpieces, Bell Bay is one of his least "modern," a tribute to classic design and use of vista that could have just as easily have been undertaken by the other great Canadian architect, Stanley Thompson. It's a comparison that would surely make McBroom proud.

BELL BAY AT A GLANCE

(800) 868–4455, (800) 565–3077,
www.bellbaygolfclub.com

Golf Course Info: Practice area, walking.

$V, 5,165–7,037 yards, four tees. *Slope rating 117–137. Course rating 70–74.*

Lodging Info: There is no lodging associated with the course, but several local establishments offer golf packages and can be found through the course's Web site or toll-free number.

Getting There: Cape Breton is five hours from Halifax, or two hours from the small airport at Sydney.

When to Go: The short golf season runs from late May through late October.

Golf Travel by Design Courses Nearby: Cape Breton Highlands (ninety minutes).

ROCKY CREST GOLF CLUB, *Muskoka, Ontario*

Thomas McBroom, known for using rock in his design, rolls out his most impressive such course to date, the aptly named Rocky Crest.

After fiddling with the massive Canadian Shield, a rock formation that lies beneath much of eastern Canada, on private and public works throughout Quebec and Ontario, McBroom mastered the Shield with his critically lauded Rocky Crest.

The 250-acre site was basically one big piece of granite, some of it covered with dirt and trees, onto which McBroom dumped more than half a million tons of sand for fairways, leaving no doubt that despite his classical roots he is a very modern designer. In this manner McBroom "painted" his bent grass fairways over much of the granite, allowing him the luxury of leaving the rock exposed—which he did early and often, using it to frame fairways and greens. The signature sixth hole features a tee shot over a 180-yard-long sheet of granite to the front edge of the fairway, one of the more unusual forced carries in the game.

Despite the predominance of rock, which McBroom does not hesitate to wash of soil to make it more apparent and attractive, he also incorporated several existing lakes and framed many holes with towering trees. He loathes repetition, and in such a setting it is easy to fall into the trap of overreliance on the very dominant natural feature, granite. By using it in different ways, however—as aiming points, frames, hazards, and backdrops—McBroom executes his self-proclaimed goal of eighteen different holes linked by a single, rocky theme.

Rocky Crest opened in 2000 and immediately jumped onto the nation's short list of best courses. Since it is technically a private club, the course, like many of McBroom's, is very well maintained, although it allows public play in conjunction with certain lodging.

ROCKY CREST GOLF CLUB AT A GLANCE

(800) 461-4454, www.clublink.com

Golf Course Info: Practice area, walking.

$$$, 5,251–6,943 yards, five tees.

Lodging Info: Rocky Crest is a private club operated by Club Link, a large Canadian golf developer. Only members and guests of one of Club Link's four area resorts can play: the Grandview Inn, Sherwood Inn, Rocky Golf Resort, and Lake Joseph Club. These can all be booked through Club Link's Web site or toll-free number.

Getting There: Rocky Crest is about 70 miles north of Toronto.

When to Go: The short golf season runs from late May through late October.

Golf Travel by Design Courses Nearby: None.

Other Notable Thomas McBroon Courses You Can Play

- **Marriott Royal St. Kitts,** St. Kitts, West Indies
- **Kytaga,** Helsinki, Finland, (thirty-six holes)
- **Deerhurst Resort,** Huntsville, Ontario (thirty-six holes, with Bob Cupp)
- **Lake Joseph Club,** Carling, Ontario
- **Hockley Valley,** Orangeville, Ontario

Mike Strantz (1957–   )
Rebel with a Cause

Controversial is an adjective Mike Strantz cannot seem to avoid. No one else designs courses that polarize visiting golfers as much, from those who love them to those who swear never to return. But it seems more of the latter are critics and more of the former golfers, because if there is one thing a Mike Strantz design is sure to do, it is become popular. Strantz has built just six courses as solo designs, and on a percentage basis, no architect in history has done better in the ratings, with half his designs landing in the Top One Hundred. In fact, two are too new to have been rated, so three out of his first four cracked the list, which is unheard of. The obvious appeal of Strantz's layouts is also the basis for criticism: His courses are bold, visual, and larger than life, taking classic features and enlarging their scale.

Vision, Illusion, Drama

The secret to Strantz's success lies in the fact that he was an accomplished artist before turning to golf course design, so he sees things from a visual perspective. His design process includes eye-level drawings of the holes before they are laid out; he builds based on what he wants the player to see. He also uses optical illusion, an element that has become virtually extinct in golf since the advent of sprinkler-head yardage marking, yardage books, and GPS systems.

Strantz broke into the business with Tom Fazio, and his first major work was at the acclaimed **Wild Dunes.** He is an excellent golfer, has traveled extensively in the British Isles, and knows his design history. While many golfers leave his courses expressing wonder and saying they have never seen anything like it before, we see traces of classic design, especially from Northern Ireland, where Strantz's favorite course, **Royal County Down,** resides. He reflects the new breed of designer incorporating classic elements into fully modern courses, and while critics cannot always accept dune-lined valleys in the inland South, we can as long as they work and fit the land beautifully—and Strantz's do.

Almost all architects try to use the predominant natural features in their work, but with Strantz this is very evident. He has created courses in very close proximity to one another that have completely different feels because the sites were different. He also emphasizes the natural features more in the form of hazards than do most architects. What we like most about Strantz's work is that he, like MacKenzie, believes beauty and golf course design are inseparable. He usually only works on one project at a time, devoting himself to it; to date he has designed nothing but public, daily fee courses, a boon to the traveling golfer. When you visit them you can expect:

HIS COURSES ARE BOLD, VISUAL, AND

LARGER THAN LIFE, TAKING CLASSIC FEATURES

AND ENLARGING THEIR SCALE.

- **A dramatic opening hole.** Being visually driven, Strantz grabs golfers' attention right away. While they are very different layouts, for instance, both Royal New Kent and Tobacco Road begin with downhill tee shots into a valley between dunes.

- **Width, on and off the fairway.** Strantz fervently believes that wider is better, so his work not only features broad landing areas but also focuses on what he calls "air width," meaning very few trees in play, which accommodates a lot of different shot shapes and encourages players to swing away on longer holes. He thinks that width is important for a course to accommodate a wide spectrum of playing abilities.

- **Deception and intimidation.** "My courses look visually intimidating, but the fairways are sometimes 80 yards wide. Once you get to where you hit your ball, you say, 'Wow, there's a lot of room out here.'" He accomplishes this in a variety of ways, such as pinching the fairway tight just in front of the tee and then widening it again, playing over a rise, or choking the beginning of the fairway with ominous hazards short of the prime landing area.

- **Varied and multiple tees.** Having built only fully modern courses, he uses four or more tee boxes on every design. But since Strantz designs his courses so the hazards and doglegs come into play at certain distances relative to the tees, it is important that you look at not just the overall length in choosing a tee, but also how far you have to carry the ball to get into position.

- **Multiple strategic options.** "For most players, the direct line to the hole is fraught with frustration and failure," says Strantz. Because he is cognizant of the different abilities of players who will be using his purely public layouts, he provides alternative paths.

Perhaps the most obvious Strantz traits are the boldness of his vision and the artistic nature of his work. Whichever of the following you visit, you are not likely to forget it.

TOBACCO ROAD, *Sanford, North Carolina*

The last place most designers would build a course is forty minutes from Pinehurst, one of the world's greatest golf destinations, but Strantz's masterpiece is more than worth the drive.

You don't *play* Tobacco Road so much as you *experience* it. You literally dive in on the first tee, hitting from an elevated ledge into a dune-lined valley pinched by mounds, making it appear much narrower than it is. Before you can catch your breath, the second shot requires you to carry a blind ridge with a tiny notch in the center, not unlike the

Known for his emphasis on visual perfection, Mike Strantz even designed beautiful cart paths at Tobacco Road. COURTESY OF TOBACCO ROAD

famed Alps hole at Prestwick. This is the start of a roller-coaster ride that requires a variety of shots, strategic thought, and complete attention, a task made nearly impossible by the imposing setting and visual drama.

In our opinion, Tobacco Road is Strantz's crown jewel to date, a course so refreshing and unique it warrants its own trip; in the entire region we'd play only Pinehurst Numbers Two and Eight before it. It also captures all the elements that Strantz believes in. While the name refers to the local tobacco-based economy, the actual site once contained a cement plant and is full of sandy, quarrylike excavations. Waste areas are the theme at Tobacco Road, but they are used in a manner different from any other course. Usually waste areas are flat expanses of sand flanking fairways. Here they're three-dimensional sandy canyons, craters, and knolls through which the course is laid out. There are no cart paths; you drive through the vast waste areas themselves, which are often built with ramps to get back to the fairway, as if the course were one vast construction site. Since you cannot always see beyond the next rise, Strantz is able to install broad expanses of grass while making it appear there is nowhere to go.

Risk-reward choices abound, such as the unforgettable fourth, a question-mark-shaped par-5 running around a deep, sandy crater. Play safely to the right and follow the lush fairway, or lay up at the edge of the crater and play an all-or-nothing second shot straight across at the green (which is closer than it appears). This hole is immediately followed by a drivable four, with a perfectly straight line from tee to green over a 300-yard waste canyon to a green with a false front. A daunting drive, it also offers a simple 2-shot alternative via a large fairway set off to the right of the hazard. Strantz continues in this vein, tempting you while also offering safe passage. Along the way he incorporates every element of the existing site, right down to the foundations of the cement factory.

The course is also filled with very modern touches. One par-3 has two different teeing areas, creating a hole that plays completely differently from day to day; another features a narrow green 60 yards wide, creating pin positions so different it might as well have two greens. The par-3 fourteenth has seven tee boxes terraced into the side of a hill, playing down over a pond to a tricky green, with yardages that can play from 80 to 204 yards. One par-4 finishes with a blind shot to a green tucked between sandy ridges. And so on, and so on. It is easy to consider these elements and conclude that Tobacco Road is gimmicky or overdone, but the fact is, every single one of these holes is thoughtfully and artfully executed, and you will want to play it again. We do.

TOBACCO ROAD AT A GLANCE

(877) 284-3762, www.tobaccoroadgolf.com

Golf Course Info: Practice area, walking allowed.

$$–$$$V, 5,094–6,554 yards, four tees. *Slope rating* 124–150. *Course rating* 66.1–73.2.

Lodging Info: There is no lodging available at the course, but chances are if you are in the area, you should be staying in Pinehurst.

Getting There: Southern Pines is served by US Airways commuter service and Amtrak. The Raleigh, Greensboro, and Charlotte airports are all within two hours. It is four and a half hours from Washington, D.C.

When to Go: Golf is played year-round, but spring and fall are high season, followed by the hot, humid summer months and the winter.

Golf Travel by Design Courses Nearby: Pinehurst (forty minutes); Tot Hill Farm (thirty minutes).

Strantz on the Cheap

All too often the traveling golfer is faced with overpriced golf or regions where all the courses are expensive. Not with Mike Strantz. To date he has done nothing but daily fee public layouts with no resort component; across the board they offer tremendous bargains. Only his two Myrtle Beach layouts, True Blue and Caledonia, break the $100 mark at peak times, but as part of a Myrtle package they can be played for much less. Royal New Kent and Stonehouse hover in the $50 range, at the very low end of courses so highly ranked, and Tot Hill Farm is simply one of the nation's best bargains, with green fees between $25 and $49.

TOT HILL FARM, *Asheboro, North Carolina*

Strantz's newest course got off to a rocky start, since the main features are exposed ledge and huge boulders.

For his latest public course, Strantz returned to the fertile North Carolina countryside near his stunning Tobacco Road. But as with his other works, proximity does not mean similarity, and Tot Hill Farm has a flavor all its own.

While Tobacco Road has an endless array of bunkers, big and small, since Tot Hill Farm is built through sandy quarries it has less than a dozen on the entire layout. Once again, Strantz tunes in to the predominant natural feature: rock, in the form of exposed ledges, rock faces, and boulders. Streams also wander through the site, creating natural waterfalls and convenient hazards. The exposed rock is used to great visual and strategic effect, creating unique hazards made of clumps of thick rough and boulders. The course also has extensive elevation changes, more than 250 feet throughout the site, which is very unusual. In comparison, the *Cascades course at the Homestead*—considered by many critics to be the prototype of mountain design—has only 230 feet. Strantz says this is possibly the best piece of land he has had to work with.

It also reflects the current change in routing style toward less conventional par arrangements. The course has five par-3s and five par-5s, but only eight par-4s—versus the usual ten. The front side includes an unusual stretch that goes par-3, -5, -5, -3, and the course closes in dramatic fashion with a par-3, -5, -4, -5 finale.

TOT HILL FARM AT A GLANCE

(800) 868-4455, www.tothillfarm.com

Golf Course Info: Practice area, walking.

$V, 4,853–6,614 yards, four tees. *Slope rating* 106–135. *Course rating* 64.5–72.2.

Lodging Info: There is no lodging associated with the course, but motels can be found nearby, and the course is about forty minutes from Pinehurst.

Getting There: Asheboro is less than half an hour from both the Greensboro and Raleigh airports.

When to Go: Golf is played year-round, but summers can be hot and humid, and winters can bring occasional frost delays and colder weather.

Golf Travel by Design Courses Nearby: Pinehurst (forty minutes); Tobacco Road (thirty minutes).

ROYAL NEW KENT AND STONEHOUSE,
Williamsburg, Virginia

Two nearby courses, as different from one another as you can imagine, stunned the golf world when both debuted on the Top One Hundred lists, serving notice that Mike Strantz had arrived.

Strantz contends that his biggest single priority on every site is to incorporate the prominent natural features, especially into his use of hazards. For proof of his convictions, look no farther than the Williamsburg area. Twenty minutes apart, these two courses bear almost no resemblance to each other, except in the use of Strantz's underlying optical design, which tricks the eye. Stonehouse is a hilly parkland course bisected with ravines; Royal New Kent, a rough, sandy, and treeless inland homage to the courses of Northern Ireland. Actually, they do have other things in common: They are both bargains and have remained wildly popular with traveling golfers.

Royal New Kent is not one of our favorite Strantz designs, mainly because of a mandate from the developer to conceal the cart paths as much as possible. The result is a course that is difficult to walk and aggravating to ride. Elevated fairways are separated from the paths by a steep slope, so once you get on the cart paths, you lose all perspective. It is even difficult to find the correct tee boxes for the next hole. As a result, much time at

Golf's Odd Couples

Mike Strantz's work is more regional than any other top architect, for the simplest of reasons: He prefers his own bed to a hotel room. While many of his peers are traveling the world by private jet designing courses from Morocco to Malaysia, Strantz, a dedicated family man, has decided not to leave home until his children head off to college. For this reason, he has created courses only in the Carolinas and Virginia, where he lives. But more interestingly, all six of his existing layouts are grouped in nearby pairs: Royal New Kent and Stonehouse outside Williamsburg; Tot Hill Farm and Tobacco Road outside Pinehurst; and True Blue and Caledonia across the street from one another in Myrtle Beach. In every single case, though, the pairs feature two radically different designs that bear little similarity. Thus they completely avoid repetition for the traveling golfer.

Royal New Kent is spent going backward or turning around. This small element, the cart path, shows how much design affects our enjoyment of the game, and in this case offsets many of the good things Strantz did on the course. Perhaps if you played it often you would unlock the secrets of its transportation routing, but the first-time visitor is constantly distracted by fear of getting lost.

Architecturally, Royal New Kent delivers a full dose of Strantz design. When he says he draws his holes from eye-level perspective, this is what he means. Standing on a tee at Royal New Kent, a narrow fairway flanked by ominous bunkers may rise over a ridge and disappear, presenting a scary and slightly uphill tee shot. In reality, the fairway opens broadly after the knoll, the hazards are short of the landing area, and there is plenty of room to play. The fairway may even go downhill, increasing the length of your tee shot. But from the tee, you see little of the hole, which unfolds as you play it. Our favorite hole at Royal New Kent is the first, from an elevated tee into a valley between faux dune slopes, re-creating the spirit of courses like **Royal Portrush.** In true Strantz fashion you have a wide landing area—but must also clear the corner of a dogleg to see the approach to the green. It immediately sucks you into the course. There are those in golf who criticize every attempt to capture the links feel in this country, especially inland; this is the main criticism that has been leveled at the course by its few detractors. But Strantz merely set out to capture the links mood, not re-create its routing, and he is aided by the very unusual fact that he had an almost entirely treeless site, a standard links characteristic rarely found in the Virginia countryside.

Stonehouse, while much less brash and dramatic, is the better course from a design and playability point of view. Its major natural features are elevation changes, ravines, and pronounced contours, slopes, and ridges. Strantz created an artful routing incorporating virtually every shift the ground made and used these to create strategic holes and force choices of path and carry. With many elevation changes between tees and greens, golfers have to repeatedly choose their irons precisely, and seek out flat landing areas and good lies. Stonehouse is a more cerebral course that quietly charms you, especially on its very strong back nine. It's also much more playable from a cart perspective than its more ostentatious neighbor.

ROYAL NEW KENT AND STONEHOUSE AT A GLANCE

Royal New Kent: (866) 284-6534 (tee times only), (804) 966-7023, www.traditionalclubs.com
Stonehouse: (866) 284-6534 (tee times only), (757) 566-1138, www.traditional clubs.com

Golf Course Info: Practice areas, walking allowed.

Royal New Kent: $–$$V, 5,231–6,985 yards, four tees. *Slope rating* 130–144. *Course rating* 70.8–74.9.

Stonehouse: $–$$V, 5,013–6,963 yards, four tees. *Slope rating* 121–140. *Course rating* 69.1–75.0.

Lodging Info: Nearby Williamsburg has lodging options at every price point, from motels to the very luxurious Williamsburg Inn, the impeccably decorated jewel in the resort's crown (800–447–8679, www.cwf.org). You'll also find a full selection of chain motels and hotels throughout greater Williamsburg, a popular tourist destination.

Getting There: Williamsburg is midway between the Norfolk and Richmond airports; it's just over an hour to either.

When to Go: Early spring to late fall. For the best weather after the crowds, try October or early November.

Golf Travel by Design Courses Nearby: Golden Horseshoe (twenty-five minutes).

CALEDONIA AND TRUE BLUE,
Pawley's Island, South Carolina

Myrtle Beach's recent renaissance can be traced to these side-by-side Strantz layouts that showed value golf could also be first-rate.

Considering that Myrtle Beach has more than a hundred public courses designed by a wide slate of big-name architects, it was a surprise to the golf community that an unknown designer could build his first course here and easily take top honors for the region. His follow-up, True Blue, is also his most controversial design.

True Blue is the only Strantz course we'd skip. Its prominent natural feature is sand, which is used to craft endless tee-to-green waste areas. Any golfer having an off day may forget that golf courses are supposed to have grass on them, because shot after shot will be played from the sandy hazards or, worse, the ample marsh. Strantz's courses are, without fail, difficult, especially from the back tees. In the classic tradition, however, he usually offers countless risk-reward choices and bailouts, so that conservative or less skilled players can choose a safer route. But from any tees, and for any ability, there are some very penal holes at True Blue, such as a near-island peninsula green jutting into a lake from the mainland on the left, with severe drop-offs in front, in back, and on the right side, and no bailout area. Island greens are by their very nature penal holes, so they are almost always short with generous and receptive greens. Not this one.

Given the long and sandy struggle that True Blue can be, it is hard to believe that a very different Mike Strantz course—his best after Tobacco Road—sits literally across the street and is the must-play course in Myrtle Beach. Caledonia Golf and Fish Club was his solo debut in 1994, and remains the highest ranked of all his layouts. Built on a former rice plantation, it oozes southern charm from its plantationlike setting, complete with lakes, streams, huge oaks, and other hardwood trees. A parkland routing on a surprisingly small lot, just 125 acres, Strantz uses every piece of wetland and adds strategic bunkers to constantly create risk-reward decisions. While Caledonia offers just as many opportunities to get into trouble as True Blue, it also features far more ways to avoid it, achieving the hard-to-reach goal of tough but fair golf. It is also a beautiful course, and not visually repetitive like its neighbor. A hole cut by a diagonal creek epitomizes the heroic carry option, while his extremely long fifteenth—a par-4 that stretches 462 yards from the tips—doglegs sharply around an enormous and deep corner bunker. To have a go at birdie, players must lay up treacherously close to the bunker, while there is plenty of room for the safer, much longer route to the right. This is classic golf, and it is classic Strantz.

Caledonia Golf and Fish Club: (888) 483–6800,
www.fishclub.com
True Blue, Pawley's Island, South Carolina: (888)
483–6800, www.truebluegolf.com

Golf Course Info: Practice areas, walking allowed.

Caledonia: $$–$$$V, 4,957–6,526 yards, four tees. *Slope rating* 113–132. *Course rating* 66.7–70.9.

True Blue: $$–$$$, 4,920–7,090 yards, five tees. *Slope rating* 112–139. *Course rating* 67.2–73.8.

Lodging Info: Pawley's Island is at the southernmost end of the Myrtle Beach strip and has some lodging of its own, most notably Pawley's Plantation, with a very good Jack Nicklaus course (800–367–9959, www.pawleysplantation.com) and Litchfield Plantation with three courses (888–714–5992, www.litchfield beach.com). These are minutes away. The rest of Myrtle is anywhere from twenty to sixty minutes away and contains more than a hundred public golf courses—and even more hotels, motels, and resorts. Almost all offer packages combining lodging and golf at lower prices than arranging them separately. Myrtle also has the best visitor bureau of any golf destination, with a detailed printed catalog of options, helpful live operators, and a very good Web site. Book your trip here and you will be able to stay and play for $40–100 per day (800–845–4653, www.golfholiday.com).

Getting There: The Myrtle Beach Airport is twenty minutes from Pawley's Island.

When to Go: Golf is played year-round, but spring is high season. Summer is hot and humid, while winter temperatures can dip into the thirties.

Travel Deals: While these are among the priciest of Strantz's designs and the upper echelon of Myrtle Beach area courses, they are still available through a number of lodging and golf packages offered by hundreds of area hotels. Some add a premium for these courses, while others offer packages specifically for the region's cream of the crop, but in any case, the packages are almost always a notable savings off the daily fee rates.

Golf Travel by Design Courses Nearby: The Dunes (forty-five minutes); Legend's Heathland (thirty minutes); Ocean course at Kiawah Island (two hours); Wild Dunes (two hours).

Tom Doak (1961–)

An Architecture Critic Who Gets Rave Reviews

I f the golf course design business was a popularity contest, Tom Doak might have trouble finding work. Before he designed his first course or built a single hole, he had established a reputation as one of the industry's most knowledgeable architectural critics. In the process he spoke his mind, often cutting his much more famous peers down to size. It would be a safe bet that some of them have not forgotten. But the only popularity that matters in golf course design is how popular layouts are with players, and based on his recent success it is unlikely that Doak will ever lack for work again. As he well knows, the industry is rife with superlatives; so many courses and holes have been described as "among the greatest on earth" that the sheer number of top courses defies description. This is partly accurate, since there are a lot of great courses—the more than a hundred in this book alone will thrill the traveling golfer. But when it comes to Doak's latest work, Pacific Dunes, it seems no superlatives are beyond reason. It is the only layout in these pages—and one of only two ever—to have received a perfect twenty-point rating from *The Golf Insider.* Some reputable, knowledgeable golf experts have called it nothing less than the best course on earth. For an architect whose work can be counted on fingers and toes, it does not get much better than that.

Talking the Talk

Doak studied landscape architecture at Cornell University and somehow managed to convince his alma mater that, after graduation, it would be a good use of the school's funds to send him on a fact-finding mission of sorts, a critical study of the great golf courses of the British Isles. During what must have been a very enjoyable year, he visited and played every course of note and some lesser tracts as well—nearly 200 in all. At the tender age of twenty-three he was put in charge of the ratings for *Golf Magazine,* which publishes the most important golf course rankings, public and private, in alternating years. He subsequently repeated his British Isles experiment with trips to the Far East, Australia, South Africa, and other far-flung golfing destinations.

But what put Doak on the map was his book *The Confidential Guide to Golf Courses,* a world atlas of the nearly 1,000 courses he has studied in person. In the guide he pulls no punches and does not hesitate to knock and even occasionally ridicule the work of his peers. The book is well executed, useful, and controversial. We don't agree with every point Doak makes, but he forcefully argues for his points of view and takes his craft very seriously. Rarely criticized by the almost universally friendly golf press, architects are not used to bad reviews—but to get them from a fellow

HE BELIEVES IN CONFRONTING THE GOLFER

VISUALLY WITH INTIMIDATING OR BEAUTIFUL

HAZARDS, BUT HE ALSO OFFERS LESS

SKILLED PLAYERS A WAY AROUND THEM.

architect is unheard of. For this reason, we are sure that more than a few designers were hoping Doak would fall flat on his face in his own design attempts.

Walking the Walk

We are happy to report that Doak disappointed them miserably, while creating enduring gems the traveling golfer will come to adore, admire, and even become addicted to. The scary part is that while Pacific Dunes would be the career layout for any designer, in this book or otherwise, it may not even be Doak's best. He has just scratched the professional surface. In years to come he will almost certainly design other masterpieces that would fit equally well with the entries to follow.

Doak's love of the British Isles is obvious in his work, which goes beyond the recent neoclassical movement to offer a minimalist, back-to-basics ethic. When you visit his courses, you can expect to see:

- **Bold, firm, undulating or crowned greens.** On many of the great courses of the British Isles, the greens are a golf hole unto themselves, with dramatic ridges and slopes, which Doak is not afraid to re-create. At his Black Forest layout in Michigan, for example, he uses severely crowned greens that fit the course perfectly. He has stated his belief that the greens should be the focal point of the course and control the way shots are played. Toward this end, his greens are often canted in one direction—intentionally set up to welcome a particular shot shape, be it fade or draw—which in turn pressures the better player to seek a particular part of the fairway from the tee.

- **Visible and dramatic hazards.** Like MacKenzie, he believes in confronting the golfer visually with intimidating or beautiful hazards, but as a devotee of playability he also offers less skilled players a way around them. His extensive bunkering replicates the historical best, especially the work of George Thomas, Alister MacKenzie, Walter Travis, and C. B. Macdonald.

- **"Theme" holes.** Doak knows as well as anyone alive what a redan hole is, and he makes his own, along with other holes that evoke features of classic golf. Not limited to a love of the links, he is equally likely to introduce the player to parkland or heathland traits.

- **Traditional construction.** Doak is not opposed to earthmoving, and in fact selected *Shadow Creek* as one of his select group of top courses in the world, shocked at how well such an artificial course could be executed. He himself moved plenty of dirt at the Legends course in Myrtle Beach. But the bulk of his designs are minimalist in terms of shaping; indeed, he built four courses with virtually no earthmoving other than irrigation ponds. He also uses old-school elements such as fescue grass, which he features on several of his designs, and firm, fast fairways and greens. This in turn leads to:

- **Ground-game-friendly designs.** By keeping fairways hard and opening entrances to "complex" green complexes, Doak encourages bump-and-

Tom Doak designed his masterpiece, Pacific Dunes, amid the rugged dunescape of Oregon's coast, the closest thing in this country to Scottish linksland.

run play. He believes golf courses should be playable no matter how much wind there is.

- **Multiple strategic options and shotmaking variety.** Doak often gives players two distinct alternatives: the newer American airborne game or a more traditional entry to the greens along the ground. But he does not stop there. More than almost any other recent designer, he sets his courses up to appreciate and reward shot shaping. While resort players can navigate the course easily enough, scratch golfers are rewarded for their ability to work the ball.

One Doak trait that is not obvious to the naked eye is his obsession with routing. He says that his firm spends much more time on the routing than most designers, trying to incorporate as many of the interesting natural features and contours as possible. Thus at Pacific Dunes, he has one of the most unorthodox routings ever built in terms of the par sequence of holes, but it was the way he thought the jigsaw puzzle of fitting holes to the land worked best. It is important to note that while Doak is well versed in tradition, and a fan of it, he is not a slave to it. He does not hesitate to embrace the newest developments in the game if he respects them. He offers, for instance, two green complexes on one hole and two tee complexes on another, both rotating from day to day, at his incredible Pacific Dunes course.

Doak's Next Challenge
Lies South of the Border

After Pacific Dunes, Tom Doak will not be intimidated when following in the footsteps of other highly acclaimed courses. His next challenge is the construction of the third course at Cábo del Sol after the highly rated Nicklaus layout and the new Weiskopf design. It is Doak's first effort outside the United States, and will be his highest-profile course besides Pacific Dunes. It will also be very different from anything in Baja. Nicklaus got what he called one of the greatest pieces of coastal land he had ever seen, and Weiskopf had similar topography, but Doak's course, to be called the Vista layout, is set on an inland mountain with more than 400 feet of elevation change—an astonishing amount for any location—and features views of the ocean for miles in every direction.

PACIFIC DUNES, *Bandon, Oregon*

Pacific Dunes has been called everything from the best links course in this country to the best course in the world, period. We will go so far as to say that along with its sibling, Bandon Dunes, there is no better thirty-six-hole resort in golf.

Mike Keiser, founder of Bandon Dunes, spent three years searching for the perfect coastal land on which to build the best links courses in the nation. He found it in remote Bandon, Oregon. The result is almost too good to be true: The first course, David Kidd's Bandon Dunes, debuted at number three on *Golf Magazine*'s list behind, just Pebble Beach and Pinehurst Number Two. Its follow-up, Doak's Pacific Dunes, is too new to have been ranked, but the golf community has universally proclaimed it much better than its companion.

As with all great links courses, the starting point is fabulous land. It is sandy and duned, with gorse, shore pines, and Scotch broom; it was also receptive to the planting of fescue grasses. Of course, it is windswept and firm, but unlike many of its Scottish counterparts it boasts stunning sea views and dramatic cliffs. In short, it is perfect for golf.

Doak's parcel has a greater variety of features and more elevation change, and in his typical fashion offers many shotmaking challenges. The course begins among the inland shore pines, reaches and follows the sea, and returns to the pines for a dramatic finish. Along the way it passes through massive dunes, raw sand scrapes of natural, grassy waste areas, and blowout bunkers that blend into the natural setting while offering beautiful visual drama. The final few holes appear carved from the earth itself, rolling through valleys and ridges of gorse and bunkers.

Pacific Dunes is so good that there is no signature hole, just one unique and thrilling challenge after another. Eleven is a short par-3 along the coastal cliffs, twelve dips back into the scrubby trees for a wonderful heathland-style challenge, and thirteen returns to the ocean for an amazing par-4, which is the longest on the course. Its green is cut into the base of a six-story dune perched atop a cliff, and nothing could make it any better.

A trend among the new architects is routings that are less symmetrical than tradition dictates, but this depends on whose tradition you mean. In the modern era, encompassing most domestic courses, a par of 72 with ten par-4s and four par-3s and par-5s has become standard. But the Ailsa course at Turnberry, perhaps the greatest links of all, with a par of 69, is more than fit to host the British Open. Great courses deviate from the norm all the time, and even unabashededly modern designer Jack Nicklaus throws in back-to-back par 3s when the Mexican coastline at *Cabo del Sol* dictates it, or a nineteenth hole as he sees fit. Mike Strantz does not hesitate to reach his par-72 with five long and short holes, and Alister MacKenzie's famous Cypress Point has both back-to-back par-3s and par-5s.

But no one takes this trend as far as Doak, who said, "We don't care about exactly what the par and total yardage are. We want every hole to be distinctly memorable." He got this at Pacific Dunes, where he used a very unconventional, nonreturning par-71 routing that stretches just 6,737 yards from the tips and includes just one par-3 and one par-5 on the front, but has four par-3s and three par-5s, with only two par-4s, on the back. It's an unheard-of mix that keeps the rhythm of the once-in-a-lifetime round alive.

A year before Pacific Dunes opened, it would have been foolish to think that Kidd's Bandon Dunes, one of the world's top courses, would be overshadowed at its own namesake resort. It would also be a mistake to miss out on Kidd's amazing design. More exposed than its sibling, it offers wider fairways and larger greens, plus pot and sod-walled bunkers throughout. It too has a slew of stunning oceanfront holes, beginning with four and five, which play along 100-foot-high cliffs. But few holes on earth rival sixteen, a par-4 requiring a heroic drive across a gorse-filled chasm to a two-tiered fairway. Reaching the more desirable upper level leaves you a short pitch to a green floating on the edge of the cliff—with nothing but the Pacific Ocean for those who go long. A par here is one you will never forget, and a trip to Bandon Dunes is one you will want to make soon. A third course is currently under way, being designed by rising star Kyle Phillips, of Kingsbarns fame.

(888) 345-6008, www.bandondunesgolf.com

Golf Course Info: Practice area, walking only, caddies available.

Pacific Dunes: $$$V, 5,107–6,557 yards, four tees. *Slope rating* 125–133. *Course rating* 71.1–72.9.

Bandon Dunes: $$$V, 5,178–7,259 yards, six tees. *Slope rating* 128–145. *Course rating* 69.7–74.6.

Lodging Info: The courses are open to the public, but the only nearby lodging is the on-site hotel at Bandon Dunes, the Lodge, which offers just twenty-one rooms and forty-eight cottages, plus two restaurants and a pub. Like the courses, it captures the British Isles atmosphere of places that exist mainly for playing golf.

Getting There: The North Bend airport, with limited commuter flights, is thirty minutes away. Eugene is two hours by car, and Portland is four.

When to Go: Golf is played year-round, but May through October is high season; rain is frequent in other months. Wind is omnipresent, but especially notable in July.

Travel Deals: These courses are so fantastic that they are bargains even at the $100-plus price tags they command. But golf gluttons can save even more: Bandon Dunes offers half-price replays and free additional golf for anyone who can tackle more than thirty-six-holes in a day.

Golf Travel by Design Courses Nearby: None.

Heathland 2: The Sequel?

After the success of Doak's Heathland layout, the first course at the Legends complex, P. B. Dye undertook the Moorland course, which is also quite a good tract. Doak returned to build a third course, the Parkland, but did not see eye to eye with the Legends developer, whose suggested changes were unacceptable to Doak, causing him to withdraw from the project. The course now lists the developer's Legend's Design Group as architect.

LEGENDS HEATHLAND COURSE,
Myrtle Beach, South Carolina

With his biggest earthmoving project to date, Doak brought his British Isles features to a flat site in Golf City, USA.

As an architecture critic, some of Doak's sternest ridicule has been directed at the countless alleged "Scottish-style" courses built in this country with little or no resemblance to the real thing. So it was a risky proposition for him to take on the same challenge—in and Myrtle Beach, of all places, a haven for parkland designs fraught with water hazards.

Ironically, the course's name is completely misleading, a fact that probably matters much more to architectural purist Doak than to the average visitor. It was intended to be a links-style course, and was originally called Linksland, but the phone operators taking reservations for the complex had trouble with pronunciation, and the name was changed to a much different meaning. The course was, and is, a tribute to links golf.

To achieve this, the first thing Doak did was to remove the trees, mostly pines, from the 175-acre site. This brings the wind into play. Doak then added gorse, heather, pot bunkers, and the usual links features. He pushed dirt to form "sand dunes"; drainage ditches became "wee burns." The greens are huge, not because Doak admires this trait, but to allow them to handle the very high volume of play that passes through the complex. Still, the greens add a traditional touch and resemble those on the Old course at St. Andrews. Like those, it is possible to stand over putts of more than 100 feet. With shaved collars and firm approaches, the course is clearly set up to facilitate the ground game; still, unlike the rock-hard greens often found on true links, these are receptive to lofted shots, and better players can stick the pins.

Perhaps the best, and most subtle, element of the course is its fairways, which have a lot more contour than the eye perceives on the tee. Like those in the Old Country, they produce some odd bounces and—in the right places—a lot of extra roll. It is worth taking the extra moment on the tee box to try to perceive the flow of the landing area in order to select the spot that will maximize your distance.

P. B. Dye's Moorland course is the other highly rated course at the fifty-four-hole complex, and it's intentionally more difficult. Bulkheaded hazards and vast bunkers are meant to be reminiscent of Pete Dye's Stadium course at PGA West, but fortunately it doesn't approach the extremes of that design and does a very effective job of balancing challenge and playability—especially important in this high-traffic resort setting. Landing areas are wide but bunkers are deep and penal, and greens are small. The result is a course that accommodates all levels of skill but resists low scores. The third course, the Parkland, is actually the longest and most difficult. Tree lined, it showcases elaborate bunkering in the style of Riviera. While it's not what Doak wanted, it is another solid layout. As a result, the Legends is one of the top complexes among the many at Myrtle Beach.

(800) 377-2315, www.legendsgolf.com

Golf Course Info: Practice areas, walking allowed.

Heathland Course: $$V, 5,060–6,785 yards, three tees. *Slope rating* 112–127. *Course rating* 69.0–72.3.

Moorland Course: $$V, 4,905–6,799 yards, three tees. *Slope rating* 118–128. *Course rating* 69.8–73.1.

Parkland Course: $$, 5,518–7,170 yards, four tees. *Slope rating* 125–137. *Course rating* 70.3–74.9.

Lodging Info: The Legends has a "Scottish-style" hotel with a pub named for Scotland's Ailsa Craig; the Gleneagles condos are another on-site option. Both are as nondescript and middle of the road as most of Myrtle Beach's vast array of lodging. For other choices contact 800–846–5552, www.golfholiday.com.

Getting There: The Myrtle Beach Airport is thirty minutes from the Legends.

When to Go: Golf is played year-round, but spring is high season. Summer is hot and humid; winter temperatures can dip into the thirties.

Travel Deals: These courses are available through a number of lodging and golf packages offered by hundreds of Myrtle Beach's hotels. These packages almost always offer a notable savings off the daily fee rates.

Golf Travel by Design Courses Nearby: The Dunes (forty-five minutes); True Blue and Caledonia (thirty minutes); Ocean course at Kiawah Island (two hours); Wild Dunes (two hours).

HIGH POINTE GOLF CLUB, *Williamsburg, Michigan*

Tom Doak learned some valuable lessons on his first design, such as not to expect a happy ending once his work is done.

Tom Doak grew up in golf-crazed northern Michigan and returned home for his very first design, High Pointe. It established him immediately as a minimalist: The only significant earthmoving was to dig an irrigation pond.

High Pointe showcases many of Doak's traits, especially around the greens. These are heavily contoured, but many are also canted or sloped to one side to force players to shape approach shots for the best results. He used fescue grass in the fairways and built them to be firm and fast to encourage the ground game. He left the natural and unusual contours in the fairways, ensuring that players would encounter many different types of lies and stances, just as on his favorite British Isles courses. In the spirit of early golf, other than the green complexes, golfers play over the terrain as nature left it. Walking is encouraged.

High Pointe opened in 1989 and immediately landed on *Golf Magazine*'s Top One Hundred, helping establish Doak's place in the field of golf design. But the course has not been maintained in the way Doak intended when he designed it, and the owners changed one hole completely. The biggest difference is that the fairways and greens have been dramatically softened in contrast to Doak's fast, firm design; this has largely eliminated the ground-game option and turned the course into a very modern stick-the-pin type of layout. This has been a sore point for Doak, but also a learning experience that many architects struggle with: Once they are done, they have no more say over how the course is handled. Maintenance styles and budgets can dramatically change a course—for better or worse.

Still, while Doak aficionados consider the course "ruined" by the changes, High Pointe is an excellent layout that captures the purity of the game. Even without the bump and run, it's well worth playing, especially since it is a tremendous bargain.

HIGH POINTE GOLF CLUB AT A GLANCE

(800) 753-7888, www.highpointegolf.com

Golf Course Info: Practice areas, walking allowed.

$V, 4,974–6,890 yards, four tees. *Slope rating* 120–136. *Course rating* 68.5–73.3.

Lodging Info: High Pointe has packages available with several inexpensive nearby hotels that, like the course itself, are true bargains. The course is outside Traverse City, which is also home to the upscale Grand Traverse Resort.

Getting There: The Traverse City airport is twenty minutes away and offers frequent commuter service in summer months.

When to Go: Golf is played from mid-April to mid-October, but June through September are ideal months.

Golf Travel by Design Courses Nearby: Black Forest (thirty minutes).

BLACK FOREST COURSE AT WILDERNESS VALLEY, *Gaylord, Michigan*

At this, Doak's most difficult creation to date, even *he* thinks it may be too tough.

Many of the more interesting stories in the history of golf course design begin with an owner asking for a difficult course. At Wilderness Valley they already had one course that was knocked for being too easy, so Tom Doak was charged with building a second layout that would not receive the same criticism. With a course rating of 75.3, he succeeded.

The name comes from the very dark trees on the site, and the course takes full advantage of the ominous woods in its defenses; the tenth hole, for example, forces a shot to be threaded between two trees. But the real star at Black Forest is the bunkering, an homage in the style of George Thomas's fabled work at Riviera. These elaborately shaped bunkers are a sight to behold, and are largely responsible for the adjective *beautiful* being so often used to describe the course. But they are less beautiful from the inside: Mere escape is an accomplishment, and there are enough of them that such feats are often required. One bunker spans 45 vertical feet. The course is also long by Doak standards and has a very unusual par of 73, featuring severely crowned greens that are hard to hold. A new fifth set of tees was just added to make the course more manageable, but even these are quite difficult for a layout playing just 4,619 yards. All in all, Black Forest is a gorgeous course, and another excellent Michigan Doak value, but high-handicappers may wish to skip it for something more manageable.

The Valley course here is also a visual beauty, due mainly to the natural setting, but has an uninspired routing that could have been stamped out anywhere. The Al Waltrous design is pleasant enough, and easy to get around, but after a round you will remember little of the experience.

WILDERNESS VALLEY GOLF RESORT AT A GLANCE

(231) 585-7090, www.blackforestgolf.com

Golf Course Info: Practice area, walking.

Black Forest: $$V, 4,619–7,044 yards, five tees. *Slope rating* 127–145. *Course rating* 70.8–75.3.

Wilderness Valley: $, 4,889–6,519, three tees. *Slope rating* 115–126. *Course rating,* 67.8–70.6.

Lodging Info: There are packages available with several nearby motels through the course.

Getting There: Gaylord is about forty minutes from the Traverse City airport.

When to Go: Golf is played from mid-April to mid-October, but June through September are ideal months.

Golf Travel by Design Courses Nearby: High Pointe (thirty minutes).

BEECHTREE, *Aberdeen, Maryland*

An unusual routing at this Middle Atlantic gem showed Doak's ability to incorporate every natural feature and foreshadowed his stunning Pacific Dunes.

There are a lot of high-end daily fee courses in the Middle Atlantic region, but from the day it opened, Beechtree was different. While many of its neighbors had a resort feel, Beechtree was clearly for "real golfers," with its extreme greens, emphasis on shot values, and premium on strategic placement and course management.

While Doak does little earthmoving, he spends a lot of time walking the land, trying to piece together a routing that maximizes every ravine, tree, and undulation on the site, and then lays his holes out accordingly. This is very much evident at Beechtree, where everything from the doglegs to the contours of the greens is driven by the lay of the land. As a result, the course has two par-3s in the first four holes and back-to-back par-5s on the front nine, nearly as esoteric as his Pacific Dunes layout.

Beechtree is one of the best examples of what Doak seeks to accomplish, and if you do not recognize these subtleties, you will have difficulty navigating the course. The fairways are fast and firm, and the classical bunkering is inspired by the most shapely work of George Thomas and Alister MacKenzie, but the heart and soul of Beechtree is its green complexes, some of which have been criticized as too severe. The green on the tenth hole, for instance, has 8 to 10 feet of elevation change and is sloped so much that a regular caddie at the course says it only has two reasonable hole locations despite its size. These slopes are exacerbated by the fact that the greens are very smooth and very fast. While occasionally frustrating, they're also among the best-maintained and truest bent grass greens we've ever seen.

The greens may be over the top, but they make Doak's penchant for shotmaking and shot shaping abundantly clear. At nearly every hole on the course, there is a right side and wrong side on which to miss; a side from which it is possible to get up and down from off the green, and a side from which it is not. To score well here, you have to appreciate the lay of the green complex—and when you miss, you have to miss where Doak wants you to miss.

BEECHTREE GOLF CLUB AT A GLANCE

(877) BEECHTR, www.beechtreegolf.com

Golf Course Info: Practice area, walking.

$$, 5,363–7,023 yards, four tees. *Slope rating* 121–142. *Course rating* 70.4–74.9.

Lodging Info: There is no lodging available at the course, but there are numerous choices in the region and in nearby Baltimore.

Getting There: Beechtree is thirty minutes from Baltimore.

When to Go: Golf is played from April through October.

Golf Travel by Design Courses Nearby: None.

Other Notable Tom Doak Courses You Can Play

- **Apache Stronghold,** Globe, Arizona
- **Vista course at Cabo del Sol,** Cabo San Lucas, Mexico

Resorts by Design

Not so long ago, thirty-six holes made a resort a golf destination—a place where people went for an extended period of time mainly to play golf. In recent years the number of multicourse resorts has boomed, and while not many can stand toe-to-toe with Pinehurst—the nation's largest, with its ninth and tenth courses under way—the number of fifty-four-, seventy-two-, and even ninety-hole resorts is growing. Some of these, like The American Club with its Pete Dye foursome, showcase the work of one designer, while others, like Reynolds Plantation, feature multiple big names. The ten resorts in this section all stand out for their array of multiple golf courses by premier designers. Any and all of them are well worth a visit.

THE LODGE AND SPA AT CORDILLERA,
Edwards, Colorado

(800) 830–6294, www.cordillera-vail.com

Colorado's premier golf resort, Cordillera has been quietly growing and cultivating a loyal following in the mountains outside Vail, the glamorous ski resort town. This culminated in 2001 with the opening of the Summit course, a Jack Nicklaus Signature design that critics are calling one of the top mountain courses in the world. Cordillera also has efforts by Tom Fazio, three-time U.S. Open Champion Hale Irwin, and acclaimed instructor Dave Pelz. The resort encompasses 6,500 acres in a stunning Rocky Mountain setting, has one of the nation's top spas, and offers lodging choices from hotel rooms to luxury homes. Plus, the resort offers golfers one of the unique benefits of golf in the Rockies: up to 15 percent increased distance on shots because of the thinner air at high altitudes! If you have always wanted to belt a 300-yard drive, Cordillera is the place.

Golf Courses

Summit: Nicklaus got the most mountainous setting at Cordillera to craft this beauty that climbs up and down among a rugged setting filled with lakes, rocks, and wildflowers. But its name comes from the nonstop views of high snowcapped summits in the area, views that Nicklaus specifically laid out his course to frame. The routing is a unique "loop," almost a perfect circle, with just one hole, the fourteenth, on the interior of the course. The rest circle the slope of the peak, affording views hole after hole in every direction.
Golf Course Info: Practice area, caddies available.
$$$$, 5,507–7,435 yards, four tees.

Mountain: Given its fine reputation in the golf travel business, it is hard to believe that Cordillera only opened its first course in 1994. The design by three-time U.S. Open Champion Hale Irwin remains Cordillera's hilliest layout. While the new Summit course wraps around the mountain, the Irwin design plunges up and down with some of the most severe elevation changes in the Rockies. For example, one par-5 plays an astonishing 620 yards from the tips, yet goes so steeply downhill that with the drop and thin air, it is considered a birdie opportunity that many guests can reach in 2. The Mountain course is built on the site of an old working ranch; antique farm machinery and other relics are scattered along the back nine, including one of the ranch's original cabins.

Golf Course Info: Practice area, caddies available.

$$$$, 5,226–7,413 yards, four tees. *Slope rating* 128–141. *Course rating* 68.0–73.6.

Valley: This Tom Fazio design sits more than 1,000 feet below the other layouts in the high-desert ecosystem, giving it a distinctive flavor that combines the look and feel of desert golf with the rolling nature of mountain golf. The site includes exposed rocks, sagebrush, and scrubby junipers, with more waste areas and fewer trees adjacent to the fairways. Like most Fazio courses, it features very wide fairways and deep, extensive bunkers; it's the most playable of the three for high-handicappers.

Golf Course Info: Practice area, walking only, caddies included.

$$$$, 5,087–7,005 yards, four tees. *Slope rating* 121–130. *Course rating* 67.2–72.2.

Short: The only one of its kind in the world, this unique ten-hole par-3 course was designed by legendary short-game scoring instructor Dave Pelz, author of *Putt Like the Pros* and several other books. Besides its fun-to-play holes stretching 100 to 200 yards from the back tees, the course is designed to test and teach all the important short-game shots, so the greens are widely varied, tiered, and contoured. They're also protected by every imaginable type of bunker—grass and sand filled—to ensure that players face putting, chipping, and pitching challenges hole after hole. The course is an important part of the Dave Pelz Scoring Game School at the resort, but is also available to all guests.

Lodging Info: Cordillera houses a limited number of guests in its fifty-six-room Lodge, built to resemble a European chateau. Cordillera is primarily a real estate community and secondarily a resort; there's also a wide selection of large luxury homes for rent. The complex includes a full-service spa, restaurants, and other summer activities, from hot-air balloon rides to horseback riding.

Getting There: Cordillera is two and a half hours west of Denver or thirty minutes from the Eagle/Vail airport.

When to Go: Golf season is brief: from May through October. The Valley course, which is lower and has sunny exposure, has a slightly longer season.

Golf Travel by Design Courses Nearby: The Broadmoor (two and a half hours).

BAREFOOT LANDING RESORT,
Myrtle Beach, South Carolina

(800) 597-8845, www.barefootgolf.com

This Myrtle Beach complex made history in 2001 when it became the first complex in the world ever to open four courses simultaneously. The seventy-two holes include layouts by modern masters Tom Fazio, Pete Dye, and rising star Greg Norman. Davis Love, who is quietly carving out a niche as a quality designer, is the fourth architect. On-site lodging is under construction, but in the meantime Barefoot Landing has quickly become Myrtle Beach's top multicourse facility.

Golf Courses

Norman Course: This player-friendly resort layout features many of the Norman signature touches, including wide fairways with little rough, shaved collars around the greens, and open approaches welcoming the ground game. There is also elaborate greenside bunkering to the sides of the greens, including a few of the sod-walled pot bunkers Norman likes to employ. He also manipulates the length of the course through hole variety to make many holes play longer than the overall yardage indicates: Two possibly drivable par-4s give Norman the extra yards to stretch longer holes, such as the 448-yard par-4 sixth.

Golf Course Info: Practice area, no walking.

$$-$$$, 4,953–7,035 yards, five tees. *Slope rating* 117–137. *Course rating* 67.8–73.5.

Fazio Course: As has been his recent trademark, the layout is entirely driven by its elaborate bunkering, and there are more traps on some holes than you would expect on an entire side elsewhere. As usual, Fazio tips the bunkers toward the player, with higher back lips to increase visibility; many cut all the way across the fairway. This breaks the holes into multiple safe landing areas, so club selection is always an issue. In keeping with the increasingly common modern trend, one hole has two greens that alternate daily. The course is not long overall, but it features some of the longest par-5s in Myrtle Beach and would be a good choice for big hitters.

Golf Course Info: Practice area, no walking.

$$-$$$, 4,820–6,834 yards, four tees. *Slope rating* 115–139. *Course rating* 68.0–73.7.

Love Course: Davis Love has done so few courses that he has yet to develop a signature style, yet his course here is a very pleasant surprise, thought by many who have played all the Barefoot layouts to be the best of the bunch. The heart of the course is its greens, which are an homage to Pinehurst Number Two, with crowned centers; in both the style and the quality of the putting surface, they're the best in Myrtle Beach. Love tried to instill a Southern flavor to the course by building "crumbling" faux ruins of a plantation home between two greens. Like Fazio, he has a hole with alternating greens.

Golf Course Info: Practice area, no walking.

$$-$$$, 5,346–7,047 yards, four tees. Slope rating 118–138. Course rating 69.8–75.1.

Dye Course: Our least-favorite course at Barefoot and one of our least-favorite

Dye designs, this is the centerpiece of the development's residential component. While the other three layouts are adjacent, the Dye course is set aside and lined with homesites. In similar fashion to his flawed **Stadium course at PGA West,** it is often impossible to see where you are supposed to aim off the tee, the design occasionally punishes shots that appear to have been struck perfectly, and unseen hazards lurk throughout. It is also by far the longest layout here, and one of the longest in the area. One positive feature is the fact that it is the only course here to allow walking.

Golf Course Info: Practice area, walking allowed.

$$–$$$, 5,021–7,343 yards, four tees. *Slope rating* 119–149. *Course rating* 69.1–75.3.

Lodging Info: Myrtle Beach has more than a hundred public golf courses and even more hotels, motels, and resorts. Almost all offer packages combining lodging and golf at lower prices than arranging them separately. Myrtle also has the best visitor bureau of any golf destination, with a detailed printed catalog of options, helpful live operators, and a very good Web site. Book your trip here and you will be able to stay and play for $40–100 per day (800–845–4653, www.golfholiday.com).

Getting There: The Myrtle Beach airport is thirty minutes from Barefoot Landing.

When to Go: Golf is played year-round, but spring is high season. Summer is hot and humid, while winter temperatures can dip into the thirties.

Golf Travel by Design Courses Nearby: The Dunes (fifteen minutes); Legends Heathland (fifteen minutes); Caledonia and True Blue (forty-five minutes); Ocean course at Kiawah Island (two hours); Wild Dunes (two hours).

HYATT DORADO BEACH/HYATT CERROMAR BEACH, *Dorado Beach, Puerto Rico*

(800) 55–HYATT, www.hyatt.com

These twin resorts sit side by side and share four classic golf courses, all designed by Robert Trent Jones Sr. Originally part of Laurence Rockefeller's posh Rockresorts chain, Dorado Beach is one of the Caribbean's classic resorts, but along with its more contemporary sibling it just underwent a $55 million top-to-bottom renovation. Everything from guest rooms to restaurants to the casino was revamped in the process, restoring some of the lost luster to this onetime hideaway for movie stars and politicians. This included a complete restoration of the four courses by Raymond Floyd, who lengthened the layouts to make Jones's original hazards play in accordance with today's improved equipment. Floyd also rebuilt worn bunkers and green complexes, and reversed the nines on the marquee Dorado East to take advantage of stronger ocean-view finishing holes and a brand-new clubhouse.

With four courses by Robert Trent Jones Sr., the Hyatt resorts at Cerromar and Dorado Beach in Puerto Rico form the largest golf complex in the Caribbean, anchored by the famed Dorado East course. HYATT DORADO BEACH

Golf Courses

Dorado East: Exactly a decade after introducing signature holes to the world at *The Dunes,* Jones was still going strong with the concept, but many think his very best is the par-5 thirteenth at the Dorado East course, site of a Senior PGA Tour event. The Z-shaped hole has a double dogleg with water short and right of the first bend and long and left of the second, en route to the green. There are three distinct routes for playing this hole, allowing golfers of all abilities to either tackle it conservatively or try for eagle or birdie. The rest of the course features very large greens, sand traps everywhere, frequent sharp doglegs, and Jones's beloved water hazards on more than half the holes. As was his style, almost all greens are elevated.

Golf Course Info: Practice area, walking allowed.

$$$, 5,805–6,985 yards, three tees. *Slope rating* 122–127. *Course rating* 70.3–72.6.

Dorado West: More difficult but similar in feel to the East, this is almost the same length and has elevated greens with equally vast and daunting expanses of sand and water. One unusual feature is its very tricky collection of par-3s. Jones often routed such holes over water hazards, but given their penal nature, they were accordingly short. Not at Dorado West, where the ninth stretches more than 200 yards with no margin for error.

Golf Travel by Design

Golf Course Info: Practice area, walking allowed.

$$$, 5,883–6,913 yards, three tees. *Slope rating* 122–127. *Course rating* 70.4–73.1.

Cerromar North: The shortest of the resort's four layouts, the North course also has ample water and sand with elevated greens, but is more wide open and straightforward. As a result, it's a more user-friendly resort course and less challenging.

Golf Course Info: Practice area, walking allowed.

$$$, 5,547–6,841 yards, three tees. *Slope rating* 124–130. *Course rating* 70.5–73.5.

Cerromar South: The longest of the four Jones courses, this is also the least treacherous. While it demands a little more distance off the tee, it is also the most forgiving, with wide fairways and hazards well out of the line of play. Like all three of the other courses, it is in better condition than ever after the recent renovation.

Golf Course Info: Practice area, walking allowed.

$$$, 5,486–7,047 yards, three tees. *Slope rating* 124–129. *Course rating* 70.0–74.3.

Lodging Info: The resorts are about 2 miles apart with connecting shuttle bus service, guests at either enjoy all privileges and shared facilities. Dorado Beach is slightly more upscale and old-fashioned, smaller and more intimate, and has the two premier golf courses. Rooms are set in two-story low-rise buildings along the beach. Cerromar Beach is a modern high-rise resort and more family oriented, with an elaborate pool complex including water slides and the world's longest river pool, as well as a casino.

Getting There: Dorado Beach is forty minutes from the San Juan International Airport.

When to Go: Golf is played year-round, but summer through fall is hurricane season. Winter months are peak season.

Golf Travel by Design Courses Nearby: None

PALM COAST RESORT, *Palm Coast, Florida*

(800) 654–6538, www.palmcoastresort.com

After several sleepy years, things are suddenly going right for this resort on Florida's northeastern coast. First, the property was acquired by Destination Hotels, a high-end golf resort company that operates the very prestigious Sunriver resort in Oregon. Destination Hotels is building a new, more upscale hotel to replace the middle-of-the-road property currently on the site. Jack Nicklaus also recently unveiled Ocean Hammock, the fifth course at the resort, to almost universal acclaim. Ocean Hammock claims to be the first true oceanfront golf course built in the state in decades, and with six dramatic holes overlooking the crashing surf of the Atlantic, it is hard to disagree. Nicklaus's course has won all sorts of awards and accolades and has even been called "the Pebble Beach of the East" by some golf writers. This may be overdoing it, but there is little doubt it is one more in his recent string of successful designs, and one of Florida's best.

Golf Courses

Ocean Hammock: Its claim to fame is half a dozen true oceanfront holes, the most in the state, dramatic one and all, but this modern Nicklaus course also includes holes along lakes, holes through sandy dunes, and wooded inland holes. It is what we have come to expect from the more recent Nicklaus designs, with great natural beauty, multiple tees for all ability levels, and dramatic closing holes. While it's a true resort course that's manageable from the shorter tees, it's also a championship-worthy test from the back. It closes with four holes Nicklaus has nicknamed the Bear Claw, including two par-4s playing 450 and 466 yards. In a throwback to early Nicklaus design, it has the highest course rating in this book from the tips, a staggering 77. Wind is also a constant factor, but despite the challenge you will find traditional Nicklaus soft touches such as his reachable par-5 and large receptive greens (www.oceanhammock.com).

Golf Course Info: Practice area, no walking.

$$$V, yards, five tees. 5,115–7,201 yards. *Slope rating* 130–147. *Course rating* 70.1–77.0.

Matanzas Woods: Until Ocean Hammock opened, this layout by golf superstar Arnold Palmer and design partner Ed Seay was the marquee layout at Palm Coast. A traditional parkland routing, it is carved from dense pine forests so that you cannot see any hole from another. Still, the real challenge is not the trees—the fairways are quite wide—but the ample bunkering and water hazards: Several holes play alongside lakes, and water reaches in front of several greens. Greens are large, allowing players to compensate for the hazards in front of the putting surface by playing an extra club on approach.

Golf Course Info: Practice area, no walking.

$$–$$$, 5,336–6,985 yards, four tees. *Slope rating* 126–132. *Course rating* 71.2–73.3.

Pine Lakes: A second Palmer and Seay design but much different from Matanzas Woods; it's similar to the duo's several private watery courses in nearby Ponte Vedra Beach. The course lives up to its name, with lakes and ponds in play on eleven holes. Fairways are narrow and lined with rows of mounds.

Golf Course Info: Practice area, no walking.

$$–$$$, 5,166–7,274 yards, four tees. *Slope rating* 124–126. *Course rating* 71.4–73.5.

Cypress Knoll: South African player and designer Gary Player laid out a serpentine course that runs along the borders of existing lakes and wetlands. It requires accuracy rather than length, because the fairways are thin and curving, presenting precise landing areas. Water is constantly in play.

Golf Course Info: Practice area, no walking.

$$–$$$, 5,386–6,591 yards, four tees. *Slope rating* 117–130. *Course rating* 69.3–71.6.

Palm Harbor: Despite its name, this design by little-known Bill Amick is a parkland course with no harbor, cut through pine and palm trees. Its main characteristic is sharp doglegs, which can be found on more than two-thirds of the holes. It is by far the shortest layout at Palm Coast.

Golf Course Info: Practice area, no walking.

$$–$$$, 5,346–6,572 yards, three tees. *Slope rating* 127–128. *Course rating* 71.2–71.8.

Lodging Info: The resort currently has an unspectacular 151-room hotel, but it offers great values by Florida standards—especially in peak season—for a course of Ocean Hammock's caliber. A more upscale and elaborate resort hotel is currently under construction. The resort also has a highly rated full-service marina.

Getting There: Ocean Hammock is thirty minutes from the Jacksonville airport, just outside St. Augustine.

When to Go: Peak season is winter, but Palm Coast is far north of most Florida resorts and can be quite cool. Prices drop in the hotter summer; spring and fall are ideal.

Golf Travel by Design Courses Nearby: TPC Sawgrass (twenty-five minutes).

HORSESHOE BAY, *Horseshoe Bay, Texas*

(800) 531–5105, www.horseshoebaytexas.com

Only a handful of architects have been chosen to execute all the courses at larger resorts, such as Pete Dye's seventy-two-holes at the *American Club* and fifty-four holes at *Casa de Campo.* Joining Dye in this elite group is Robert Trent Jones Sr., who laid out four courses at the twin Hyatt complexes in Puerto Rico and fifty-four of the toughest holes he ever designed at the Horseshoe Bay resort in Texas. His monopoly will be broken in 2003, when a fourth course, designed by Jack Nicklaus, is scheduled to open.

The resort is set in the Lonestar State's "hill country," an area outside San Antonio formed by an ancient geological uplifting that is a magnet for the state's top-quality golf courses. The three layouts span a fifteen-year segment later in Jones's career and reflect the touches that made his courses recognizable—and that made them tough. Off the course, Horseshoe Bay is a giant landscaping project filled with boulders, streams, ponds, and waterfalls, all mixed with tropical plants and colorful birds, including many macaws. You'll also find a marina on huge Lake LBJ, several elaborate pool complexes, and a large number of condos and hotel rooms to choose from.

Golf Courses

Slickrock: The resort's developer loved water features, and this fit well with Jones's pioneering use of them on the golf course. As a result, Slickrock, the first course at the resort, built in 1974, had some of the most cutting-edge water features of its time. The most obvious is a 100-foot-high human-made waterfall on the signature fourteen hole, which features a special "wet cart path" under the cascade that golfers drive along through the fall's basin. The waterfall must also be carried off the tee, just one of the myriad hazards at the difficult layout, which—despite these challenges—is now the resort's easiest course. It is relatively flat with wide fairways and large greens, though a substantial number of large fairway and greenside bunkers await you. Besides its plentiful bunkers, the course makes great use of the native granite outcroppings and water hazards, which are in play on thirteen holes.

Golf Course Info: Practice area, no walking.

$$–$$$, 5,377–6,384 yards, four tees. *Slope rating* 70.2–72.6. *Course rating* 117–127.

Ramrock: The second layout Jones designed and the toughest at the resort, this is much different from its predecessor. Nearly all the fairways are sloped, and the course has substantial elevation changes, including uphill approaches (as was Jones's style), on many holes. There are fewer fairway bunkers here but the landing areas are tighter, ten holes have water, a dry creekbed is in play on a third of the holes, and the greens are much smaller and well bunkered. Jones, the first builder of the island green, incorporates one here that stretches a terrifying 191 yards from the tips.

Golf Course Info: Practice area, no walking.

$$–$$$, 5,306–6,926 yards, four tees. *Slope rating* 129–140. *Course rating* 70.0–74.5.

Applerock: One of the last great courses Jones designed, this is another very stiff challenge that plays a yard short of 7,000 from the back tees. Severe elevation changes and sloped fairways are the rule. An example of Jones's penchant for uphill approach shots and penal water hazards is found on the sixteenth, in which players cross a stream off the tee and again at the base of a green sitting 50 vertical feet above the fairway. Overall, however, you'll find considerably less water and fewer bunkers than on its siblings; the challenge comes from length, elevation change, and the difficulty in finding a flat lie on the course.

Golf Course Info: Practice area, no walking.

$$–$$$, 5,509–6,999 yards, four tees. *Slope rating* 118–139. *Course rating* 69.3–74.0.

Saddlerock: A Jack Nicklaus Signature course is expected to open in mid-2003, and at approximately 7,100 yards will be the resort's longest.

Lodging Info: The resort has 200 rooms in two complexes. The Inn sits at the marina, and offers both hotel rooms and one- to three-bedroom condos. The Adventure Inn has condos converted to larger hotel rooms. There are elaborate water sports and pool offerings, an equestrian center, a spa, and a large tennis facility.

Getting There: The resort is 85 miles from San Antonio and four hours from Dallas or Houston.

When to Go: Golf is played year-round, but peak season is March through October, and many nongolf facilities shut down the rest of the year. Because of the blistering Texas summers, spring and fall are ideal.

Golf Travel by Design Courses Nearby: None.

GREENBRIER, *White Sulphur Springs, West Virginia*

(800) 624–6070, www.greenbrier.com

One of the nation's grand old golf resorts, the Greenbrier has a loyal following of summer guests who partake not only of golf but also of the many other sporting distractions that make the property one of a kind. The resort offers falconry, a Land Rover off-road driving school, an equestrian center, a large tennis facility, and an elaborate shooting club, plus miles of hiking and biking trails, all on a staggering 6,500 acres. The choices of lodging are equally comprehensive, from somewhat dated and very standard hotel rooms to bungalows, cabins, and deluxe homes. The Greenbrier has won both a Mobil five-star and AAA five-diamond rating. Guests participate in a Modified American Plan that includes meals.

Golf Courses

Greenbrier: The Seth Raynor course was redone by Nicklaus at the height of his fearsome design style, and was made even more menacing since he was charged with toughening the layout specifically for the 1979 Ryder Cup. The result is a fairly long course with tight rolling fairways, frequent elevation changes, and elevated, well-bunkered greens. To make matters more challenging, water hazards appear on more than half of the holes. What makes the course so interesting is that it blends the strategic design style popular in the early twentieth century with the modern emphasis on the power game and use of water hazards, as exemplified by the final hole, a par-5 that plays nearly 640 yards from the tips. Elevated greens protected by deep bunkers encourage high, lofted approach shots.

Golf Course Info: Practice area, walking allowed.

$$$, 5,346–6,572 yards, three tees. *Slope rating* 127–128. *Course rating* 71.2–71.8.

Old White: The original layout at the Greenbrier was a C. B. Macdonald design, and for most of its routing it reflects the classical influences of the Scottish courses Macdonald studied. It is truly strategic, emphasizing position off the tee, and features small, sloped greens, often protected by deep bunkers but almost always allowing a bump-and-run ground approach to the putting surface. A notable exception is the unusual par-3 finishing hole that plays over a pond to the green—a penal design out of character with Macdonald's penchant for redans and other classic 1-shotters.

Golf Course Info: Practice area, walking allowed.

$$$, 5,179–6,652 yards, three tees. *Slope rating* 119–128. *Course rating* 69.1–70.0.

Meadows: Bob Cupp almost completely rebuilt what was known as the Lakeside course, a Dick Wilson design that was renamed the Meadows. Despite its moniker, the course features water hazards at every turn, including three ponds bulkheaded with stone walls that Cupp inserted in front of greens. He also planted some 200 trees to give the course a more woodsy, private feel. Despite the water, it has the widest fairways of the resort's three courses and is the most forgiving off the tee, especially from the front tee boxes.

Golf Course Info: Practice area, walking allowed.

$$$, 5,001–6,807 yards, three tees. *Slope rating* 115–132. *Course rating* 68.0–72.4.

Lodging Info: The resort has 643 rooms, including more than 70 guest houses, to choose from. All guests are on a meal plan that includes breakfast and dinner.

Getting There: US Airways offers seasonal service right to the resort, and Amtrak serves the White Sulphur Springs train station. It is about four and a half hours from Washington, D.C.

When to Go: Golf is played year-round, weather permitting, but the real season is April through November—it frequently snows in winter.

Golf Travel by Design Courses Nearby: The Homestead.

THE HOMESTEAD, *Hot Springs, Virginia*

(800) 838-1766, www.thehomestead.com

A short drive from the **Greenbrier** lies another grand old golf resort, the Homestead. Each has its own equally adamant group of supporters, but the Greenbrier clearly has the edge in off-course facilities, with virtually every activity and type of lodging you could imagine. On the course the competition is much closer. Still, with one of the nation's first mountain courses—even today considered among the best—and other layouts by Donald Ross and Robert Trent Jones Sr., the Homestead may have a slight edge.

Like its rival, the Homestead offers Modified American Plan packages that include lodging and dining; it's also equally formal, with jacket and tie required at dinner in many restaurants. Incidentally, both resorts claimed local star Slammin' Sammy Snead as their own.

Golf Courses

Cascades: This layout by Golden Age designer William Flynn is an American classic, and while Flynn assisted at both Pine Valley and Merion—and would go on to lay out the second course at the **Marriott Seaview**—this was his first high-profile solo effort. The course's main feature is that it is hilly, but far more so than most "hilly" courses. Nearly every shot played is up or down, and usually from an uphill, downhill, or sidehill lie. One of the reasons it gets rave reviews is that it requires golfers to hit every club in their bag during a round, but also requires constant consideration of how the lay of the land will affect the outcome of each swing. In addition, it is carved from thick woods and demands accuracy with narrow fairways that climb and drop—while often simultaneously doglegging. Greens are medium-sized, fast, and well protected by bunkers. What keeps the course from over-powering players is the fact that it is relatively short; as such, it becomes a strategic effort. It also reminds us that well before the likes of Mike Strantz and Tom Doak, the land often dictated unusual routings. The course closes par-3, -5, -5, -3.

Golf Course Info: Practice area, walking allowed, caddies.

$$–$$$, 4,967–6,679 yards, three tees. *Slope rating* 124–137. *Course rating* 70.3–73.0.

Lower Cascades: Robert Trent Jones was brought in to do a sequel to the well-received Cascades, and surprisingly, it is one of his gentlest efforts. It too is relatively short, and while he incorporates a meandering stream through-out the back nine to satisfy his need for water hazards, the main defense is an abundance of his large fairway bunkers. This combined with the non-demanding length, creates an unusual Jones course: It rarely requires a driver, and it rewards those who go shorter off the tee but keep their ball in the fairway. The fairways are wider than at the Cascades; as long as you keep the ball out of the large bunkers, you can do well here.

Golf Course Info: Practice area, walking allowed, caddies.

$$–$$$, 4,686–6,579 yards, three tees. *Slope rating* 110–127. *Course rating* 66.2–72.2.

Old: The first layout at the resort was done by none other than Donald Ross, but unfortunately almost no touches of his original routing remain; the course has been tinkered with constantly since before the turn of the twentieth century. It was most recently renovated by Rees Jones and is a true resort course, the shortest and easiest at the Homestead. Ironically, the redesigns have featured "Ross-style" crowned greens, which might lead players to think they are original. The Old course features one of the shortest par-4s you will see—just 298 yards from the back tees and downhill all the way—but it finishes with a small, domed, and hard-to-hold green in the style of Pinehurst Number Two.

Golf Course Info: Practice area, walking allowed, caddies.

$$–$$$, 4,852–6,211 yards, three tees. *Slope rating* 115–120. *Course rating* 67.9–69.7.

Lodging Info: The rooms are all in the main building, an imposing redbrick edifice that has been welcoming guests since Thomas Jefferson stayed here. Rooms in the older wing are very traditional and have limited amenities, while the newer wing features more modern lodging with fireplaces, wet bars, and other extras. Meal plans are available.

Getting There: It is about five hours from Washington, D.C.

When to Go: Golf is played year-round, weather permitting, but the real season is April through November—it frequently snows in winter.

Golf Travel by Design Courses Nearby: The Greenbrier.

WALT DISNEY WORLD, *Orlando, Florida*

(407) W–DISNEY, www.disneyworld.com

"The Happiest Place on Earth" may be better known for its fireworks display and rides like Pirates of the Caribbean, but with ninety-nine holes and its own PGA tournament, it's also one of the largest golf resorts in the world. Off the course, nothing on the planet can compare to Disney's facilities, which include nearly thirty hotels, more than 250 restaurants, four huge theme/amusement parks, a working movie studio, and endless nightlife, entertainment, and sporting diversions.

Disney has also attracted some of the game's top architects, including Pete Dye, Tom Fazio, and the less heralded but quite successful Joe Lee. In fact, at Disney, Lee quietly outshines his big-name neighbors. Regardless of which you prefer, however, there are four very good courses and a nine-holer perfect for introducing the family to the game.

Golf Courses

Palm: The premier Disney layout, this Lee design uses its main feature, water, to create a "target-style" layout akin to desert golf, but more penal. There are four holes like this, broken into landing areas from tee to fairway and fairway to green by water. Yet while this is both scary and beautiful, none of the carries is onerous. You'll also find an abundance of bunkers, very good greens, and the largest natural grass practice range we've seen. The closer here is a very good, but very challenging par-4 with an island green that, at 454 yards, has been ranked the fourth most difficult hole on the entire PGA Tour.

Golf Course Info: Practice area, no walking.

$$$, 5,311–6,957 yards, four tees. *Slope rating* 124–133. *Course rating* 68.7–73.

Magnolia: Another Lee design adjacent to the Palm, Magnolia is a very similar but less intimidating routing with less water, especially in the line of play. There is still abundant opportunity for errant shots to splash down, but far fewer forced carries. An exception is the memorable par-3 sixth, which not only features a lengthy carry over a lake but also protects the green with a famous bunker carved in the shape of Mickey Mouse's head. This is the longest course at Disney. Both courses have an entertaining mix of wooded and water holes, all with ample bunkers, and both feature a strong closing stretch. The facility also includes Oak Trail, a nine-hole walking course popular with families.

Golf Course Info: Practice area, no walking.

$$$, 5,232–7,190 yards, four tees. *Slope rating* 123–133. *Course rating* 69.1–73.9.

Eagle Pines: Dye and Fazio shared the work at what Disney promotes as its marquee facility, with a newer clubhouse and a high-end daily fee feel. Eagle Pines is Pete Dye's effort, reminiscent of the Carolina sandhills with sandy waste areas bordered by tall native grasses. It is a visually strong course, and in a unique touch, dark straw made of pine needles is used to line holes, creating both additional waste area and stark optical relief. It is the shortest of the eighteen-hole layouts at Disney, but counters with water on a whopping sixteen holes. In the Dye tradition, the four tees are quite separated, allowing the course to cater to players of all abilities. Ironically, the waste-area style is more in keeping with Tom Fazio, who created the course next door.

Golf Course Info: Practice area, no walking.

$$$, 4,838–6,772 yards, four tees. *Slope rating* 111–131. *Course rating* 68.0–72.3.

Osprey Ridge: Fazio uses mounding as the defining feature at this layout built through existing wetlands, which he tried to leave intact. Since the wetlands border nearly every hole, the rows of rolling mounds along the edges of the corridors of play create a containment area, helping keep errant shots in play. The course is good looking and a sound routing, but in a bit of a departure from his usual style, Fazio has installed huge greens. On the same scale as those at St. Andrews, these are easy to hit but leave open the possibility of 3 and even 4 putts from 150 feet away.

Golf Course Info: Practice area, no walking.

$$$$, 5,402–7,101 yards, four tees. *Slope rating* 121–135. *Course rating* 68.9–73.9.

Lake Buena Vista: This stand-alone course is the third Joe Lee design and the least interesting of all the Disney layouts. It is the only one with housing—and lots of it, detracting from an otherwise beautiful natural setting. While it's carved through wetlands and glades with an old Florida feel that reminds players of what the state was once like, the houses and an uninspired routing weaken the course.

Golf Course Info: Practice area, no walking.

$$$, 5,194–6,819 yards, four tees. *Slope rating* 120–128. *Course rating* 68.2–72.7.

Lodging Info: Walt Disney World offers almost thirty resorts within its vast boundaries, including everything from a hotel for military veterans and a campground to several luxury properties. The best of the upscale choices are the Boardwalk, Grand Floridian, and Contemporary resorts. A wonderful middle-of-the-road choice is the Wilderness Lodge, and among the value properties we like the Caribbean Beach resort. About a third of the hotels within Disney World are not owned by the resort; guests of these do not receive Disney benefits, which include free transportation by bus, boat, and tram within the property and—more important—free taxi service to and from the golf courses. There are a host of other benefits, too, including early theme park admission and charge privileges, so we see no reason to stay at a non-Disney hotel within Walt Disney World.

Still, there are much less expensive choices outside the complex, and guests get only a slight discount on green fees.

Getting There: Disney is less than thirty minutes from the Orlando airport, one of the easiest to reach in the world.

When to Go: Golf is played year-round, but winter can get chilly and even see frost delays. Busy seasons for the theme parks and golf are opposite: The latter is slow in summer, when it is hot and school vacation keeps the parks full, but the courses are crowded in winter when the parks are emptier.

Golf Travel by Design Courses Nearby: Grand Cypress.

SANDESTIN, *Destin, Florida*

(800) 277-0800, www.sandestin.com

Situated in a part of the Florida panhandle known best for its unique bright white sand beaches, Sandestin has quietly evolved from a sprawling mix of residential, hotel, and golf facilities into one of Florida's top golf resorts. Far from a household name, the resort is closer to Alabama than to the part of Florida most people visit, yet recent changes have ensured that it will soon attain the status it deserves. Canada's Intrawest, the world's most successful ski resort developer and the force behind the planned villages and golf resorts at Whistler, British Columbia and Mont Tremblant, Quebec, purchased Sandestin several years ago. Since then it has brought in Robert Trent Jones Jr. to design the acclaimed Raven layout and built a pedestrian resort village similar to its ski towns up north. With a wide range of lodging, dining, and activities, some of the world's best beaches, and first-class sport fishing, plus four very good golf courses by the likes of Jones Jr. and his brother Rees Jones, Sandestin is well worth a visit. It is also one of Florida's best golf values.

Golf Courses

Burnt Pines: The premier tract at Sandestin is the semiprivate Burnt Pines, open only to members and resort guests. It was designed by Rees Jones during his mounding phase, many holes feature fairways lined with rolling mounds serving to frame the target area and contain balls. Burnt Pines is a very attractive course that occupies a lot of real estate, yet is blissfully secluded and almost free of homes. The front play through a pine forest, and the back, along a bay. The layout showcases several Jones traits, such as elevated tee boxes and clear views of the holes, plus raised green complexes accepting bump-and-run approaches. The long-term plan is that when the course reaches its membership goals, it may become private and stop allowing resort guests to play.

Golf Course Info: Practice area, walking allowed.

$$–$$$V, 5,096–6,996 yards, four tees. *Slope rating* 122–135. *Course rating* 68.7–74.1.

The Raven: Robert Trent Jones Jr. designed two courses in Arizona, one in Colorado and one in West Virginia using this name, which has become sort of

Laid out carefully through an environmentally sensitive area, Rees Jones's Burnt Pines is one of four top courses available to guests at Florida's Sandestin resort. REES JONES INC.

a brand within his brand. Both Arizona courses—the Raven at Sabino Springs and the Raven at South Mountain—have been among the highest-rated courses in that golf-crazed state. Yet what has really set them apart is their landmark high-end daily fee service, a trend also evident at Jones's latest Raven creation, opened in 2001. Instead of forecaddies, "player assistants" roam the course with radio headsets, keeping their eyes on shots, raking bunkers, even running back to the pro shop should players run out of balls. The course incorporates the marshy land from the former third nine at the resort's Baytowne layout. It winds through wetlands with long wooden boardwalks for carts, featuring water in play on eleven holes. But there are only two forced carries on the course, including the stunning sixth, a par-3 over water to a green framed by shapely bunkers. In a nod to very contemporary design trends, the course features nineteen holes, with two different par-3 sixteenth holes that alternate daily.

Golf Course Info: Practice area, no walking.

$$–$$$V, 6,910 yards, four tees. *Slope rating* 137. *Course rating* 73.8.

Baytowne: The original course at Sandestin, created by Tom Jackson, this twenty-seven-hole design lost nine holes when the Raven was built next door. The course is now what used to be the Harbor and Dune nines, and is Sandestin's "resort-style" course and its easiest, since there are wide fairways and no forced carries. Still, there is lateral water on more than half the holes, including every hole on the harbor side. The few holes without water are heavily wooded, because the course cuts through thick pine forests. Fairways are rolling with a surprising amount of undulation. Baytowne is a bit of a hidden gem, far superior to the many similar resort courses throughout flattish Florida.

Golf Course Info: Practice area, no walking.

$$V, 4,862–6,890 yards, four tees. *Slope rating* 114–127. *Course rating* 68.1–73.4.

The Links: Jackson's second course at Sandestin has one thing in common with its sibling: lots of water, in this case on thirteen holes, occasionally on both sides of the fairway. For this reason the name *Links* is far from historically accurate, but Jackson does incorporate a few authentic elements, with no forced carries and open fronts allowing bump-and-run shots on nearly every hole. Greens are large and flat, offering a welcome respite from missed shots ending up in lakes; they're often offset diagonally to create risk-reward choices between a running and a lofted approach. The ninth, a par-5 curving along the river, is an homage to the famous eighteenth at Pebble Beach.

Golf Course Info: Practice area, no walking.

$$V, 4,969–6,710 yards, four tees. *Slope rating* 115–124. *Course rating* 68.7–72.8.

Lodging Info: Sandestin has a wealth of lodging options, from a Hilton hotel on the premises to 750 condos in numerous complexes, plus town homes and the 150-room Baytowne Inn. The newly opened Village at Baytowne offers several additional lodging choices; more are under construction.

Getting There: The resort is about ninety minutes from Pensacola.

When to Go: Golf is played year-round, but winter can get chilly; spring and fall are ideal.

Golf Travel by Design Courses Nearby: None.

AMELIA ISLAND PLANTATION, *Amelia Island, Florida*

(800) 874-6878, www.aipfl.com

Although overshadowed by Pete Dye's two TPC courses at nearby **Sawgrass,** Amelia Island has two fine Dye courses of its own, plus another wonderful layout by Tom Fazio. The courses are set amid the 1,300-acreresort, which is full of oak, palmetto, and pine trees, with both marsh and ocean exposure—a little bit of everything needed to craft first-rate golf courses. Add luxurious accommodations at both the resort's hotel and in numerous rental condos and homes, along with a world-class tennis facility and beautiful beaches, and it becomes hard to understand why Amelia Island gets so little press.

Golf Courses

Long Point Club: Somehow Fazio manages to roll all the island's features into one. While the back-to-back par-3s playing along the Atlantic coast on the front are the most memorable, those routed through the forests, over marshland, and around lakes are equally compelling. Variety and beauty are the themes at this Fazio gem. It's a bit of a departure from his usual style, featuring several long forced carries and relatively little bunkering. In keeping with the varied nature of the layout, the nines are quite different as well, with the front narrower and shorter, and the back much more exposed to ocean winds.

Golf Course Info: Practice area, no walking.

$$-$$$, 4,927–6,775 yards, four tees. *Slope rating* 122–135. *Course rating* 70.2–73.0.

Ocean Links: Dye originally designed a twenty-seven-hole layout for Amelia Island, and his Oceanside nine was combined with a new nine by Bobby Weed to form the Ocean Links course. The original Dye nine was quite short by his current standards; to make up for this he used small greens, oceanfront holes exposed to wind, and many of his nefarious bunkers. With the new addition, the course has an impressive five holes on the water, plus ten more that incorporate lakes or marshes, making it a good place to lose some golf balls. While the shortest of the three layouts here, the course is fraught with penal hazards and demands accuracy at every turn, including the closer—a short par-3 that, in typical Dye fashion, plays to a peninsula green surrounded by water.

Golf Course Info: Practice area, no walking.

$$-$$$, 4,550–6,301 yards, four tees. *Slope rating* 115–134. *Course rating* 66.4–70.3.

Oak Marsh: The combination of Dye's original Oak Marsh and Oyster Bay nines, it features his trademark bulkheaded greens and water hazards throughout. It also has narrow fairways and small greens, many large bunkers, and trees encroaching on play, making it a short, placement-oriented course, very much in the spirit of his early Harbour Town success. The Oyster Bay nine has four holes laid out right through the marshes with challenging forced carries from the back tees, very reminiscent of Dye's more famous *Ocean course at Kiawah Island.*

Golf Course Info: Practice area, no walking.

$$-$$$, 4,983–6,502 yards, four tees. *Slope rating* 119–130. *Course rating* 67.1–71.7.

Lodging Info: The Amelia Island Plantation includes the new 250-room Amelia Inn & Beach Club, as well as varied assortment of higher-end condos and villas. There is a new full-service spa and one of the nation's highest-rated tennis centers. There is also a Ritz-Carlton on the island.

Getting There: Amelia is 30 miles from Jacksonville.

When to Go: Peak season is winter, but Amelia is far north of most Florida resorts and can be quite cool. Prices drop in summer; spring and fall are ideal.

Golf Travel by Design Courses Nearby: None.

Appendix

The Golf Insider's Top Ten Favorite Golf Travel by Design Courses

1. Pacific Dunes, Bandon Dunes, Oregon
2. Royal County Down, Northern Ireland
3. Spyglass Hill, Pebble Beach, California
4. Whistling Straits, The American Club, Kohler, Wisconsin
5. The Links at Spanish Bay, Pebble Beach, California
6. Moonah Course, Mornington Peninsula, Australia
7. Prestwick, Prestwick, Scotland
8. St. George's Hill, Weybridge, England
9. Tobacco Road, Sanford, North Carolina
10. Reflection Bay, Las Vegas, Nevada

Resources for Learning More About Golf Course Architecture

Books

Rough Meditations, by Bradley Klein, Sleeping Bear Press, 1997. A collection of musings by Klein, a respected architecture critic and editor for *Golfweek.*

Some Essays on Golf Course Architecture, by Harry Colt and Charles Allison, Charles Scribner and Sons, 1920. The first book on the subject by the father of parkland golf (out of print).

Masters of the Links, edited by Geoff Shackelford, Sleeping Bear Press, 1997. A collection of design essays by the likes of Ben Crenshaw, Tom Doak, Pete Dye, C. B. Macdonald, Alister MacKenzie, and A. W. Tillinghast.

The Anatomy of a Golf Course, by Tom Doak, Lyons & Burford, 1992. The first book by über-critic and next-generation designer Doak.

The Confidential Guide to Golf Courses, by Tom Doak, Sleeping Bear Press, 1996. Doak's ratings and comments on hundreds of courses worldwide.

The Spirit of St. Andrews, by Alister MacKenzie, Sleeping Bear Press, 1995. Reprint of MacKenzie's in-depth examination of St. Andrews and general musings on his designs and those of his contemporaries.

Golf Has Never Failed Me, by Donald Ross, Sleeping Bear Press, 1996. New printing of "lost" commentaries on golf and design by America's first master.

Golf Course Design, by Geoffrey Cornish and Robert Muir Graves, John Wiley & Sons, 1999. The two expert designers who teach Harvard's seminar in golf course design and have laid out hundreds of courses share a vast amount of their knowledge.

Golf by Design: How to Lower Your Score by Reading the Features of a Course, by Robert Trent Jones Jr., Little, Brown, 1993. A comprehensive look at golf course design and how it affects the playing of the game by one of its most prolific architects.

Discovering Donald Ross: The Architect and His Golf Courses, by Bradley Klein, Sleeping Bear Press, 2001. A new look at Ross's style and a course-by-course examination.

The Architects of Golf, by Geoffrey Cornish and Ron Whitten, HarperCollins, 1993. The history of golf course design and an encyclopedic listing of courses and designers (out of print).

The Art of Golf Design, by Michael Miller and Geoff Shackelford, Sleeping Bear Press, 2001. Prints of oil paintings of important golf holes by acclaimed landscape artist Miller accompanied by descriptive text from Shackelford.

Golf Architecture in America, by George Thomas Jr., Sleeping Bear Press, 2001. Reprint of the classic book with drawings, photos, and commentary on America's earliest great courses.

The Links, by Robert Hunter, Sleeping Bear Press, 2000. Reprint of the classic book on the courses of the Golden Age of Golf Architecture in America.

Toronto Terror: The Life and Works of Stanley Thompson, by Jim Barclay, Sleeping Bear Press, 2000. The definitive biography of Canada's greatest designer.

The World Atlas of Golf: The Greatest Courses and How They Are Played, by Pat-Ward Thomas, Herbert Warren Wind, Charles Price, Peter Thomson, and Derek Lawrenson, Thunder Bay Press, 1998. Coffee table book examining a broad collection of the world's great courses, including many overseas.

Web Sites

www.golfdesign.org: Home site of the American Society of Golf Course Architects, with member listing, bios, and links to sites of individual designers. Architect's Corner features commentary and essays by dozens of top designers.

www.golfclubatlas.com: Site dedicated to the examination of individual courses with frequent guest interviews by designers and critics including

Tom Doak, Mike Strantz, and others. Also features detailed analysis of a broad slate of top courses, public and private, around the world.

www.thegolfinsider.com: Home site for *The Golf Insider* newsletter, including excerpts from current issues and detailed index of past topics.

www.eigca.org: Home site of the European Institute of Golf Course Architects, with member listings and additional information.

Museum

Golf House: The museum of the United States Golf Association at its headquarters in Far Hills, New Jersey, has an extensive library collection of original documents including actual hand-drawn golf course designs by Donald Ross, A. W. Tillinghast, Walter Travis, and others. These and other design related items rotate in and out of the museum's ongoing displays. There are also short-term special exhibits on design topics, such as a recent six-month display of paintings and photographs highlighting the Golden Age of American Golf Course Design. Call (908) 234–2300 or visit www.usga.org for more information.

The Golf Insider Index of Featured Resorts and Courses

The following guide lists all courses and resorts included in this book that have been covered in past issues of *The Golf Insider,* a critical newsletter devoted to golf travel topics. Profiles include features on specific resorts, course reviews as part of regional features, highlights of new courses, and special reports on important individual courses. Each also includes detailed travel, dining, and lodging information and tips. Back issues are individually available for $10 each; one- and two-year bound compilations of back issues are available for $69.95 and $119.95, respectively. To order, call toll-free at (877) 526–6331 or visit www.thegolfinsider.com.

May 2000: Princeville, Hawaii; Kauai Lagoons, Hawaii; The American Club/Whistling Straits, Wisconsin; Great White Course at Doral, Florida; Stoke Park, England.

June 2000: Royal Portrush, Northern Ireland; Royal County Down, Northern Ireland; Walt Disney World, Florida; The Greenbrier, West Virginia.

July 2000: Tobacco Road, North Carolina; Le Geant/Mont Tremblant, Quebec; Marriott Seaview, New Jersey; Irish Course at Whistling Straits, Wisconsin; Naples Grande, Florida.

August 2000: Ocean Course/Kiawah Island Resort, South Carolina; The Sagamore, New York; The Raven at Sandestin, Florida.

September 2000: Desert Springs Marriott, California; Greg Norman Course at PGA West, California; The Experience at Koele/Lanai, Hawaii.

October/November 2000: Reflection Bay, Nevada; Rio Secco, Nevada; Las Vegas Paiute Resort, Nevada; Ocean Hammock, Florida; Sandestin, Florida.

December 2000/January 2001: Valderrama and Sotogrande, Spain.

April/May 2001: Banff Springs, Alberta; Jasper Park Lodge, Alberta; Chateau Whistler/Whistler Resort, British Columbia; Pine Hill, New Jersey.

June 2001: Prestwick and Southwestern Coast of Scotland; Ted Robinson Jr. Guest Architecture Column.

July 2001: Bandon Dunes/Pacific Dunes, Oregon.

August 2001: Cabo del Sol/Palmilla/Eldorado, Mexico; The Broadmoor, Colorado; Grand Cypress, Florida; Blackstone National and Pine Hills, Massachussetts.

September 2001: Moonah Course and the Mornington Peninsula, Australia; Ocean Course at Half Moon Bay, California; Wolf Course at Las Vegas Paiute Resort, Nevada.

October/November 2001: The Dunes, South Carolina: Bear's Best, Nevada; Bear Trace Trail at Ross Creek, Tennessee; Horseshoe Bay, Texas; Barefoot Landing, South Carolina.

December 2001/January 2002: Nicklaus/Weiskopf Courses at Vista Vallarta, Mexico; Four Seasons Punta Mita, Mexico; TPC Sawgrass, Florida.

February/March 2002: Eden Course at St. Andrews, Scotland; Phoenician, Arizona; Doonbeg, Ireland.

April/May 2002: Algonquin, Canada; Links at Crowbush Cove, Prince Edward Island; Reynolds Plantation, Georgia; Shadow Creek, Nevada; Cascata, Nevada.

June 2002: Royal New Kent and Legend of Stonehouse, Virginia; Golden Horseshoe Gold Course, Virginia; The Balsams, New Hampshire.

July 2002: Sunningdale, England; Wentworth, England; St. George's Hill, England; Stoke Park, England.

Indexes

Alphabetical Index

D

Dancing Rabbit, 103
Deerhurst Resort, 227
Desert course, Cabo del Sol, 211–12
Desert Springs Marriott, 137, 139–41
Donald Ross Memorial Course, Boyne Highlands, 32
Doonbeg, 88, 181–82
Dorado Beach, 89, 255–57
Dorado East, Hyatt Dorado Beach, 256
Dorado West, Hyatt Dorado Beach, 256
Doral, 185
Dunes, The, 75–77
Dunes course, PGA West, 118
Dye Course, Barefoot Landing Resort, 254–55

E

Eagle Pines, Walt Disney World, 265
Eden course, St. Andrews, 42–44
El Conquistador, 157
Eldorado, 132–33
Elks Run, 188
Emerald course, Wailea, 171
Experience at Koele, The, 137–39, 175

F

Falcon's Fire, 203
Fazio Course, Barefoot Landing Resort, 254
Fazio Course, Treetops Resort, 103
Fountain Grove Resort, 145
Four Seasons Emerald Bay, 188
Four Seasons Hualalai, 134
Four Seasons Nevis, 164–66, 214

G

Gold course, Wailea, 171
Golden Horseshoe Gold course, 83–84
Grand Cypress, 125–27

Grayhawk, 103
Great Waters, Reynolds Plantation, 134, 197
Great White course, Doral, 185–87
Green Gables Golf Course, 70–71
Greenbrier, 261–62
    Meadows course, 261
    Old White course, 261
Greg Norman Course at PGA West, 118, 179–81, 185

H

Half Moon Bay, 146, 151, 153–54
Harbour Town, 104, 106, 119
Heather course, Boyne Highlands, 89
High Pointe Golf Club, 247–48
Hockley Valley, 227
Homestead, The, 33, 233, 262–64
    Cascades course, 233, 262–63
    Lower Cascades course, 263
    Old course, 33, 263
Horseshoe Bay, 89, 259–61
    Applerock, 260
    Ramrock, 260
    Saddlerock, 260
    Slickrock, 260
Hyatt Cerromar Beach, 255–57
    Cerromar North, 257
    Cerromar South, 257
Hyatt DFW Bear Creek, 145
Hyatt Dorado Beach, 255–57
    Dorado East, 256
    Dorado West, 256
Hyatt Regency Hill Country, 157

I

Indian Wells Resort, 145
Inn of the Mountain Gods, 145

J

Jack Nicklaus Tournament Course, PGA West, 118
Jasper Park Lodge, 61, 65–67, 69, 168, 223
Jockey Club, The, 58–60

Golf Travel by Design Courses by Region

United States

Northeast
  Maryland
    Beechtree, 250
    Links at Lighthouse Sound,
      The, 152
  Massachussetts
    Blackstone National, 199
    Crumpin-Fox, 81
    Pinehills, 199
  New Hampshire
    Balsams, The, 26
  New Jersey
    Marriott Seaview, 28
    Pine Hill, 102
  New York
    Sagamore, The, 24

South
  Alabama
    Robert Trent Jones Golf
      Trail, 84
  Florida
    Amelia Island Plantation, 268
    Grand Cypress, 125
    Great White course at
      Doral, 185
    Naples Grande, 195
    Palm Coast Resort, 257
    Sandestin, 266
    Tiburon, 187
    TPC Sawgrass, 112
    Walt Disney World, 264
    World Woods, 100
  Georgia
    Oconee course at Reynolds
      Plantation, 196
  North Carolina
    Pinehurst Number Eight, 96
    Pinehurst Number Seven, 192
    Pinehurst Number Two, 20
    Tobacco Road, 230
    Tot Hill Farm, 233

South Carolina
  Barefoot Landing Resort, 253
  Caledonia, 237
  Dunes, The, 75
  Legends Heathland
    course, 246
  Ocean course, Kiawah
    Island, 110
  Palmetto Dunes, 155
  Palmetto Hall, 155
  True Blue, 237
  Wild Dunes, 99
Tennessee
  Bear Trace Trail, 127
Virginia
  Golden Horseshoe Gold
    course, 83
  Homestead, The, 262
  Royal New Kent, 234
  Stonehouse, 234
West Virginia
  Greenbrier, 261

Midwest
  Michigan
    Bay Harbor, 149
    Black Forest course at
      Wilderness Valley, 248
    Donald Ross Memorial Course
      at Boyne Highlands, 82
    High Pointe Golf Club, 247
    Shepherd's Hollow, 150
  Wisconsin
    American Club, The, 107

West
  Arizona
    Phoenician, The, 142
    TPC Scottsdale, 208
    Troon North, 207
  California
    Desert Springs Marriott, 139
    Greg Norman Course
      at PGA West, 179
    La Quinta/PGA West, 117